ABROAD AT HOME

**THE 600 BEST INTERNATIONAL TRAVEL
EXPERIENCES IN NORTH AMERICA**

New Bedford, Massachusetts, celebrates its Portuguese roots with Madeira Feast.

ABROAD AT HOME

THE 600 BEST INTERNATIONAL TRAVEL EXPERIENCES IN NORTH AMERICA

NATIONAL GEOGRAPHIC

WASHINGTON, D.C.

Byodo-In Temple,
Valley of the
Temples Memorial
Park, Oahu, Hawaii

CONTENTS

Front cover: (top) Japanese Tea Garden, San Francisco; (bottom left to right) True Grain Bread bakery, Cowichan Bay, B.C.; St. Louis Cathedral, New Orleans; seared scallops, Avant Tapas and Wine, Buellton, California; lavender farm, Sequim, Washington.

Back cover: (left to right) Kee Beach, Kauai, Hawaii; tulips in Washington Park, Albany, New York; Thomas Jefferson Memorial, Washington, D.C.; Caribana parade, Toronto.

Dining alfresco on rue du Petit-Champlain, Quebec City

INTRODUCTION

When I lived in Queens, New York, one of the world's most diverse neighborhoods, I'd make a walk around a grab bag of global cultures just to get to the subway. In a ten-minute stroll, I'd pass street carts selling Salvadoran cornmeal *pupusas* and Mexican carne asada tacos, and shops filled with Tibetan noodles, Argentine steaks, Indian saris, Bollywood DVDs, cheap Uruguayan cream-filled pastries, dangling chicken feet, and brightly colored bottled potions seen through the office windows of Amazonian witch doctors. I never went into one of the South American healers for a consultation—we do live with some regrets, don't we?—but I always veered that way to see who might be in.

That's New York. People expect to encounter different cultures in different ways. But as I ventured beyond my international urban mecca and through the pages of this book, I was amazed (and delighted) to see how much of that sense of the world you can feel all across the United States and Canada, perhaps in your own backyard.

I see this book as a dream trip planner for making, at the very least, detours into "other worlds" on any North American journey. No matter where you go, there's something surprising around the corner. Because, yes! I want to hear Brazilian fado singers in Newark's Ironbound; join a Laotian street party in Philadelphia; take sausage-making classes in the Ozarks; try Lebanese lamb dumplings in Michigan's Mideast mecca; or nibble on freshly harvested truffles in Oregon as if I were in the French Périgord, along with judging who has the best, most authentic bowl of Vietnamese pho (noodle soup): southern California, Montreal, or—gulp—Orlando?

Experiencing the world at home is fascinating, fun, and real. And more important, put together, these experiences add up to a fuller understanding of what the United States and Canada really are. Much more than advertised.

ROBERT REID
Offbeat Observer,
National Geographic Travel

CHAPTER 1
NORTHEAST

Boston's Italian
St. Anthony's Feast

FRENCH ACADIA

Expelled from Nova Scotia by the British during the French and Indian War, Francophone Acadians laid down new roots in Quebec, Louisiana, and elsewhere. Some were drawn to the fertile basin of the St. John River Valley, in what is today Aroostook County, Maine. You'll find their legacy in villages including Van Buren, Madawaska, and Frenchville.

WHAT TO SEE: Stroll through the unique stacked and pegged, or *pièce-sur-pièce*, houses and potato barns built by early émigrés in Van Buren's Acadian Village to get a sense of 18th-century Acadian life. Tour the village's Morneault House, one of the area's oldest, and note the nautical details like "ship's knees," supportive beams that Acadian boatbuilders adapted for landlubbing carpentry.

WHAT TO EAT: *Ployes*, buckwheat flour pancakes, are the all-purpose Acadian staple. Eat them dressed up or down—with a pat of butter or as the old-timers do, spread with molasses. "You can also wrap ice cream in them and drizzle with chocolate sauce, my personal favorite," says Janice Bouchard of the buckwheat-producing Bouchard Family Farm. At Dolly's Restaurant in Frenchville, slather salty pork *creton* or rib-sticking chicken stew on made-to-order ployes. Or check out the Ployes Festival in Fort Kent.

INSIGHT · Valley French

Get in your *char* (car) and drive past fields and fields of *patates* (potatoes). You're in the St. John River Valley, fertile in a rich regional lexicon. Valley French is a distinctive patois of standard French, Quebecois expressions, English, and terms used by the area's indigenous people. "Valley residents are in an unusual case in which the [U.S. and French Canadian] border shifted around them," says James Myall, coordinator of the Franco-American Collection at Lewiston-Auburn College.

The town is the proud record holder of the world's biggest ploye, roughly 12 feet in diameter!

■ *Essentials:* Acadian Village, 859 Main St., Van Buren, tel 207-868-5042, connectmaine.com/acadianvillage; Dolly's Restaurant, 17 U.S. Rte. 1, Frenchville, tel 207-728-7050; Ployes Festival, held annually in Aug., fortkentchamber.com/events/events.html

Cooking a giant *ploye* (buckwheat pancake), Fort Kent

Acadian Village
in St. John Valley

You Could Be In . . . NEW ZEALAND

White Mountains, New Hampshire
The lupine-carpeted White Mountains look every bit like New Zealand's Lake Tekapo.

Sweets and scones at Dunbar Tea Shop on Cape Cod

CAPE COD, MASSACHUSETTS
ENGLISH TEA

In 1773 America, the greatest tea guzzlers were arguably Boston Harbor's fish. Though the Boston Tea Party helped ignite the American Revolution, today the steamy beverage no longer boils patriotic blood and, in fact, is widely consumed throughout New England in British-inspired tea parlors.

WHAT TO DO: Fancy a cuppa and a wee scone? Pop into Dunbar Tea Shop in Cape Cod's oldest town of Sandwich and one of America's finest tea establishments, the cover model for the book *The Great Tea Rooms of America*. The wood-paneled tea parlor is steeped in history: In the 18th century the room was a gentlemen's smoking den. Today the pipe smoke has been replaced with the swoon-inducing scent of freshly baked scones, the tingling of teaspoons on blue-and-white Canton saucers, and the quiet murmur of ladies and gents taking their afternoon tea in style. Something about a dreary wet day curled up by the fireplace, sipping English breakfast poured from a teapot swathed in a pink, *toile de Jouy* cozy simply warms the crumpets of the soul.

BEYOND TEA: For appetites rumbling for something more than a dainty cup of tea, the teahouse delivers. How about a pint of malty Old Speckled Hen or a glass of Cider & Black, a cocktail of English Woodpecker hard cider with a dash of Ribena, a beloved British soda made from black currant? The Cumberland Crumpet Melt, with cheese bubbling over roasted chicken and cranberry jam, is sure to satisfy.

■ *Essentials:* Dunbar Tea Shop, 1 Water St., Sandwich, tel 508-833-2485, dunbartea.com

DIGGING DEEPER

"For they said, it was a shame to quarrel upon Christmas Day." Indeed only merriment and delight abound during the Yuletide season at Dunbar, when costumed performers read from Dickens's *A Christmas Carol* on Sunday evenings throughout December.

AZOREAN LEGACY

Azoreans started coming to New England in the 19th century, after working as crew members on American whaling ships voyaging to the far-flung Atlantic islands. The boats would stop off in the Azorean islands off the coast of Portugal, stock up on provisions, and often pick up a few seaworthy islanders before heading out to sea again. Sometimes, the new shipmates stayed aboard to the voyage's end, settling in New England. Today, Fall River holds the largest Portuguese population in the United States.

WHAT TO SEE: Admire the sleek lines of the large-scale Azorean whaleboat model at the Azorean Whaleman Gallery, the only permanent exhibit honoring Portuguese patrimony in the United States, at the New Bedford Whaling Museum.

WHAT TO EAT: If there were ever an Eataly of Portuguese food, Fall River's Portugalia Marketplace would be it. The former mill turned specialty grocer houses everything from great barrels of fava beans to fluffy sugar-dusted fried dough known as *malassadas*. But one product in particular reaches cult status here. "Portugalia is an homage to salted cod," says Maria Lawton, area resident and author of *Azorean Cooking*. "They have a whole separate room devoted to all different cuts of *bacalhau*. You want cod cheeks? They've got 'em."

REGATTA TIME: The sound of a horn ripples across Buzzards Bay. The yellow flag snaps to attention. Sleek hulls in blue, yellow, pink, and red streak across the water as their sun-beaten rowers pound out stroke after stroke, each boat vying to eke out a lead. This is the annual

MORE • Portuguese Festivals

Feast of the Blessed Sacrament: Specially imported Madeira wine and grill-your-own *carne de espeto* sirloin skewers fuel this New Bedford, Massachusetts, century-old festival. *First weekend in Aug., portuguesefeast.com*

Boston Portuguese Festival: Lusophone luminaries descend on Boston for two months of Portuguese heritage, arts, and culture, culminating in a Day of Portugal Parade. *Various events April–June, bostonportuguese festival.org*

Portugal Day NY: A 5-mile run for adults and a kids' race in Manhattan's Central Park followed by music. *June, portuguesecircle.com/portugaldayny*

Portugal Day Festival: This two-day, Newark, New Jersey, festival wraps up with a night of dancing to traditional Portuguese fado. *Weekend closest to June 10, portugaldaynewark.com*

International Whaleboat Regatta, held alternate years in nearby New Bedford and the Azores in Portugal.

■ *Essentials:* New Bedford Whaling Museum, 18 Johnny Cake Hill, New Bedford, tel 508-997-0046, whalingmuseum .org; Portugalia Marketplace, portugaliamarketplace.com; International Whaleboat Regatta, held in September every other year, New Bedford, whalingmuseum.org

Azorean boats race on the Acushnet River.

AROUND THE WORLD IN
BOSTON

A young reveler aboard a St. Patrick's Day float, South Boston

My Neighborhood

JAMAICA PLAIN

I think there are only four Ecuadorians besides me in all of Boston, and three of us are in Jamaica Plain. We have people from all over the planet here. People from the Dominican Republic, Puerto Rico, El Salvador, Colombia, Mexico, Haiti, India, Vietnam, Laos. In the '70s, there were a lot of Irish and Italian people here. Then in the '80s and '90s, Latinos and African Americans began moving here. Now the baby boomers are coming back. Old Stag Tavern, which used to be a very traditional bar, is now Coco's, and it attracts a Latino crowd for live music and merengue dancing. I like to cook food from the Andes, and there are several bodegas here where I buy ingredients like [the fruit] *naranjilla* and *tomate de árbol* [tamarillo].

DANILO MORALES
Jamaica Plain Neighborhood Development Corporation

Italian Sausages and Celebrations

St. Anthony's Feast proudly weighs in as New England's largest Italian celebration. For four days in late August, the neighborhood is a riot of Catholic masses and Italian street food. It all crescendos with a ten-hour procession of the icon of Saint Anthony under a deluge of confetti. You'll find *arancini* (fried rice balls), *zeppole* (Italian donuts minus the holes), and cannoli at this *grandissimo* Italian street feast. Boston's historic North End struts its Italian stuff, both edible and spiritual, with other fests during its high feast season in August. At the Fisherman's Feast, streamers fall from the sky, trumpets blare, and a statue of the Madonna is paraded through the streets of Little Italy. Immigrant fishermen brought the tradition to Boston over a century ago from the Sicilian town of Sciacca. All the pious, calorie-busting mayhem is "for the same reason," says Fisherman's Feast chairman Domenic Strazzullo. "We're here to keep our heritage alive." *St. Anthony's Feast, third weekend in Aug., saintanthonysfeast.com; Fisherman's Feast, last weekend in Aug., fishermansfeast.com*

Lithuanian Social Hub

Lithuanian food is the sort that warms the belly and invites merry conversation between mouthfuls of *balandeliai*, meatballs stuffed in cabbage. On weekends the basement of the Lithuanian Club serves as both authentic Lithuanian restaurant for foodies in the know and a social hub of the Lithuanian community. Conversations in English and Lithuanian flow in this decidedly no-frills setting. Think office chairs and nary a tablecloth with a little oomph from imported Švyturys beer. On Sundays the kitchen draws a steady stream of regulars from nearby St. Peter Lithuanian Parish, the city's last remaining Lithuanian church. "After the 10:30 Lithuanian Mass, the devotees religiously head over to the club for special dishes only made on Sunday," says

St. Anthony statue,
North Boston

Boston's Chinatown—the only one left in New England

church secretary and organist Daiva Navickas. The Sunday special includes *cepelinai*, juicy potato dumplings stuffed with minced meat, the so-called national dish of Lithuania. The club also hosts Lithuanian bands and performers in its auditorium. Plan a visit to the Lithuanian Parish around the holidays for bilingual Christmas carols and a traditional meatless Christmas Eve feast, open to all. "Christmas Eve for Lithuanians is like Thanksgiving for Americans," Navickas says. *South Boston Lithuanian Club restaurant, 368 W. Broadway, tel 617-268-1055, open Sat.–Sun., sblca.org; St. Peter Lithuanian Parish, 75 Flaherty Way, tel 617-268-0353, stpeterlithuanianparish .org*

Polish Kielbasa Link
Wedged between South Boston and Back Bay, the so-called Polish Triangle (now more of a sliver than it once was) is the go-to spot for Polish ingredients, particularly kielbasa, some of which is made locally in a handful of delis. Dorchester's Baltic European Deli sells house-made kielbasa. Beyond the cases of densely packed sausages, explore aisles of Polish treats like sauerkraut and *krowki*, semisoft milk toffee candies. Going on 80 years old, D&J European Market and Delicatessen churns out its fair share of kielbasas, but the real showstoppers are the baked goods, like homemade swirly *babkas* coffee cakes and raspberry-filled sugar-dusted doughnuts, and liverwurst sandwiches

drizzled with Polish mustard. For a sit-down meal, venture into Café Polonia across the street. The atmosphere screams "Polish mountain cottage," a cozy place to tuck into hearty *bigos* (meat and cabbage stew) and potato pancakes stuffed with goulash. *Baltic European Deli, 632 Dorchester Ave., South Boston, tel 617-268-2435; D&J Market, 120 Boston St., Dorchester, tel 617-436-9766; Café Polonia, 611 Dorchester Ave., tel 617-269-0110, cafepolonia.com*

Kung Fu Flicks
Grab a folding chair and settle in for an outdoor Chinese movie at the annual Films at the Gate event in Chinatown. Every year, cinephiles gather for three nights of free outdoor screenings

The Main Neighborhoods

Little Italy
Throughout Boston's North End
BEST BET: Gorging on cannoli at Mike's Pastry

Polish Triangle
Polish enclave wedged between Dorchester and South Boston
BEST BET: Seasonal blueberry pierogies at upscale Café Polonia

Allston
Dozens of ethnic restaurants around intersection of Brighton and Harvard Aves., including Brazilian, Thai, and Malaysian
BEST BET: Afghan comfort food like *kaddo* (baked pumpkin with seasoned beef) at Ariana

Chinatown
Sixty-some Asian restaurants and bakeries on and around the Beach Street commercial area
BEST BET: Herbal remedies at Nam Bac Hong

Jamaica Plain
Diverse population in Boston's "Emerald Necklace" neighborhood, south of Brookline
BEST BET: International fare along Centre and South Streets

of Chinese-language (with English subtitles) and classic kung fu flicks. "You'll see faces from all over Boston's neighborhoods," says co-founder Sam Davol. Despite the bare-bones setting—metal folding chairs, shaky screen, and street noise—the event fills up. "You could have a better AV experience in your living room, right? Well that's not why people come. They love movies. But more importantly, they love watching movies together." Folding chairs are first come first serve, so consider bringing your own tailgating chair. Or visit in August, when the frenetic neighborhood

of Chinatown gets an extra dose of energy during the August Moon Festival, when vendors and visitors pour into the streets to celebrate the end of the harvest and the lunar cycle. *Films at the Gate, Hudson St. between Beach and Kneeland Sts., one weekend in Aug. or Sept. (check website), filmsatthegate.org; August Moon Festival, Sun. closest to Aug. 15, bostoncentral.com*

K-Pop and Korean Soul Food

Give your taste buds a workout with a trip through Allston's Korean offerings like finger-licking garlic

soy chicken wings at Bonchon or bubbly tofu soups at Kaju Tofu House, dubbed the city's best Korean restaurant by *Boston Magazine*. When local Kathy Chang misses home, she heads to Myung Dong. "In Korea, you can go to places called *pojangmacha* late night and grab some *anju* [drinking snacks] and *soju* [a Korean spirit traditionally made from rice]. I love Myung Dong because they serve a lot of that 'street' food." The casual, collegiate decor—bar stools, white string lights, and Korean flags—lends itself to communal feasting

on juicy *Ddok Bokghi*, elongated, stir-fried rice cakes with carrots and onions smothered in a red pepper sauce. Wrap up the night by belting out some K-pop tunes with friends in your own private karaoke room at DoReMi, a "Korean institution" says Chang. *Bonchon, 123 Brighton Ave., Allston, tel 617-254-8888, bonchon.com; Kaju Tofu House, 58 Harvard Ave., Allston, tel 617-208-8540; Myung Dong Restaurant, 90 Harvard Ave., Allston, tel 617-206-3229, myungdong1stave.com; DoReMi, 442 Cambridge St., Allston, tel 617-783-8900, doremikaraoke.net*

Fresh bread delivered to Little Italy in Boston

Irish O'Party

Boston's considerable Irish-American population, along with the rest of the city's revel-ready, take to the streets of Southie to celebrate their Irish heritage. Everyone's Irish on St. Paddy's Day, right? Begun in 1784, the current incarnation of the Saint Patrick's Day Parade has been running annually since 1901. Listen for the jubilant crooning of the uniformed and kilted Boston Police Gaelic Column of Pipes and Drums as the officers blast their way through town. Pub-crawl your way along the parade with a mandatory pit stop at Blackthorn Pub, where you'll meet some serious footie fans and Irish Americans raising a hearty "*Sláinte!*" toast to the Emerald Isle. Nearby Shenannigans might be the best sponge for all that whiskey and Guinness, serving up rib-sticking Irish fare like shepherd's pie, and bangers and mash. As for the rest of the city, beware: "It's mayhem and it's not just a day, it's a whole week," says St. Paddy's Day veteran and local graduate student Charlotte Lockhart. "Everything and anything is green. It's like Boston's version of Mardi Gras." *Saint Patrick's Day Parade, southbostonparade.org; Blackthorn Pub, 471 W. Broadway, South Boston, tel 617-269-5510, blackthornboston.com; Shenannigans Irish Pub & Restaurant, 332 W. Broadway, tel 617-269-9509, shenannigansirishpubbostonma.com*

Walking Map *Little Italy*

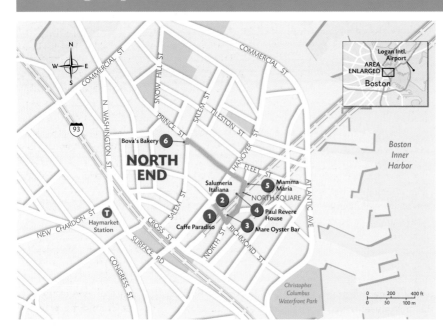

Littleᴛ Italy's densely packed cafés and eateries make it the ideal destination for a foodie stroll.

1 | Fuel up for your stroll along Little Italy's cobbled streets with a cappuccino and a filled-to-order cannoli at third-generation **Caffe Paradiso** (*255 Hanover St., tel 617-742-1768, caffeparadiso.com*).

2 | Continue up Hanover and take a right onto Richmond Street, where you'll find **Salumeria Italiana** (*151 Richmond St., tel 617-523-8743, salumeria italiana.com*), filled to the brim with Italian specialties like squid ink pasta, salted anchovies, and cured meats.

3 | All this shopping should whet your appetite for some Prosecco and *frutti di mare* at the sustainably sourced **Mare Oyster Bar** (*135 Richmond St., tel 617-723-6273, mareoysterbar .com*).

4 | From there turn left onto North Square, where you'll pass the **Paul Revere House** (*19 N. Square, tel 617-523-2338, paulreverehouse.org*).

5 | If it's dinnertime, you may be lured in by the osso buco or lobster agnolotti at **Mamma Maria** across the square (*3 N. Square, tel 617-523-0077, mammamaria.com*).

6 | From here, window- and menu-shop your way along Prince Street until you reach the 24-hour **Bova's Bakery** for a sweet treat (*134 Salem St., tel 617-523-5601, bova bakeryboston.com*).

"Epsom Races: Preparing to Start" by James Pollard, Yale Center for British Art, New Haven, Connecticut

INTERNATIONAL ART GALLERIES

Mine Aboriginal myths in Virginia or grab a selfie with an Egyptian goddess in San Jose.

■ Yale Center for British Art

Hogarth, Gainsborough, and Turner are some of the English artists you'll discover in this splendid collection in New Haven, Connecticut, spanning the 16th century to the present day—the largest collection of its kind outside the United Kingdom.
britishart.yale.edu

■ El Museo del Barrio

An eye-popping display of Latino, Caribbean, and Latin American art hide behind a neoclassical Fifth Avenue, Manhattan facade—ranging from ancient Santos carvings to ritual masks to provocative pop art. The museum also hosts the annual Three Kings Day Parade, ushered by 12-foot-tall painted puppets.
elmuseo.org

■ National Museum of African Art

Try to plan a visit around a few of the continual live events at this Washington, D.C., museum (part of the Smithsonian), from Kenyan hip-hop musicians to Ethiopian dance troupes. Want to know more about one of the museum's more than 9,000 objects? Schedule a consultation in advance with a curator to learn about two of them. "We are the only museum in North America (and one of very few anywhere) devoted solely to the arts of Africa," says museum curator Bryna Freyer.
africa.si.edu

■ Kluge-Ruhe Aboriginal Art Collection

Tucked in among tidy Jeffersonian buildings in Charlottesville, Virginia, lies a treasure trove of Australian Aboriginal art that goes back 40,000 years. In one gallery, explore the creation myth of the Wagilag Sisters, from the serpent who swallowed them whole to the itchy, stinging caterpillars that brought them back to life. Elsewhere, see paintings on leaves and bark.
kluge-ruhe.org

■ Asian Art Museum

A gilded bronze Buddha dated 338 is the crown jewel of San Francisco's Asian Art Museum's world-famous collection. More than 18,000 objects represent 6,000 years of culture.
asianart.org

■ Rosicrucian Egyptian Museum

From humble beginnings—a single Sekhmet (lion goddess) statue—an impressive Egyptian art museum was born in San Jose, California. Among the ancient mummies on display are those of a cat and a five-year-old girl.
www.egyptianmuseum.org

■ Royal Ontario Museum

Gaze at the magnificent "Paradise of Maitreya" and be grateful. A century ago, the Yuan dynasty–era Buddhist mural narrowly escaped destruction and was saved by very dedicated monks. It is now the prize of the Bishop White Gallery of Chinese Temple Art in Toronto, Canada's Royal Ontario Museum.
rom.on.ca/en

NEW HAVEN, CONNECTICUT

ITALIAN FARE

If there were ever a New World capital of pizza, New Haven would be it. Italian immigrants began pouring into the region in the late 19th century, finding work in New Haven's shirt factories. By the early 1900s, three industrious families created "apizza," as New Haven–style pies are called—legacy that would span nearly a century.

WHAT TO EAT: The best known apizza is undoubtedly Frank Pepe's. The house specialty has been the same since Italian immigrant Pepe opened a New Haven institution in 1938: white clam pizza—nothing but freshly shucked little neck clams, shredded cheese, olive oil, oregano, and *lots* of garlic atop a toasty, charred crust. Still, says Pepe devotee Jessica Kagan Cushman, "There's nothing better, in my humble opinion, than a bacon and onion Pepe's pizza with a pitcher of beer." No-frills Modern Apizza draws acolytes for its simple tomato pies on one end of the pizza spectrum, and meat-laden "Italian Bomb" on the other. At cash-only Sally's, neither the place nor the pies have changed much since Sal Consiglio founded Sally's in 1938.

JOINING IN: For the full Italian fix, visit in June for the four-day, more-than-century-old St. Andrew Apostle Society's Italian Feast. Of course, food plays a major part in the action, from fried dough and calzones to fried clams

INSIGHT · Pizza Parlance

You may have noticed New Haven residents have their own way of talking. It's "apeetz," not pizza, "mootz," not mozzarella. *Capisce?* The particular pronunciations are vestiges of the original *Napoletano*-speaking Italian immigrants and fathers of New Haven apizza. "It's a case of retrograde assimilation," says Italian professor and New Haven resident Giuseppe Gazzola. "People heard '*a pizza*'—'a' for the singular feminine article of the Neapolitan dialect—and thought it was one word: *apizza*."

and calamari, specialties of the group's adopted coastal Italian city of Amalfi.

■ *Essentials:* Frank Pepe Pizzeria, multiple locations, tel 203-865-5762, pepespizzeria.com; Modern Apizza, 874 State St., tel 203-776-5306, modernapizza.com; Sally's Apizza, 237 Wooster St., tel 203-624-5271, sallysapizza.com; St. Andrew's Italian Feast, ssaanewhaven.com

These days, Pepe's grandkids run the Frank Pepe Pizzeria in New Haven.

Brick oven–fired pies at Modern Apizza, New Haven

You Could Be In . . . AMSTERDAM

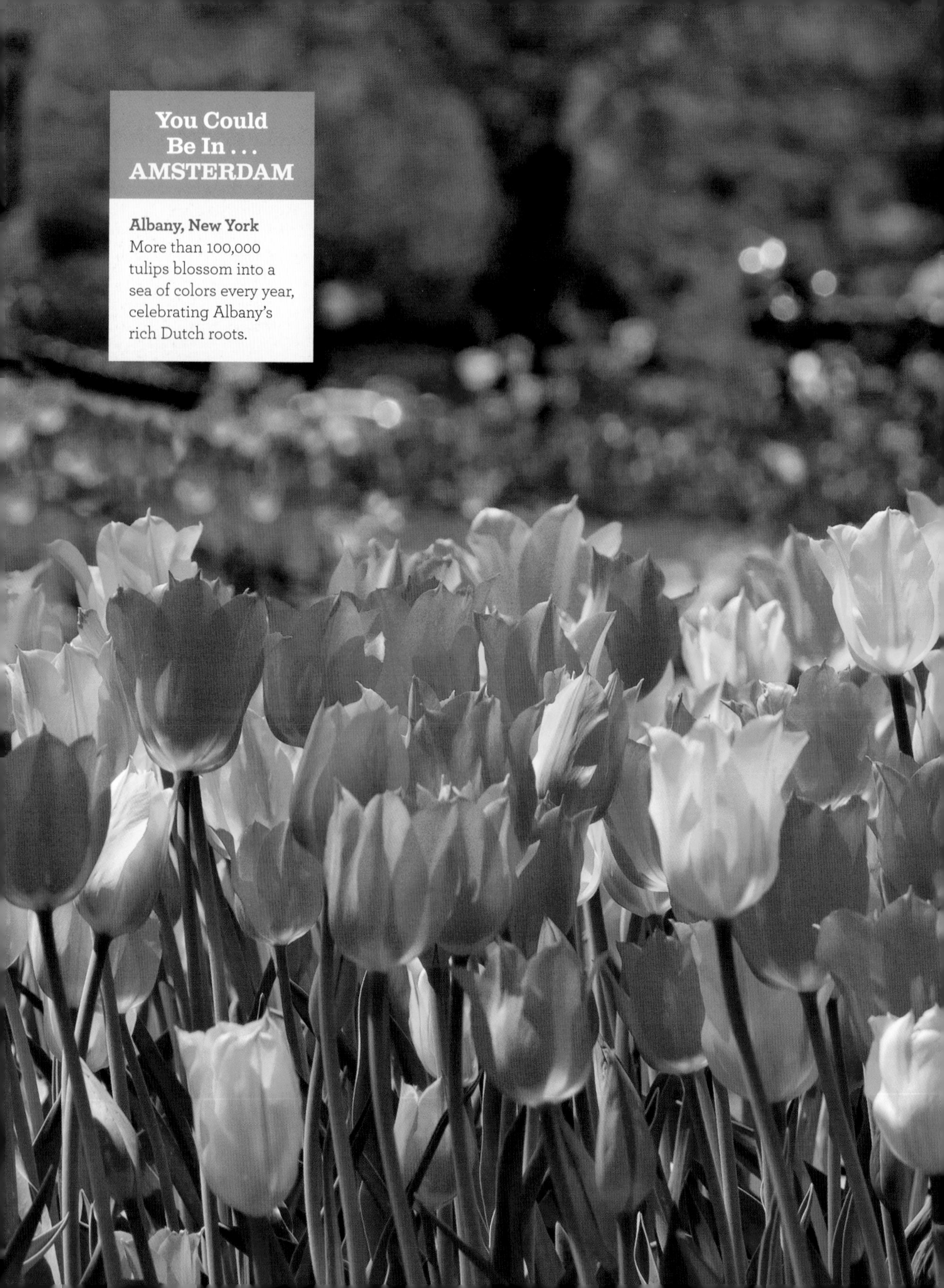

Albany, New York
More than 100,000 tulips blossom into a sea of colors every year, celebrating Albany's rich Dutch roots.

AROUND THE WORLD IN
NEW YORK CITY

Greek Orthodox
Easter service,
St. Demetrios
Cathedral, Astoria,
Queens

My Neighborhood

FLUSHING, QUEENS

My family is from the city of Xi'an in China. My first introduction to Flushing was in 1999. We'd drive down from Connecticut just to go shopping, eat, and get my hair cut. My head's shape is apparently too Asian and I can never get a decent haircut at a regular American barbershop, so I would get a $6 haircut at this dive-y Chinese hair salon in Flushing called Five Star Beauty Salon. I went through all my phases of hair experimentation as a teenager there. I still go to the same spot, visiting the same barber for the same price. On these trips, I'd also gorge on authentic Chinese food. We would go grocery shopping for snacks and specialty condiments like black rice vinegar to bring back with us until our next visit.

JASON WANG
CEO, Xi'an Famous Foods

Everybody Say *Opa!*
Streets and storefronts of Astoria, Queens, are infused with Greek culture and shops throughout the year, but the community *really* comes out to play every May. That's when members and neighbors of the 80-plus-year-old St. Demetrios Cathedral celebrate the annual Greek Festival. Don't be shy when the dancing begins. Students at the parish parochial school are happy to teach you what it takes to link arms and join the fun. After working up an appetite, work your way through the food options—from souvlaki and gyros to the sweet delight of *kourabiedes,* ground almond cookies covered in confectioners' sugar. If you have kids in tow,

it'll be tough to pry them away from the carnival rides but it's worth a try. The flea market area is filled with Greek arts, crafts, and lots of music. Want some Greek to go? "If you are looking for Greek ingredients, you must visit Titan Foods," says Dan Saltzstein, New Yorker and a travel editor at the *New York Times.* "A stunning selection. The variety of fetas and olive preparations alone will blow your mind."
The Greek Festival, St. Demetrios Cathedral, 30-11 30th Dr., Astoria, tel 718-728-1718, saintdemetriosastoria .com; Titan Foods, 2556 31st St., Astoria, tel 718-626-7771, titanfoods.net

Mile of Cultures
New York City's Museum Mile stretches along

Fifth Avenue from 82nd Street straight on up to El Barrio, aka Spanish Harlem. And that's where El Museo del Barrio awaits. Founded in 1969 by a group of *puertorriqueños* dissatisfied with the lack of Latino works in the city's museums, the museum immerses visitors in the importance, beauty, and influence of Hispanic and Caribbean artists on the city and the world. Wander through the rich history of Latin artists from pre-Columbian works to contemporary artists. In town in spring or summer? Head out into the streets on a guided tour that, quite literally, walks you into a deeper understanding of the neighborhood and the Puerto Rican community that has called

All ages ring in the
Chinese New Year,
New York City.

The savory side of Spanish Harlem's Puerto Rican Festival in the Big Apple

it home since just after World War II.
El Museo del Barrio, 1230 Fifth Ave., tel 212-831-7272, elmuseo.org

Russian Pointe
Watch the next generation of acclaimed Russian dancers—the American division—sashay their stuff onto the stage with an annual performance of Tchaikovsky's *The Nutcracker*. The school also holds recitals during its yearly Children's Festival. Brighton Beach itself is quite the place to behold. One New Yorker asked a friend visiting from St. Petersburg, Russia, what surprised him most about the city. "His out-of-left-field response was 'Brighton Beach,'" Natalia Yamrom says. "The one thing he absolutely could not have imagined was a thriving Russian/Soviet culture of the '70s and '80s."

The Nutcracker and Children's Festival, 2001 Oriental Blvd., Brooklyn, tel 718-769-9161, brightonballet.com

Too Français
Disappear off to France just blocks from Bloomingdale's. Few buildings anywhere in the world spill over with as much local pride—for a place that's not really local—than the Upper East Side's French Institute Alliance Française. Housed in an elegant historic building, the institute offers French art shows, films, discussions, wine tastings, and more. And come Bastille Day, there's no better place to be in the city; the free annual street fair, held on a Sunday near July 14, celebrates French Independence Day with music, drinks,

and plenty of *fromage, bien sûr!*
Alliance Française, 22 East 60th St., tel 212-355-6100, fiaf.org

Alt St. Paddy's
Manhattan's massive St. Patrick's Day parade is legendary and, at times, controversial. For a more personal feel, head out to the Irish strongholds of Sunnyside and Woodside in Queens for the annual St. Pat's for All parade. Then it's off to a local pub you go—there are plenty of them—for some traditional Irish music, singing, food, and a well-poured Guinness (something that doesn't happen quite as easily in the crazy crowded pubs around the Manhattan parade route). A good bet for food: Donovan's Pub at 57-24 Roosevelt Ave. Though known for its burgers, it's the classic

The Main Neighborhoods

Astoria
Broadway between 31st and Steinway Streets
BEST BET: Fried calamari and grilled octopus at Taverna Kyclades

Little Odessa by the Sea
Russian shops and restaurants that pepper Brooklyn's Brighton Beach
BEST BET: The Millennium Theatre for Russian concerts and plays

Korea Way
32nd Street between 5th Avenue and Broadway
BEST BET: Stepping into the Jade Igloo sauna at Juvenex Spa

Little Italy
Bumped up against Manhattan's Chinatown
BEST BET: A warm loaf of bread from Parisi Bakery

Little Poland
Polish bakeries and restaurants in Greenpoint, Brooklyn
BEST BET: The white borscht plate at Lomzynianka Restaurant

shepherd's pie you'll want to order.

St. Patrick's Day parade, stpatsforall.com

Hidden Korea

It's easy to just . . . not see it. But that would be a shame. Manhattan's Koreatown is wedged into and between office buildings—some of the restaurants are far from restauranty on the outside—just blocks from Macy's, Penn Station, Madison Square Garden,

and the rest of midtown madness. But it's a land of its own. Watch for signs offering karaoke, Korean fried chicken, BBQ, and more. Oh, wait: Unless you read Korean, you might not understand the signs; the neighborhood businesses definitely cater to those far from home. But all are welcome (though ordering may, at times, require a bit of language-difference pantomime). One of the neighborhood

restaurant mainstays is Hanbat, which serves a traditional Korean menu, complete with the customary predinner parade of tiny dishes called *banchan.* Korean food newbies (or those just really fond of crispy rice) should order *bibimbap,* a dish of meat, vegetables, and egg that's served in a sizzling hot stone bowl. Don't touch it—but dig right in. Thanks to round-the-clock hours, Hanbat

satisfies at whatever hour the rest of your Big Apple adventures finish up. *Hanbat, 53 W. 35th St., tel 212-629-5588, hanbatnyc .com*

Italy Reboot

Arthur Avenue, a four-block stretch of the Belmont section of the Bronx, has been an Italian enclave for decades. Italy's green, white, and red flag flies proudly, and eavesdroppers would do well to learn

Walking Map *Little India*

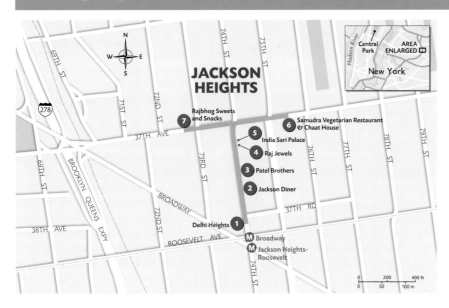

W hether visitors are shopping for a sari, stunning hand-worked gold jewelry, springtime Indian mangos (devotees track their arrival), or just a quick snack of sweet and spicy *papri chaat,* Jackson Heights's Little India delivers.

1 | **Delhi Heights's** menu features an extensive selection of Indian and Himalayan dishes (*37-66 74th St., tel 718-507-1111, delhiheights.us*).

2 | The neighborhood's best known restaurant, **Jackson Diner** focuses mostly on dishes from

North India (*37-47 74th St., tel 718-672-1232, jack sondiner.com*).

3 | Be careful not to spend all your money at marvelous **Patel Brothers** on spices, dal, jars of ghee, and copper water glasses (*37-27 74th St., tel 718-898-3445, patelbros.com*).

4 | At **Raj Jewels,** 22k gold (and diamonds and gemstones) is worked into intricate marvels (*37-11 74th St., tel 718-426-1459, rajjewels.net*).

5 | Even Mother Nature might be jealous of the range of colors available at **India Sari Palace** (*37-07 74th St., tel 718-426-2700*).

6 | **Samudra Vegetarian Restaurant & Chaat House** is one of the neighborhood's newest and best additions (*75-18 37th Ave., tel 718-255-1757, samudravegetarian.com*).

7 | Indian sweets lean very sweet—and colorful. One of the best selections is at **Rajbhog Sweets and Snacks,** which also sells savory treats from an always busy counter (*72-27 37th Ave., tel 718-458-8512, rajbhog.com*).

Italian if they really want to understand the conversations that flow through the neighborhood. "Walking down Arthur Avenue feels like stepping back in time," says Sunset Park, Brooklyn resident Jen Wittlin. "It has not seemed to change since the 1950s. I almost wouldn't be surprised to see Frank Sinatra crooning in one of the formal Italian dining rooms that line the street. But what I really go for is the pizza."

Arthur Avenue Retail Market (launched by Mayor Fiorello LaGuardia himself in 1940), a covered, indoor complex that, somehow, has an outdoor vibe, anchors the neighborhood. The multivendor market sort of feels like you're walking through the center of a small town in Italy. The sounds, sights, and smells are the same: men sitting with coffees, jawing over the day's events; extra chairs at tables loaded down with packages from the day's shopping; the scent of Italian food staples swirling into a delightfully heady aroma that leaves visitors both hungry and satisfied. Vendors include sausage makers, bakers, butchers, fresh pasta makers, delis, fish markets, cheese shops, and on and on. Locally made mozzarella hews to centuries-old techniques from the old country. *Arthur Avenue Retail Market, 2344 Arthur Ave., Bronx, closed Sun., arthuravenuebronx .com*

Lovable Jerk

Those shy about spice should grab some extra tissues (there will be tears) and venture forth anyway for this essential Jamaican-in-NYC experience: a plate lunch at Peppa's Jerk Chicken. Influential Big Apple food critic Robert Sietsema once wrote, "Brooklyn is the jerk capital of the world, more so than even Jamaica itself." And he named Peppa's as one of his go-tos. The constant stream of diners in and out of this not-so-fancy storefront would seem to agree.
Peppa's Jerk Chicken, 738 Flatbush Ave., Brooklyn

Brooklyn's Borscht Belt

Nobody in Greenpoint would blink an eye if you tried to pay for a pierogi with a złoty—granted they (probably) wouldn't accept the Polish currency. After browsing the neighborhood's stores, with many signs in Polish and newsstands filled with Polish-language newspapers and magazines, it's easy to forget you're in Brooklyn (until a decidedly American hipster resident shows up as a reminder). But locals both new and old country know Manhattan's cupcake trend could never hold a sugar crystal next to the Polish bakeries around Greenpoint. Fuel any walking tour

An Italian market on Arthur Avenue, the Little Italy of the Bronx in New York

Pulaski Day Parade
in New York City

of Greenpoint's lovely streets, filled with historical architecture including the former home of the Polish Legion of American Veterans, with *paczki* (Polish doughnuts) from Rzeszowska Bakery, a hearty rye bread from Old Poland Bakery & Restaurant, or, if you lean savory, some of NYC's best stuffed cabbage at Northside Bakery. For the General Casimir Pulaski Memorial Day Parade in October, which honors a Polish nobleman who fought—and died—for the United States during the Revolutionary War, follow the locals "into the city," as outer borough residents say, for the 80-plus-years-strong main

event. Over in Manhattan you'll see dancers make their way along Fifth Avenue while doing some of Poland's five national dances—from the *mazur,* a sprightly dance, to the group dance (listen for the clicking of their heels) of the *krakowiak.* But back in Greenpoint, where Old World Polish Pulaski Day bumps up against all things hip, expect twists on the theme, like borscht cook-offs with, of course, locally grown beets. *Rzeszowska Bakery, 948 Manhattan Ave., tel 718-383-8142; Old Poland Bakery & Restaurant, 190 Nassau Ave., Brooklyn, tel 718-349-7775; Northside Bakery, 190 Nassau Ave.,*

Brooklyn, tel 718-349-7775; General Casimir Pulaski Day Parade, pulaskiparade.com

Back to the Beginning
No single building details the connection between continents and the way their people shaped NYC quite as much as the Lower East Side's Tenement Museum. Guided tours of the apartment of a family of sweatshop workers and a German family's saloon make it clear that the promise of a new life in America has always come at a hefty price.

Taste the area's legacy with a stop at the 100-year-old Russ & Daughters for some appetizing, distinctly New

York City experience. "The Lower East Side holds a special place for all New York Jews," says the *New York Times'* Saltzstein. "Of course, it's wildly different now—filled with chic shops and a throbbing nightlife scene. But Russ & Daughters is an oasis from all that—a temple to smoked fish, the best in the city. And its new café, a few blocks away, captures those old-school charms wonderfully." *Tenement Museum, 97 Orchard St., tel 212-982-8420, buy tour tickets in advance through tenement.org; Russ & Daughters, 179 E. Houston St., russanddaughters .com*

Skewers of grilled meat delivered tableside at Brasilia Grill, Newark

NEWARK, NEW JERSEY
TASTE OF BRAZIL

Portuguese immigrants began pouring into Newark's Ironbound neighborhood in the early 20th century, paving the way for their Brazilian brethren. At the heart of the Lusophone legacy lies Ferry Street with its many Portuguese bakeries and Brazilian eateries.

JOINING IN: In June, catch a performance by folk dancers at the Dia de Portugal and dance the night away to soulful fado singing. For a dose of samba spirit, hit September's Carnival-style Brazilian Day Festival. "Brazil is a huge country, so the festival has national foods of all kinds: barbecue from the gauchos [cowboys] of the south, African- and Indian-influenced foods from the northeast, and a European mix from the southwest," says Leo Ferreira, journalist at *Brazilian Voice*.

WHAT TO EAT: Don't call yourself a carnivore until you've been to a Brazilian *churrascaria*, the heavyweight of all steakhouses. The best part about these buffet-style meat meccas is that you're not even expected to stand up to get the good stuff. Like any good *rodizio* (all-you-can-eat Brazilian eateries), waiters at Newark's Brasilia Grill deliver skewer after skewer of salty grilled meat, and

INSIGHT · Tony Turf or Surf

Lately Newark's Ironbound district has been shedding its Tony Soprano gruff in favor of a more cosmopolitan air. Take **Manu's Sushi Lounge,** which pegs itself as a Japanese-Portuguese-Brazilian fusion restaurant (not so far off what you might find in sushi-loving São Paulo). Carnivores will be happy to find Brazilian skewered beef *picanha* on the menu, and an extensive selection of raw fish will appease the sushi fiends. *90 Ferry St., Newark, tel 973-465-5600, manussushilounge.com*

slice them tableside to your heart's content. Whenever you're ready to wave the white flag of surrender, stick up the little sign on your table that reads "no more." If you don't, the meat will just keep coming.

■ *Essentials:* Dia de Portugal, portugaldaynewark.com; Brasilia Grill, 99 Monroe St., Newark, tel 973-589-8682, brasiliagrill.net

Lively folk dancing at Newark's Portuguese Festival

LITTLE LIMA

In the Peruvian enclave of Little Lima on Paterson's west side, it's easier to find fresh seafood seviche, yucca, and *lomo saltado* stir-fry than a Big Mac. The neighborhood abuts Little Italy and a diverse community of Puerto Ricans, Argentinians, and African Americans, a multicultural mix that echoes Lima's. Thanks to its history of textile and manufacturing jobs, Paterson has been enticing Peruvians from Lima's barrios since the 1950s. "Everything I can find in my country, I can find in Paterson," says New Jersey Peruvian immigrant Gisela Ochoa. "We feel like we are in Lima."

WHAT TO EAT: You may want to brush up on your Spanish before sampling one of Little Lima's dozens of locally owned restaurants. Modern Peruvian food incorporates a unique blend of ancient indigenous foods with European, African, and Asian influences. Jade Garden, a Chinese-influenced Peruvian *chifa* restaurant, serves dishes like *arroz chaufa* (fried rice) with *sopa wonton* (wonton soup). But for more traditional fare like *papa a la huancaina* (boiled potatoes in a cream sauce) and seviche (a seafood dish "cooked" in lime), head to fan favorite La Tia Delia. (See also page 35 for Peruvian rotisserie chicken recommendations in Paterson and elsewhere.)

IN THE KNOW: With some 30,000 Peruvian immigrants—the highest percentage in the United States for a

MORE · Peruvian Hubs

Pachamama Peruvian Arts, New York City: A collective of folklorists, instrument makers, dance instructors, and Andean musicians offer free after-school arts programs throughout the city. *pachamamaperuvianarts.org*

Kaypi Perú at the National Museum of the American Indian, Washington, D.C.: From pisco sour–making classes to movie screenings, this weeklong annual summer festival runs a Peruvian gamut of fun. For more information, go to Facebook and search "Kaypi Peru Festival." *nmai.si.edu*

Peruvian Canadian Cultural Association, Edmonton, Alberta: Edmonton's Peruvian families banded together to form Aculpeca. Dance lessons and performances showcase the history, traditions, arts, crafts, language, and culture of Peru. *aculpeca.com*

city its size—Paterson even has a branch of the Peruvian Consulate General downtown.

■ *Essentials:* Jade Garden, 927 Main St., tel 973-279-1333; La Tia Delia at 28 Market St., tel 973-523-4550

Respect for the Peruvian national anthem, Paterson

Spit-roasted
Peruvian chicken

PERUVIAN CHICKEN

Chow down on the best of the crisp and juicy South American import.

■ **Leña y Carbon**
Eschewing the modern gas-fired rotisserie, Paterson, New Jersey's Leña y Carbon, which translates to "firewood and charcoal," deploys both in its custom brick oven–producing chicken infused with a unique smoky taste.
359 Union Ave., Paterson, N.J., tel 973-653-9380, and 44 Market St., Passaic, N.J., tel 973-928-4144

■ **D'Carbon Pollos a la Brasa & Parrillas**
Residents rave about the crispy skin and moist, flavorful meat of the blackened *pollo a la brasa* served with zesty Peruvian fried rice at this Paterson neighborhood favorite. Dine in or take out at this cash-only chain.
587 River St., Paterson, N.J., tel 973-278-6505

■ **Sardi's**
Sardi's slow-cooked rotisserie chicken makes it Maryland's most popular Peruvian eatery. Point and choose from sides like fried yucca and Peruvian corn to accompany the plentiful portions.
10433 Baltimore Ave., Beltsville, Md., tel 301-595-3222, and 430 N. Frederick Ave., Gaithersburg, Md., tel 301-977-3222, sardis chicken.com

■ **El Pollo Rico**
Long lines are the norm at this Washington, D.C.–area, worth-the-wait, fast food–style joint. Regular clientele can't get enough of the consistent and tender chicken or the two complementary dipping sauces: a spicy crushed jalapeño spread and a mild mayonnaise. Plantains and empanadas round out a true feast best washed down with Inca Kola.
Multiple locations in the Washington, D.C., area, welovethischicken.com

■ **D'Candela**
D'Candela was the first to introduce many Chicagoans to *pollo a la brasa*, but "it's still the best," says Chicago-based food writer Mike Sula; its "chicken is particularly plump and juicy." This upscale restaurant caters to a largely Peruvian crowd and boasts an extensive menu, but rotisserie chicken—bathed overnight in a blend of 15 ingredients—is the star.
4053 N. Kedzie Ave., Chicago, Ill., tel 773-478-0819, dcandela.com

■ **San Fernando Peruvian Roasted Chicken**
Posters of Machu Picchu adorn these tiny establishments where golden brown skin and fall-from-the-bone chicken keep Seattleites coming back for more. Creamy cilantro and fiery orange habañero dipping sauces add an extra kick.
900 Rainier Ave., Seattle, Wash., and 20815 67th Ave. W., Lynnwood, Wash., tel 206-331-3763

■ **Pio Peruvian Rotisserie Chicken**
Don't be fooled by its strip mall setting in Calgary, Canada. Loyal customers tromp through the wintry snow to revisit this eatery's golden brown and succulent chicken. A passionate Peruvian family churns out their *pollo a la brasa* with love. "Mom's in the kitchen, I'm up front, my Dad helps with tables, and my brother works on the weekend," says manager Sandra Mora. "We import hard-to-find ingredients and grow our own black mint. The only thing you'll find bottled up in our kitchen is ketchup."
2929 Sunridge Way N.E., Unit 104, Calgary, Alta., tel 403-681-7378, pioperu .com

AROUND THE WORLD IN
PITTSBURGH

The Australian Nationality Room in Pittsburgh's Cathedral of Learning

From Baptist to Brews
It's Friday night in Pittsburgh and time for church. Not so fast. St. John the Baptist Church, a 20th-century house of worship for Pittsburgh's Irish and Scotch Catholic families, is now a bastion of beer. At Church Brew Works, plop down on refashioned pews to chow down on pierogies, a nod to the city's Polish heritage. Take a moment to study the original stained-glass windows that still bear the names of the families who commissioned them. "Generations of people who worshipped here and got married here are now coming back to show their grandchildren this place," says Patti Goyke, who has worked at the brewery for nearly two decades.

Church Brew Works, 3525 Liberty Ave., tel 412-688-8200, churchbrew.com

Global One-Stop
Explore 29 cultures in 29 rooms. Designed by architects from around the world, the Nationality Rooms at the University of Pittsburgh offer an efficient and eye-popping way to discover the amazing variety of immigrants drawn to the potato-bearing, steel-milling landscape of Allegheny County over the decades. Step into the English room and enter a 16th-century House of Commons. Go Byzantine in the Russian room, where needlepoint *vishivka* tapestries adorn the walls, while the blue, wedding cake–like columns in the Indian room evoke a courtyard

in the ancient city of Nalanda. In December, international holiday flare and ethnic edibles are added to the mix. *Nationality Rooms at the University of Pittsburgh, 4200 5th Ave., tel 412-624-6001, tour.pitt.edu/ tour/nationality-rooms or nationalityrooms.pitt.edu*

Italian From Scratch
Rounds of floppy dough are tossed in the air with a flick of a wrist before being topped and slipped into a sizzling, wood-fired brick oven for just 90 seconds. That's all it takes for a crispy, toothsome Neapolitan pizza at Mt. Lebanon's Il Pizzaiolo. The menu lovingly covers the full Italian, with antipasti and handmade pastas followed by *secondis* of *branzino* (sea bass) and

"People think cars and flowers are beautiful. I see a basement full of hanging sausages and think, 'Well, this is beautiful.' I remember as a kid when my non-Italian friends would come over and see sausages hanging in the basement. They'd be all weirded out. Now making your own sausages and wine is popular again, things Italians have been doing for hundreds of years. Last year we made 300 pounds of sausage for my son's communion. This kind of cooking is something we grew up with. My kids love it. If I don't keep the sausages locked up they'll be gone in a split second. I do my cheese shopping at my favorite place: Pennsylvania Macaroni Co. *(2010-2012 Pennsylvania Ave., pennmac .com)*. They've got imported prosciutto, and their cheese selection is just unbelievable."

JACK DE LEONIBUS
Editor of Ciao Pittsburgh *(ciaopittsburgh.com)*

veal Milanese. What isn't made from scratch is imported from Italy. In summer, dine alfresco on the patio, sipping *limoncello* liqueur among the lemon trees. *Il Pizzaiolo, 703 Washington Rd., Mt. Lebanon, and 8 Market Square, Mt. Lebanon, tel 412-344-4123, ilpizzaiolo .com*

Bavarian Brews and Bites

Hear that rumble? That would be a fleet of antique Porsches and Volkswagens revving their engines in the annual German Parade & Auto Display in the traditionally German-speaking neighborhood of Deutschtown. The event is also a rare opportunity for the public to dine at the members-only, Swiss heritage club Teutonia Männerchor, which hosts a post-parade, sausage-laden buffet. Throughout the year, simulate a Bavarian feast at German brewpub Max's Allegheny Tavern for savory schnitzel, buttery spaetzle, and steins of beer.

Want to stay in the neighborhood? Check into the 1848 Priory Hotel, once home to Benedictine monks and hub of Deutschtown's European immigrant community. *German Parade & Auto Display, a Sat. in Sept., deutschtown.org; Teutonia Männerchor, 857 Phineas St., tel 412-231-9141, pghmannerchor.com; Max's Allegheny Tavern, 537 Suismon St., tel 412-231-1899, maxsallegheny tavern.com; The Priory Hotel, 614 Pressley St., tel 866-377-4679 or 412-231-3338, thepriory.com*

Jewish Body and Soul Food

Once upon a time Murray Avenue and Forbes Street, the commercial arteries of Squirrel Hill, were chockablock with Jewish businesses. Though the neighborhood has diversified over the decades, Squirrel Hill still boasts a handful of kosher eateries. At Smallman Street Deli, shop for take-out options like smoked fish and thinly sliced salami, or chow down one of the city's best Reuben sandwiches. At new kid on the block, Nu, slurp away aches and pains with a bowl of "Jewish penicillin," otherwise known as chicken ball soup. *Smallman Street Deli, 1912 Murray Ave., tel 412-421-3354, smallmanstreetdeli.wix .com/smallmanstreetdeli; Nu Modern Jewish Deli, 1711 Murray Ave., tel 412-422-0220*

Sample beer and schnitzel at Max's Allegheny Tavern in Pittsburgh's Deutschtown.

Main Fountain
Garden at
Pennsylvania's
Longwood Gardens

LONGWOOD GARDENS, KENNETT SQUARE, PENNSYLVANIA
OLD WORLD GARDENS

Watch as a graceful *corps de* 750 fountains leaps and shoots glowing water straight into the air, dancing in sync to a sound track of classical music. As the music reaches a crescendo, a flurry of fireworks erupt in the sky, a spectacle designed to rival the splendid fountain shows at Versailles. Here at Longwood Gardens, the musical fountain shows light up the sky on evenings throughout summer.

IN THE KNOW: The gardens and the mansion evoke the highly manicured, sprawling estates of the Old World. Pierre S. du Pont, American entrepreneur and great-grandson of the DuPont company founder, developed the gardens with the care of a dedicated botanist and the flair of a globe-trotter, inspired greatly by his travels in Europe. "[The] fountains combine the ornamentation of Italian waterworks, the grandeur of French gardens, and the illuminated spectacle found in the world's fairs," says executive director Paul Redman.

WHAT TO SEE: Today over 1,000 acres of woodlands, meadows, and gardens invite visitors from around the world. Wander through the exquisite Italian Water Garden, designed to resemble Italy's Villa Gamberaia outside Florence with some 600 jets of water. Or weave your way around giant herbaceous rabbits in the seasonal topiary garden. In the bonsai room, admire the precision and scale of this miniature seasonal forest. In winter, the inspiration turns to the tropics, with the Orchid Extravaganza's colorful and exotic blooms from such far-flung places as New Guinea and Ecuador.

■ *Essentials:* 1001 Longwood Rd., Kennett Square, tel 610-388-1000, longwoodgardens.org

DIGGING DEEPER

Down the road from Longwood in Brandywine Valley, Pierre du Pont's cousin Alfred built the Louis XVI–style Nemours Mansion and Gardens. Tap your inner French aristocrat at the lavish spread, a gift to his second wife Alicia, including its formal parterre gardens. *nemoursmansion.org*

The Winterthur Museum's Fraktur Hall, Wilmington, Delaware

FOREIGN ROOMS IN AMERICA

Wander around a Venetian palazzo; whet your appetite in a medieval dining room.

■ **Winterthur**
Yet another du Pont manse turned museum, Winterthur in Wilmington, Delaware, is exceptional for its comprehensive survey of American antiques over 150 years. In the Fraktur Room, admire examples of German-influenced furniture, and take a peek at the pieces of fraktur, decorative documents used to commemorate life events such as births. "Many, many Pennsylvania German families had fraktur in their homes, although they didn't display them on the wall," says Lisa Minardi, assistant curator.
5105 Kennett Pike, Wilmington, Del., tel 302-888-4600, winterthur.org

■ **Peacock Room, Freer Gallery of Art**
The resplendent blue-and-gold Peacock Room has had many lives: from London dining room to private Detroit residence to Washington, D.C.'s Freer Gallery of Art, where it now harbors a bevy of Asian ceramics. Time your visit for the third Thursday of the month, when the shutters are opened and the Peacock Room spreads its proverbial wings.
1050 Independence Ave S.W., Washington, D.C., tel 202-633-1000, asia.si.edu

■ **The Ringling**
Venice meets Sarasota, Florida, in the mansion cum European palace by the water built by 1920s circus royalty John and Mable Ringling. As on Venice's Grand Canal, the view from the water is best, showcasing the "rich color of terra cotta with the intense blue sky and the shimmering of light on the glazed surfaces," says curator Ron McCarty.
5401 Bay Shore Rd., Sarasota, Fla., tel 941-359-5700, ringling.org/ca-dzan

■ **Hearst Castle**
Though this San Simeon, California, castle feels fit for a king, the private quarters of publishing tycoon William Randolph Hearst are just that: private. Compared with the rest of the house, Hearst's bedroom was modest in scale, though the decor was anything but. The 14th-century paneled ceiling came all the way from Spain. The Gothic library showcases Hearst's sizable collection of Greek amphora.
750 Hearst Castle Rd., San Simeon, Calif., tel 800-444-4445, hearstcastle.org

■ **The Naust, Danish Canadian National Museum**
Behold this vessel of pillage and plunder. Inside the Naust, a traditional Danish boathouse at the Danish Canadian National Museum, you'll find the replica Viking ship *Freydis Joanna.* "It was built the way they would have 1,000 years ago," says curator Faye Kjearsgaard. "No power tools. Just one great big huge oak tree."
Range Road 31, Dickson, Alta., tel 403-728-0019, danishcanadians.com

■ **Gubbio Studiolo, Metropolitan Museum of Art**
Cozy and Renaissance collide at the tiny Gubbio Studiolo, a room that was once in an Italian palace now tucked into New York City's massive Metropolitan Museum of Art. The 15th-century sanctuary delights with trompe l'oeil cabinets and intricately carved walls.
1000 5th Ave, New York, N.Y., tel 212-535-7710, metmuseum.org

AROUND THE WORLD IN
PHILADELPHIA

The Shofuso Japanese House and Garden, Fairmount Park, Philadelphia

My Neighborhood
UPPER DARBY

Everything Italian
Crusty breads, redolent cheeses, plump tomatoes—at the Italian Market you'll find every ingredient you need for a Mediterranean picnic. The alfresco market, open seven days a week, is the oldest in the United States, serving Philadelphia foodies since the 1880s. Today the market overflows with cured meats, hand-rolled pasta, fresh fish, and more. During May's Italian Market Festival, a marching band blazes the trail as roughly two dozen life-size statues of saints are rolled along Montrose Street. The procession makes a ceremonious pit stop on 9th Street for the Blessing of the Market before ending at St. Paul Catholic Church. *Italian Market, 919 S. 9th St., tel 215-278-2903,* *italianmarketphilly.org and italianmarketfestival.com*

Mellow Japanese Immersion
Built in Japan in the 1950s and brought to the United States for an exhibit, the Shofuso Japanese House is as authentic as they come. Study the elegant movements of classical Japanese dance or the history and etiquette of traditional tea ceremonies here in one of the many courses offered throughout the year. Wander its tranquil gardens and contemplate the meaning of life as you toss bits of bread to the gaping-mouthed koi fish below you. Over in Fairmount Park, celebrate the coming of spring at the Subaru Cherry Blossom Festival when the park bursts into a sea of cotton candy pinks. *Shofuso House, Horticultural Dr., tel 215-878-5097, japanesehouse.org; subarucherryblossom.org*

Latino Arts and Sounds
Graffiti is all grown up in Philadelphia's Puerto Rican and Latino community of Fairhill, where brilliantly hued murals splay across civic spaces. The best bet is to take a tour with the much lauded Mural Arts Programs to fully appreciate—and locate—the murals. Then pop into the third generation–run Centro Musical for live Latin music or pick up some reggaeton albums. *Mural Arts Program, tel 215-925-3633, muralarts.org/tour; Centro Musical, 464 W. Lehigh Ave., tel 215-425-7050*

Growing up, nobody in my family talked about our Irish heritage. When I asked my Aunt Grace about being Irish, she told me, "It doesn't matter. We're American." Had I not gone to Ireland and met my Irish relatives, I wouldn't think we had any Irish traditions at all. But then I realized every time we visited family, we'd go straight into the kitchen and have tea and cake. That's very Irish. Delaware County is called the 33rd county of Ireland, and there are lots of Irish people in Upper Darby, bordering West Philadelphia. At the Irish Coffee Shop here *(8443 W. Chester Pike)*, you'll hear conversations going on all around you in Irish. They serve a proper Irish breakfast with eggs, sausage, rashers (aka bacon), fried tomatoes, mushrooms, black sausage, baked beans, Irish soda bread, bangers, black and white puddings—the carnivore special!

DENISE FOLEY
Founder,
IrishPhiladelphia.com

Mummers Parade

More than 10,000 costumed mummers march proudly in Philly's annual Mummers Parade, Philly's own wacky brand of Carnival. This ancient and most festive tradition of ringing in the New Year has roots in the Old World, brought over by Swedish immigrants. Over the years, comic clubs were formed to lampoon local politicians and officials. Multiple 64-piece string bands, whose combined costumes cost in the tens of thousands, contribute the upbeat soundtrack to the festivities. The rest of the year, get a taste at the Mummers Museum, featuring costumes, oral histories, and live music in summer. *phillymummers.com; Mummers Museum, 1100 South 2nd St., 215-336-3050, mummersmuseum.com*

Comme les Français

A mob is forming and you need to decide which side you're on: Are you a cake-tossing French revolutionary or a cake-eating loyalist? Either way, gussying up is strongly encouraged during Bastille Day (July 14) at the Eastern State Penitentiary Historic Site. And not just any old cake. "Tastykake's butterscotch krimpets are a Philly favorite, and they're quite aerodynamic," says Nicole Fox of Eastern State Penitentiary. "People get here early to claim a spot in the Tastykake splash zone. They bring butterfly nets, bucket hats, and baskets to increase their odds." After the beheadings, storm the neighborhood of Fairmount for French wine and dinner specials in the name of *liberté, égalité, fraternité*. *Eastern State Penitentiary, 2124 Fairmount Ave., tel 215-236-5111, easternstate.org/bastille-day*

Laotian Street Party

From the outside you might take it for a themed restaurant, but the multicolored Lao Buddhist Temple in North Philly is actually the religious core of the city's Laotian population. During the New Year's Celebration (traditionally observed in mid-April by Laotians, Thais, and Cambodians), the temple bursts with fresh flowers and hums with prayers before flooding the streets for the parade of Nang Songkran, or the New Year Princesses. To ensure a prosperous year, the princesses escort the severed head of King Kabinlaphom, part of Laotian Buddhist lore. The parade devolves into a block party buoyed by live Laotian pop music and some seriously flavorful street eats, like fermented lemongrass sausage, and sour and spicy papaya salad. *Lao Buddhist Temple, 335 E. Chew Ave., tel 215-621-7133, parade on April 15 or 16*

Flamboyant costumes in Philadelphia's Mummers Parade

You Could Be In . . . PARIS

Philadelphia, Pennsylvania
The Barnes Foundation in Philadelphia has an extensive collection of works by French masters like Cézanne.

AROUND THE WORLD IN
BALTIMORE

Greek Independence Day Parade in Baltimore

Pierogies Plus
Despite the proliferation of standard-issue bars and seafood restaurants in gentrified Fell's Point, there's still some Polish left in the old neighborhood. Holy Rosary Church continues to offer Mass in Polish thrice weekly, and Polish delis have managed to fend off modern incursions. Eastern European beauties work the counter at Krakus Deli, a Polish general store where Polish is still the lingua franca. Try specialties like the house-smoked kielbasa or potato pierogies. For a sit-down meal, sidle up to a table at Ze Mean Bean Café for "Slavic Night" Thursdays and order a heaping plate of pierogies with a bowl of chunky borscht. For special Polish dill pickles

and "not the grocery store kind," Baltimore graphic designer Carla Tomaszewski recommends Sophia's Place, Polish Deli. "It's also a really nice lunch counter where you can have a sit-down meal served on Polish china." At the summer Polish Festival in Timonium, just north of the city, folk dancers in traditional garb twirl across the exhibition hall at the Maryland State Fairgrounds. Proceeds help fund the Christmas caroling when Polish songs fill the streets of Fell's Point every December 23.
Krakus Deli, 1737 Fleet St., tel 410-732-7533, krakusdelibaltimore .com; Ze Mean Bean Café, 1739 Fleet St., tel 410-675-5999, zemeanbean.com;

Sophia's Place, 1640 Aliceanna St., tel 410-342-6105, sophiaspolishdeli .com; Polish Festival, 2200 York Rd., Timonium, Md., pcamaryland.org

Going Greek
The drippings of rotisserie chicken and roasted lamb with lemony potatoes marinate the atmosphere at the Greek Folk Festival, a star on Baltimore's calendar of ethnic festivals. Pick up a few dance cues from the Hellenic Golden Coins, a folk troupe, and fuel up on succulent street food like gyros. Upstairs in the cultural center, warm the soul with dishes that your *yia-yia* (grandmother) might have made, like pastitsio, a pasta casserole, and moussaka,

I'm first-generation Greek but I grew up in Los Angeles so I actually married into Greektown. If you really want to feel how Greek Greektown is, you go to St. Nick's. My wife and I were married there 12 years ago. I was waiting in the church, and she was up the street getting ready at the house with her bridesmaids. Then the entire Greek community walked her down from the house with clarinet music. Businesses come and go here, but the two main staples are Acropolis and Ikaros Restaurants on opposing corners of Eastern Avenue. It's every immigrant's dream to move up from row houses to owning a house with a big yard and a picket fence. The Latinos today are the Greeks of yesterday and the Germans before that.

SAM RADDOPOULOS
St. Nicholas Greek Orthodox Church entertainment director

a baked eggplant dish. Learn to stuff your own grape leaves at a cooking demo led by volunteers from St. Nicholas Greek Orthodox Church. "People in this congregation really know how to cook Greek food," says Maria Salpeas, church secretary. St. Nicholas is the cornerstone of Baltimore's Greek community and the site of the blue-and-white-streaked Maryland Greek Independence Day Parade in March. Pop in for dinner at no-frills BYOB restaurant Samos for Greek *mezedes* (appetizers) like shrimp with grilled *halloumi* cheese and spanakopita (spinach pie) followed by main dishes of roasted lamb and grilled skewers. *Greek Folk Festival, greekfolkfestival.org; Samos, 600 Oldham St., tel 410-675-5292, samos restaurant.com*

BYOPasta

Pack some pasta and channel your inner Fellini at the Little Italy Open Air Film Festival on Friday evenings through July and August, where Italian-language films (with subtitles) and Italian-American classics (like *Moonstruck*) are screened on the outside wall of the popular Italian restaurant Ciao Bella. Many local restaurants offer take-out specials for the occasion, perfect for dining alfresco. For arguably the best edibles in the area seek out Trinacria, an Italian deli and gourmet grocery that has been in Baltimore for over a century. Find racks and racks of oils, vinegars, capers, and sun-dried tomatoes as well as hot-pressed paninis and mortadella-stuffed sandwiches. *Little Italy Open Air Film Festival, Friday evenings in July and Aug., little italymd.com; Trinacria, 406 N. Paca St., tel 410-685-7285, trinacria baltimore.com*

Rolling Oktoberfest

Ever wondered what it would be like to drink beers with 16 of your best friends all sharing the same bike? Charm City Pedal Mill offers just such an experience with its 16-person bicycles. Like the comical beer bikes of Germany's Oktoberfest parades, group biking is paired with group beer guzzling. Choose from private or public bike tours—private if you can field your own bike team, public if you want to make new friends—and booze cruise your way through Fell's Point beer halls. *Charm City Pedal Mill, tel 443-956-6455, charm citypedalmill.com*

Baltimore's Little Italy Open Air Film Festival

CHAPTER 2

SOUTH

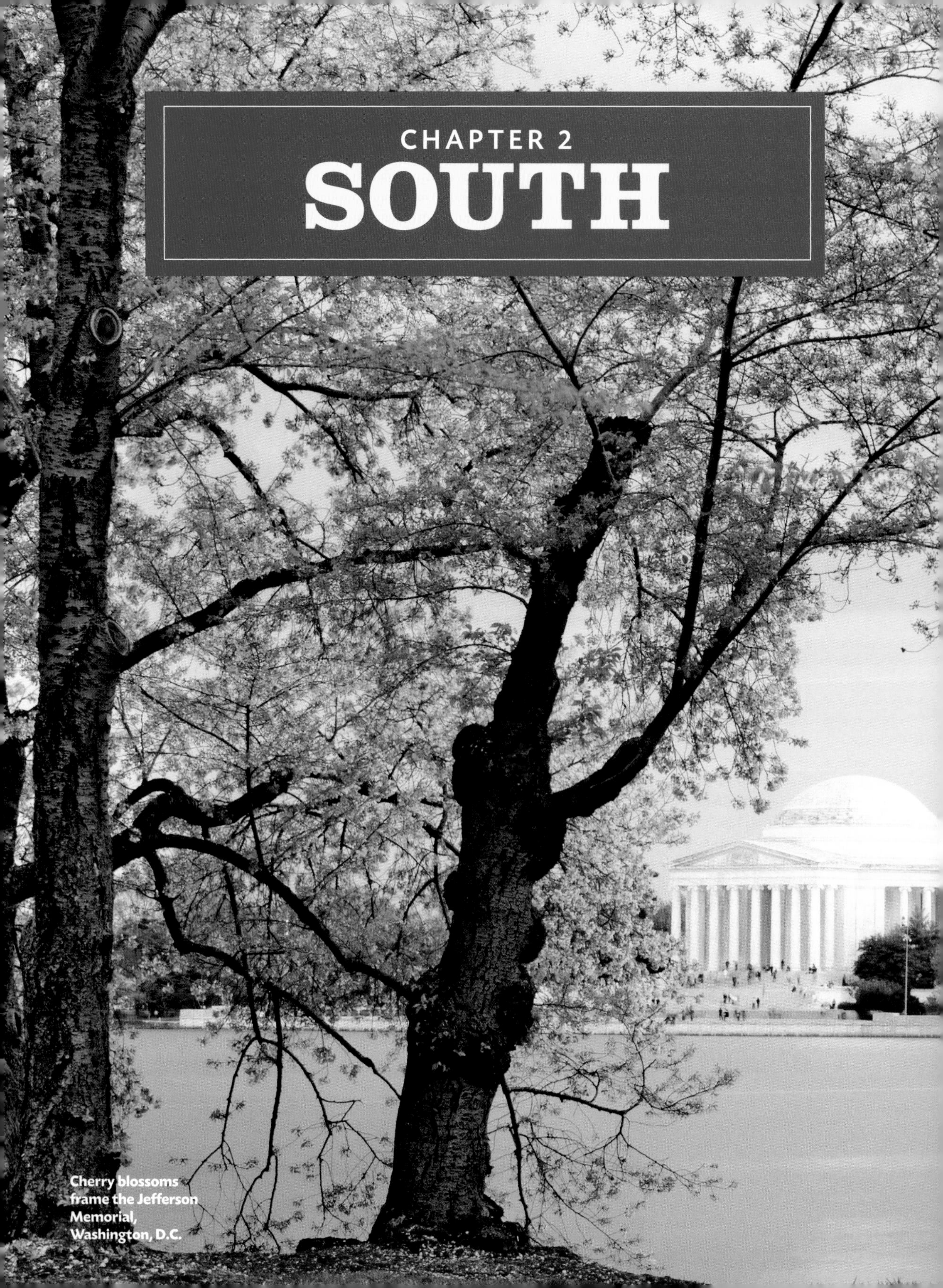

Cherry blossoms
frame the Jefferson
Memorial,
Washington, D.C.

WASHINGTON, D.C.

African Drum Circle in Meridian Hill Park

Piece of Italy

Entering A. Litteri in D.C.'s Noma neighborhood, you may very well think you've just entered a garlic-infused, wine- and pasta-packed grocery off the Piazza della Signoria in Florence. The 80-some-year-old deli and market, started three generations ago by brothers-in-law Mariano DeFrancisci and Antonio Litteri, specializes in house-made Italian sausages and massive vats of oils and vinegars. Saturdays are "old family" day, when Italians who once lived in the neighborhood make the pilgrimage from suburbia to stock up for the week on Old World goods. "It's hidden behind white-green-and-red doors," says Caroline Hickey, project manager for National Geographic Travel Books and a neighborhood resident. "You have to know it's there."
A. Litteri, 517-519 Morse St., N.E., tel 202-544-0183, alitteri.com

Ethiopian Fare

For an authentic bite of Ethiopian eats, head to Habesha Market and Carry-out. "It's the trendiest spot for both Ethiopians and non-Ethiopians to get fresh food and still make it back before their lunch hour expires," says Menna Demessie of the Society of Ethiopians Established in the Diaspora. The nation's capital is also a capital of Ethiopian eats, with what some say is the second largest population of Ethiopians outside Addis Ababa. For a full immersion, take the "Little Ethiopia" tour with DC Metro Food Tours. *Habesha Market and Carry-out, 1919 9th St. N.W., tel 202-232-1919, habeshamarket.com; DC Metro Food Tours, 809 Princess St., Alexandria, Va., tel 202-683-8847, dcmetrofoodtours.com*

Pho-tastic!

You won't hear or read much English at the Eden Center, a de facto meeting place for the mid-Atlantic's booming Vietnamese community in suburban Falls Church, Virginia. You'll think you've landed in a Saigon strip mall. Wander through nooks and crannies of the 100-plus Vietnamese restaurants, bakeries, and provision

I used to hate going [to Eden Center] as a kid. After church, all my friends would go to Dunkin' Donuts and McDonald's, and we'd go to Eden Center. I thought it was so weird. My father—a Vietnamese refugee who came to America in the 1970s—would hold court there all afternoon, sipping *café sua da,* iced coffee with condensed milk. But as an adult, I've come to appreciate the ethnic enclave. Now, it's my go-to place for comfort foods—bubble tea, pho, *bánh mì* (baguette). I go two or three times a week! My father? He is still there every Sunday. He's like the don of the place. He knows everybody. Dad finds all the hidden spots, and then I photograph the menus (often in Vietnamese) and tell my Yelpers "Papa V's Favorites."

KIMBERLY VAN SANTOS
Yelp's community manager

The dragon, an
arresting feature
of D.C.'s Chinese
New Year Parade

Kite flying at the annual April festival

stores, stopping by Hai Ky Mi Gia for egg noodle soup with duck, or Huong Viet for *bun thit nuong* (grilled meat on noodles). Fiery lion dances course through the center during the annual Tet and Moon Festivals, while the annual memorial for Vietnamese American Freedom Fighters Day honors Virginia's uniformed veterans in a stately ceremony. *Eden Center, 6751 Wilson Blvd., Falls Church, Va., tel 703-204-4600, edencenter.com*

From Russia With Love
Step inside Russian restaurant Mari Vanna and enter a dollhouse curated by your dear, sweet babushka, replete with floral sofas, nesting dolls, and lace doilies. Slavic dishes like borscht and *pelmeni* (dumplings)

are washed down with house-infused vodka at this St. Petersburg-Muscovite chainlet. It's said to be the favorite hangout of Capitals Russian hockey star Alexander Ovechkin, who orders the borscht. "It feels like home," he told the *Washington Post*. "It feels like Russia." *1141 Connecticut Ave. N.W., tel 202-783-7777, marivanna.ru/washington*

Block Party
A man hand-pulls noodles in the window of tiny Chinatown Express, just steps from the colorful Friendship Arch, signaling that although D.C.'s Chinatown may not be the largest around, it's tenaciously clinging on with its staunchly authentic businesses. Pop in to no-frills China Boy, where a loyal following of takeout diners flocks

for heaping bowls of beef *chow foon*. Got a craving for salted duck eggs? New Da Hsin Trading Co. has a neighborhood monopoly on Chinese snacks, souvenirs, and herbal remedies. Browse a mind-boggling selection of teas and Buddha statuettes. *Chinatown Express, 746 6th St. N.W., tel 202-638-0424, chinatownexpressdc.com; China Boy, 817 6th St. N.W., tel 202-371-1661; New Da Hsin Trading Co., 811 7th St. N.W., tel 202-789-4020*

Pretty in Pink
On a magical sunny day in March or April, when the cherry blossoms reach their peak, head to the Tidal Basin to join the throngs in the Japanese tradition of *hanami* ("viewing flowers"). Washington's sakura trees, a diplomatic

Little Ethiopia
A dozen restaurants on U and 9th Streets N.W.
BEST BET: Ethiopian spices and the *awaze tibs* (sautéed beef with sauce) at Habesha Market

Eden Center
120 Vietnamese shops at Eden Center in Falls Church, Va.
BEST BET: Reveling in "Tet" Lunar New Year

Chinatown
Twenty Chinese and other Asian restaurants on H and I Streets, between 5th and 8th Streets N.W.
BEST BET: Dragon dances and fire-crackers during the annual Chinese New Year Parade

Koreantown
Korean shops along Little River Turnpike, Annandale, Va.
BEST BET: Korus Fest at Bull Run Regional Park for K-pop karaoke

Salvadorean Enclave
Restaurants and street vendors around Mount Pleasant and Columbia Heights
BEST BET: Pork-filled *pupusa* tortillas at Gloria's Restaurant in Columbia Heights

gift from Japan to the people of the United States, are celebrated in a monthlong National Cherry Blossom Festival. Events include a kite festival, live traditional and J-pop performances, and a Rokkaku Battle, where enthusiasts fly special hexagonal Japanese fighter kites. *nationalcherry blossomfestival.org*

Francophile Fest
The Hillwood Estate, Museum and Gardens transform into an 18th-century French court for Bastille Day, France's national holiday. Actors in frilly period costumes prance around the manicured French parterre gardens while white-faced mimes delight crowds with their exaggerated gesticulations. Did you spot that Marie Antoinette look-alike with her beehive coiffure? She might just show you how to apply the most seductive *mouche*, or beauty mark. Inside the mansion, explore the astonishing collection of Fabergé eggs and antiques—including two commodes by Louis XVI's cabinetmaker—all collected by cereal heiress Marjorie Merriweather Post, founder of the estate. *Hillwood Estate, Museum and Gardens, 4155 Linnean Ave. N.W., tel 202-686-8500, hillwoodmuseum.org*

Globe-Trot
One minute you're ducking the high kicks of a Brazilian capoeira master, the next you're smacking your lips at the bitter saltiness of Australian Vegemite (either you'll love it or you'll hate it), then you're cleansing your palette with a juicy glass of Argentinian Malbec. Let your eyes, ears, and nose lead you around the world during Passport DC, an annual event when the capital's myriad embassies fling open their doors to visitors and offer a glimpse into each culture. Stroll down Embassy Row and take in the distinctive architecture of each diplomatic mansion. Inside you'll find everything from Indonesian dancers to Ethiopian coffee. *Embassy Days takes place over two Saturdays in May and is part of the monthlong Passport DC, culturaltourismdc.org*

Walking Map *Embassy Row*

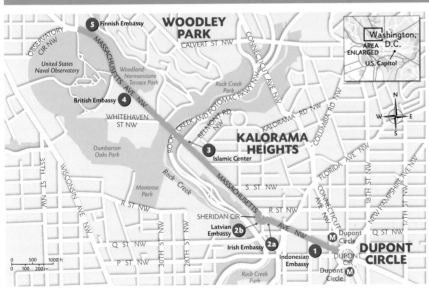

3 | After the circle, to the right, stands the **Islamic Center,** a practicing mosque and historic building open to the public (*2551 Massachusetts Ave., tel 202-332-8343, theislamiccenter.com*).

4 | Continue across the Massachusetts Avenue Bridge over Rock Creek Park; to the left is the brick **British Embassy** with a statue of Winston Churchill outside the gate (*3100 Massachusetts Ave.*).

5 | Follow Massachusetts Ave. around the Naval Observatory to the modern, glass, LEED-certified **Finnish Embassy** (*3301 Massachusetts Ave., tel 202-298-5800, public tours once a month, finland.org*).

The capital city's so-called "Embassy Row" offers a unique chance to tour the globe in just a few blocks.

1 | Walk west, up Massachusetts Ave. from Dupont Circle, and the Dupont Circle Metro stop. On the left is the **Indonesian Embassy,** formerly the Walsh Mansion (*2020 Massachusetts Ave., tel 202-775-5200, weekday tours, embassyof indonesia.org/wordpress*).

2 | Follow Massachusetts Ave. around Sheridan Circle past the stone, French-influenced **Irish Embassy,** and the Spanish mission-style **Latvian Embassy** (*2234 Massachusetts Ave.; 2306 Massachusetts Ave.*).

Not for the squeamish: Garra rufa fish perform this pedicure.

GLOBAL BEAUTY SECRETS

Revel—or recoil—from these exotic and sometimes strange beauty treatment imports.

■ **Doctor Fish**
This is not for the faint—or the ticklish—of feet. At doctor fish spas, schools of tiny carp nibble the dead cells right off your toes, leaving smooth skin in their itty-bitty wake. The piscine treatment from Turkey and Asia has spread to a handful of U.S. states. Yvonne's Day Spa in Alexandria, Virginia, claims it was the first.
Yvonne's Day Spa, 8643 Richmond Highway, Alexandria, Va., tel 703-799-3708, yvonnesalon.com; Doctor Fish spas around the U.S.: doctorfishmassage.com/location

■ **Geisha Facial**
Sit back, relax, and let the fecal matter of Japanese bush warblers seep into your pores. *Uguisu no fun,* or the "Geisha Facial," uses a mask of bird droppings

to soften and brighten skin. For trend writer Alix Strauss, one Geisha Facial at New York's Shizuka Day Spa was enough. "My skin did feel brighter and softer but this definitely seemed like more of a unique experience . . . like a beautification rite of passage."
Shizuka New York Day Spa, 7 W. 51st St., New York, N.Y., tel 212-644-7400, shizukany.com

■ **Eyebrow Threading**
Believed to have originated in India thousands of years ago, threading uses rolled strands of cotton to pluck and shape eyebrows. The trend is catching on in North America: In the past decade, the threading powerhouse S.H.A.P.E.S. Brow Bar has grown from a single kiosk in a Chicago mall to a nationwide franchise of more than 65 salons.

S.H.A.P.E.S. Brow Bar, multiple locations, shapesbrowbar.com

■ **Henna Body Art**
Intricate, rust-colored tattoos have long graced the limbs of brides in the Middle East and South Asia. The characteristic ruddy dye from the henna plant is temporarily tattooed onto feet, hands, and bellies, a practice known as *mehndi.* Today, henna artists can be found in nearly every major North American city. Find one near you through Henna Heals, a Toronto-based organization that lists reputable artists working with all-natural ingredients. The organization also helps pair cancer patients with artists who create henna crowns.
Henna Heals, 888 Dupont St., Unit #308, Toronto, Ont., hennaheals.ca

■ **Speleotherapy**
Inhale deeply and let your lungs fill with restorative, salty air. If a ham can be cured in a salt shed, than a person can be cured in a salt cave, right? At Chicago's Galos Salt-Iodine Caves visitors recline for 45-minute intervals in the mineral-rich microclimate, said to improve lung function. Customer Janet Wright, a Chicago-based psychic, concurs. She takes the plunge with her husband "for the relaxation, like a mini, mini vacation that's very cheap," she says. The wonders of "speleotherapy"—curing in caves—were first touted in 1843 by a Polish physician (who noted that salt miners had unusually low rates of respiratory disease).
Galos Caves, 6501 W. Irving Park Rd., Chicago, Ill., tel 773-283-7701, galoscaves.com

VIRGINIA PIEDMONT AND MARYLAND
ENGLISH-STYLE RACING

On a warm spring day in the Virginia countryside, genteel ladies and gents don Barbour jackets, oversize hats, and herringbone flat caps to sip bourbon, or perhaps champagne, and watch sleek stallions tear across a grassy field. Indeed, with its rolling green hills punctuated by ancient stone walls, the Virginia—and Maryland—countryside is a natural fit for English-style horse racing.

WHAT TO SEE: The races come in all shapes and sizes: From a backyard point-to-point like the fall and spring races at Ben Venue Farm in Rappahannock County, to the $75,000-purse Maryland Hunt Cup steeplechase in Worthington Valley. Winners of the latter automatically qualify to compete in the English Grand National in Liverpool.

For a more traditional take, seek out smaller races like those in Middleburg or Montpelier, Virginia.

IN THE KNOW: Like the champagne-fueled car "boot" picnics of English so-called point-to-points, tailgating at American races often involves lavish spreads of charcuterie, cheeses, and cocktails served from the trunk of an SUV. For some, the tailgating is the raison d'être, particularly at races with larger purses like the Virginia Gold Cup. "You know how the saying goes," says Will O'Keefe, racing vice president of the Virginia Steeplechase Association and

INSIGHT · What's the "Point"?

The story goes that steeplechase racing officially began in the 1750s in Ireland when two foxhunters started bragging about whose horse was faster. To settle the dispute, they picked two churches as landmarks and raced from steeple to steeple, from "point to point." Over the ensuing decades, the sport gained traction in Britain and eventually made its way to America. According to some accounts, the earliest recorded point-to-point in the New World was held in 1834 in Washington, D.C.

longtime race announcer. "Who invited these horses to our cocktail party?"

■ *Essentials:* Middleburg Fall/Spring Races, Glenwood Park, Middleburg, Va., tel 540-687-6545, middleburgspring races.com; Old Dominion Races at Ben Venue, 38 Ben Venue Rd. (Rte. 729), Flint Hill, Va., tel 540-364-7457; general steeplechase info, tel 540-439-3820, centralentry office.com

The Middleburg Spring Races in Virginia

You Could Be In . . . INDIA

Wheeling, West Virginia
The ornate Palace of Gold near Wheeling recalls the Mogul palaces of Rajasthan.

HELVETIA, WEST VIRGINIA
SWISS APPALACHIA

Fleeing drought in their homeland in the 1860s, Swiss immigrants eventually landed in West Virginia, whose mountains, fir forests, and burbling streams reminded them of home. They called their settlement Helvetia, Latin for Switzerland. Though their Swiss-German language has mostly fallen by the wayside, the community—less than 60 people total—is still characterized by a Swiss-laced resourcefulness and optimism.

WHERE TO EAT: The Swiss touch is visible throughout the tiny village: flowers decorating the entrance bridge, shops such as the Honey Haus (serving tea and selling locally produced honey, jams, and jellies), the Kultur Haus (housing a mask museum, general store, and post office), and the Hutte Swiss Restaurant, with a Sunday *Berner Platte*, a Swiss-style buffet that leaves little to be desired, including bratwurst and sauerkraut, house-made applesauce and sausages, and apple butter and cheeses.

JOINING IN: For a chance to chat up the locals—and beat the snow—time your visit for a square dance (first Saturday of every month), where folk musicians keep time for waltzes and old country polkas. The dances are especially lively during the Helvetia Fair, a homey, heritage fête with

INSIGHT · Short but Sweet

Fasnacht, a Swiss version of Carnival, lives on in Helvetia. It centers around a parade of revelers in handcrafted masks. "It's a short parade; if you blink you'll miss it," says postmaster Heidi Arnett. Nevertheless, the best maskmakers are rewarded with a mini Swiss flag, and at the end of the night, Old Man Winter is set ablaze. Check out the masks year-round at the Kultur Haus.

lots of *fahnenschwingen*, Swiss flag-waving. Listen for the *yodel-ay-hee-hoos*, the triumphant blaring of alpenhorns, and the jingle of Bernese mountain dogs pulling little carts in the "Alpine" parade.

■ *Essentials:* Honey Haus, helvetiawv.com; Kultur Haus, kulturhaus.helvetiawv.com; Hutte Swiss Restaurant, 1 Main St., tel 304-924-6435; Helvetia Fair, helvetiawv.com

Old Man Winter gets a Swiss send-off at Helvetia's Fasnacht.

"[The Fasnacht festival is] a madhouse as far as sitting down and talking to people." —POSTMASTER HEIDI ARNETT

Alpenhorns at the
Swiss National Day
celebration in Helvetia

Hauck's Handy Store, site of the annual Dainty Contest, Louisville

LOUISVILLE, KENTUCKY
GERMANTOWN

It looks like much ado about not much. But crowds line up along the barriers anyway, so you look closer at the action. A player positions himself behind the chalk line etched across the street. He has three chances to whack a little wooden peg from the ground with his stick to send it catapulting down the street. The farthest flung peg wins. Welcome to a hard-core game of Old World dainty, the pride of Kentucky's Germantown.

A BIT OF HISTORY: It's always been a simple game, played by children in the streets back in Germany and brought by immigrants to Kentucky in the 19th century. Over the decades the sport became little more than a nostalgic memory of a simpler time with simpler tastes. That longing for the past spurred two friends and Germantown residents to research and revive the lost art of dainty.

JOINING IN: Today the tongue-in-cheek Schnitzelburg World Dainty Championship is the undisputed highlight of the summer, as spectators and competitors flock to the stoop of Hauck's Handy Store, a historic landmark still operated by the original owner and Dainty Championship co-founder George Hauck. The simple act of whacking a peg is a source of great pride for the community.

Though the name *Germantown* remains, only a few businesses are still around that reflect the town's heritage. Luckily, Eiderdown Restaurant on Goss Avenue dishes up a menu billed as "European-inspired Southern" with a nod to Bavaria in its beer cheese, spaetzle, and extensive draft beer list.

■ *Essentials:* World Dainty Championship, at Hauck's Handy Store, 1000 Goss Ave., tel 502-637-9282, last Mon. in July; Eiderdown Restaurant, 983 Goss Ave., tel 502-290-2390

DIGGING DEEPER

There's only one stipulation to compete in the Dainty: You have to be of age. "George Hauck told me although it's a child's street game, he wanted 'children' ages 45 and older to be able to participate," says Lisa Pisterman, local historian and author.

SCOTTISH HIGHLAND GAMES

On a warm June day, the noble rumble of bagpipes fills the air as tartan-clad men and women showcase their strength and aptitude at the Highland Games. No, you're not in Scotland; this is Glasgow, a small town in rural, southern Kentucky. Named for its Scottish settlers, this Appalachian village breathes Smoky Mountain air and Celtic heritage.

JOINING IN: The games, which began here in the mid-1980s, now attract some 20,000 people for a weekend of good clean competition and merrymaking. The festivities kick off with a jig during the Friday night ceilidh, or Scottish folk concert. The pinnacle of the physical tests is undoubtedly the caber toss, when muscular men compete to lift a tall bare tree trunk, much like a telephone pole, shuffle forward with it, and then hurl it into the air so it flies end over end. Longtime Glasgow resident Cassandra Gray fondly recalls the early days of the games. "We loved introducing our children to this different cultural tradition, especially the Scottish dancers," she says. "So beautiful! The bagpipers made such an impression on our daughter [that] she had a bagpiper at her wedding." Everyone is welcome to the Tartan Ball, where the dress is black tie—tuxedo or formal highland dress for men, and gown with tartan sash over left shoulder with a brooch for women.

MORE · Scottish Festivals

St. Andrew's Society of Detroit Highland Games: Claims to be the oldest *continuous* games in North America. The regalia of the fully festooned pipe and drum soloists and bands is spellbinding. *highlandgames.com*

Caledonian Highland Games, San Francisco, California: Throwing heavy objects as far or as high as possible basically sums up the competition; these games are billed as America's oldest. *thescottishgames.com*

Highland Games, Victoria, British Columbia: Tartans take over the coast-perched town of Victoria every May for its Highland Games, running for over 150 years. The Scottish fun includes a whisky tasting school with a variety of Scotch single malts. You can bet it's popular. *victoriahighlandgames.com*

■ *Essentials:* glasgowhighlandgames.com

Glasgow's Highland Games

KENTUCKY DOWN UNDER

Hop right this way! At the Kentucky Down Under (KDU) Adventure Zoo, snuggle with velvety-furred, hand-raised joeys and go eye to eye with six-foot-long woma pythons. "Kids learn that not all snakes are bad, that they serve a purpose in nature," says local realtor Brian Dale. Have a laugh with a cackling kookaburra, the so-called "Bushman's alarm clock" and member of the kingfisher family. In the aviaries, stand still as rainbow lorikeets swoop down to roost on your head and shoulders and sip from the cup of nectar you're holding. Don't be offended if they leave a little "souvenir" behind.

WHAT TO SEE: The park also hosts demonstrations in various aspects of Australian life, like sheep shearing—the goal being to shear the wool in one unbroken pelt—and didgeridoo playing. Kids get to learn fun facts about dingoes through interaction with hand-raised ones: They can't bark, only howl. Each year, one baby kangaroo is selected to be hand-raised for outreach programs with kids, who delight in watching the joey take its first hops. You'll see kangaroos along the "Outback Walkabout" and it will be obvious which are the most curious critters. Watch your back pocket lest a kangaroo purloin your car

INSIGHT · A Spelunking Zoo?

The original attraction was Mammoth Onyx Cave, filled with the usual suspects of stalactites, stalagmites, and cave draperies. When Bill and Judy Austin recently took over, they wanted to set it apart from other caves in the region. Their vision: Surround it with creatures from Judy's native Australia. The new name was a natural. "With Judy being from 'Down Under' and the caves actually *being* down under, the name was a double entendre," says Dale. *Aha!*

keys! The park has begun to branch out to other species, including Shire draft horses, the world's largest breed, and stubby-legged miniature ponies, which make for an amusing sight when they pal around together.

■ *Essentials:* Kentucky Down Under, 700 L and N Turnpike Rd., Horse Cave, Ky., tel 270-786-1010, kdu.com

Friendly Australian lorikeet parrots at Kentucky Down Under

"When you handle a kangaroo [you] appreciate the animal's personality." —HARVEY DOUGHERTY OF KENTUCKY DOWN UNDER ADVENTURE ZOO

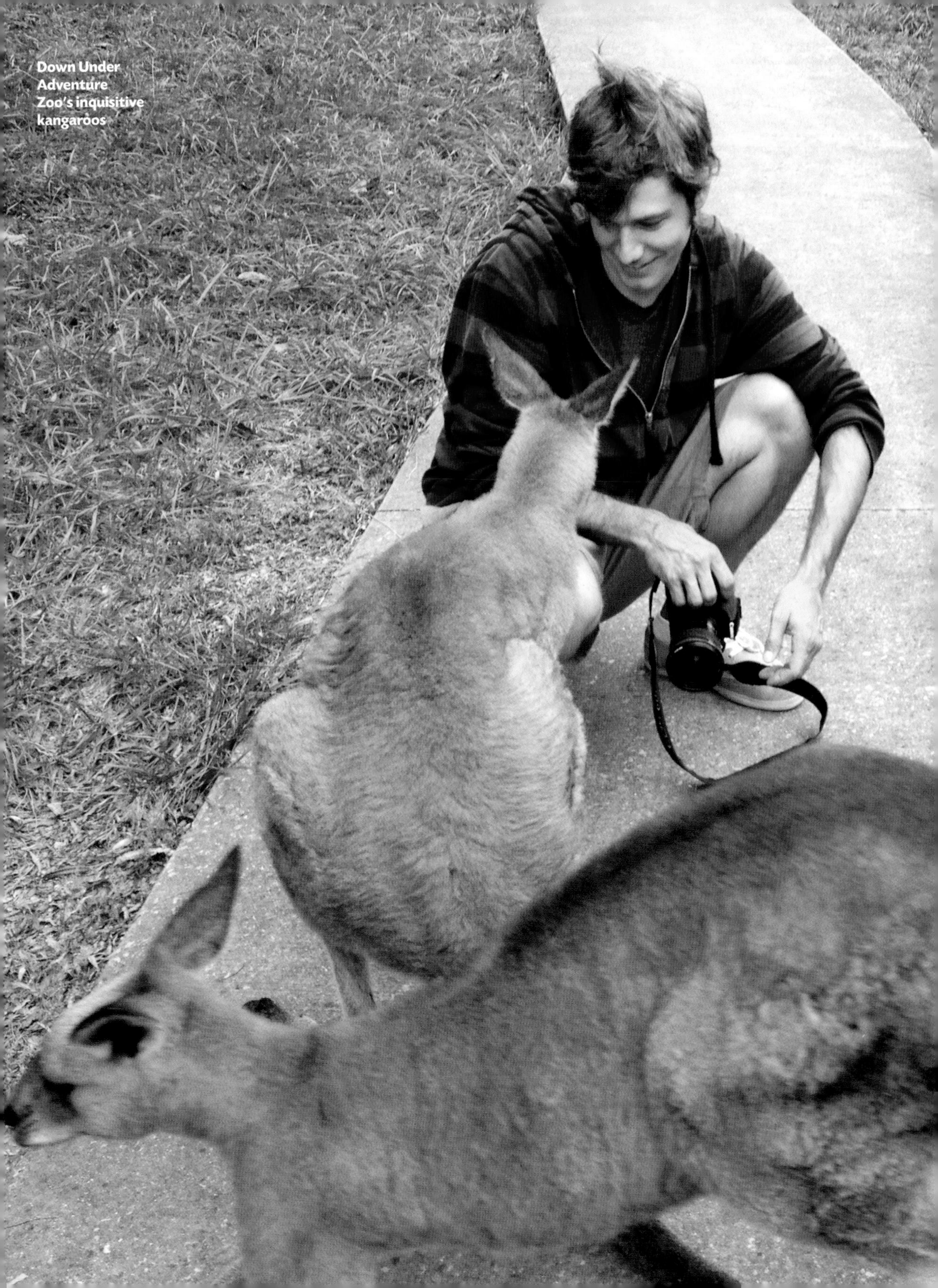
Down Under Adventure Zoo's inquisitive kangaroos

You Could Be In . . . FRANCE

Asheville, North Carolina
The Loire Valley seems near at hand at the sprawling, château-style Biltmore Estate in Asheville.

Fresh artisan breads at La Farm Bakery, Cary, North Carolina

FRENCH CAFÉS AND BAKERIES

Find your bliss at these destination pâtisseries.

■ **La Farm Bakery**
Centuries-old French techniques rule at La Farm Bakery in Cary, North Carolina, where chef-owner Lionel Vatinet hails from La Rochelle, France. Sourdough *boule* bread is the house specialty, which, like all their breads, is made with time-tested traditional ingredients, none of that bleached, bromated flour nonsense.
4248 N.W. Cary Pkwy., Cary, N.C., tel 919-657-0657, lafarmbakery.com

■ **Maison Villatte**
French chef Boris Villatte whips up flakey, buttery *pain au chocolat* in his Falmouth, Massachusetts, Maison Villatte that is among the culprits to blame for the lines on weekends. Maison Villatte's seasonal fruit tarts are not to be missed.
267 Main St., Falmouth, Mass., tel 774-255-1855

■ **Bien Cuit**
You've never seen bread this pretty in your life. The baguettes at Bien Cuit in Brooklyn, New York, are so photogenic that they landed on the cover of *Bon Appétit*'s "Best Baguettes in America" issue. You cannot go wrong with the French staples here, but be sure to sample the signature *miche* bread, fermented for a whopping 68 hours. You won't be disappointed.
120 Smith St., Brooklyn, N.Y., tel 718-852-0200, bien cuit.com

■ **Ken's Artisan**
Giant boules of traditional fresh *levain* bread give the semi-industrial decor of Ken's Artisan in Portland, Oregon, a touch of French rusticity. The open kitchen allows customers in line to watch the next day's buttery croissants being rolled out and the bread

dough being kneaded. In January, pick up a *gâteau des rois,* France's traditional cake for the Epiphany. "I can *ooh* and *ahh* and say it's better than Paris, but it really is!" says Lindsey Cressman, who fondly remembers working at Ken's a decade ago.
338 N.W. 21st Ave., Portland, Ore., tel 503-248-2202, kensartisan.com

■ **L'Amour du Pain**
The *saucisson* brioche at L'Amour du Pain in Boucherville, Quebec, may look like a typical loaf—that is until you slice inside and find a sausage has been baked into it. Sample myriad traditional *viennoiserie*—pastries made with the croissant-like French dough. Word to the wise: L'Amour du Pain is one of a slew of Québécois bakeries that participate in the annual Fête du Croissant, offering croissants for a

(Canadian) dollar a pop.
393 rue Samuel de Champlain, Boucherville, Que., tel 450-655-6611, lamour dupain.com

■ **Maison Christian Faure**
If the elegant curls of chocolate that coif the éclairs at Maison Christian Faure in Montreal, Quebec, seem like the work of an artiste, you're not far off the mark. French pastry chef Christian Faure is a MOF (Meilleurs Ouvriers de France), an honor bestowed on the best of the best in French artisan trades. Mille-feuille and seasonal fruit tarts fill the glass cases in the parlor and boutique, while students learn to whip up picture-perfect *macarons* at the pastry school upstairs.
355 Place Royale, Montreal, Que., tel 514-508-6453, maisonchristian faure.ca

Sweetgrass baskets made from native bulrush at Charleston's City Market

NORTH/SOUTH CAROLINA AND GEORGIA
GULLAH AND GEECHEE CULTURE

Down in the brackish low country of the southern United States, a rich Creole culture known as Gullah in the Carolinas and Geechee in Georgia, is still thriving, intact thanks in large part to the geographic isolation of its barrier islands along with recent initiatives. In 2006, Congress formalized the importance of the region by designating the Gullah Geechee Cultural Heritage Corridor to recognize the rich culture and its importance in American history. The Gullah language blends English with strong undercurrents of the African languages spoken by slaves who were brought over to work on rice plantations. Linguists have noted strong ties between Gullah and languages of the rice-growing coasts of Sierra Leone.

WHERE TO EAT: Soulful dishes like "okra perlou," a rice stew seasoned with pork, have earned Mount Pleasant's Gullah Cuisine national acclaim. For a more down-home meal, order up a plate of crispy fried shrimp at Beaufort's bare-bones diner LT's Home Cooked Meals. "The food is good and LT is a character," says Bill Rauch, Beaufort's former mayor. "If you are looking to hear someone cuss in Gullah, LT is your man."

JOINING IN: At the annual Gullah Festival in Beaufort, South Carolina, listen to Gullah tales recounted by "Aunt Pearlie Sue," aka Anita Singleton-Prather, a Gullah advocate and entertainer, and peruse the wide selection of tightly handwoven sweetgrass baskets, a traditional Gullah craft akin to the *shukublay* baskets of Sierra Leone.

■ *Essentials:* Gullah Geechee Cultural Heritage Corridor, tel 843-818-4587, gullahgeecheecorridor.org; Gullah Cuisine, 1717 U.S. 17, Mt. Pleasant, S.C., tel 843-881-9076, gullahcuisine.net; LT's Home Cooked Meals, Sea Island Pkwy., Beaufort, S.C., tel 843-524-3122; Original Gullah Festival of South Carolina, one weekend in May (check website), theoriginalgullahfestival.org

DIGGING DEEPER

You may luck out and encounter plenty of Gullah speakers on your own—listen for expressions like "tek'e foot een 'e han," which means "to run or to leave quickly." Or you may want to try joining a reputable group like Charleston-based Gullah Tours for greater access. *gullahtours.com*

AFRICAN VILLAGE

Driving north from picturesque Beaufort, South Carolina, through the expanses of low country and driveways lined with grand, Spanish moss-draped oak trees, you'll stumble upon a sign that is likely to pique your interest: "African Village of Oyotunji. As Seen on TV." Once you reach the village, another placard greets you: "NOTICE: You are leaving the US. You are entering the Yoruba Kingdom." Not technically, of course. But philosophically, you've left the United States.

IN THE KNOW: Here the houses are low and thatched. Men in traditional African *fila* hats and women in colorful dresses of guinea brocade and billowing *gele* head wraps go about their daily life, adhering to West African Yoruba traditions. A smattering of families live or have houses at the Yoruba Kingdom of Oyotunji African Village, created in 1970 by an African-American priest called King Oba Efuantola Oseijeman Adelabu Adefunmi I. The village is part of an effort by the Detroit-born leader to foster African Yoruba culture in the United States.

JOINING IN: The best time to go is the end of May for the Egungun Festival, when priests and initiates invoke the spirits of their ancestors. Designated dancers masquerade through the village to the accompaniment of drums, their bodies and faces entirely covered in exquisitely

INSIGHT · Yoruba Mecca

Not surprisingly, the Yoruba village has been the subject of interest for theologians and scholars outside the community. "The whole culture of Yoruba is based on ancestral connections," says Eric "Omawale" Brown, who is currently undergoing initiation into the men's society. "The most interesting thing I've seen is that people of all faiths—Rastas, Jewish people, Muslims— they all come here looking for ancestral connections."

embroidered robes. Visitors are encouraged to shop at the Trader's Bazaar, "an authentic African market," where you'll find orisa bead jewelry and other handicrafts. For the full effect (and a chance to talk to the elders), stay a weekend in the village in its simple hostel-like accommodations, Ile Afrique.

■ *Essentials:* Oyotunji African Village, 56 Bryant Ln., Sheldon, S.C., tel 843-846-8900, weekday visitors and large groups should email info@oyotunji.org to book ahead, oyotunji.org

Honoring the god Shango in Oyotunji African Village

"At Oyotunji, you'll forget you're in the U.S. You'll believe you're in Africa." —OMO OBA OLANIYAN OLASOWO, RESIDENT OF OYOTUNJI

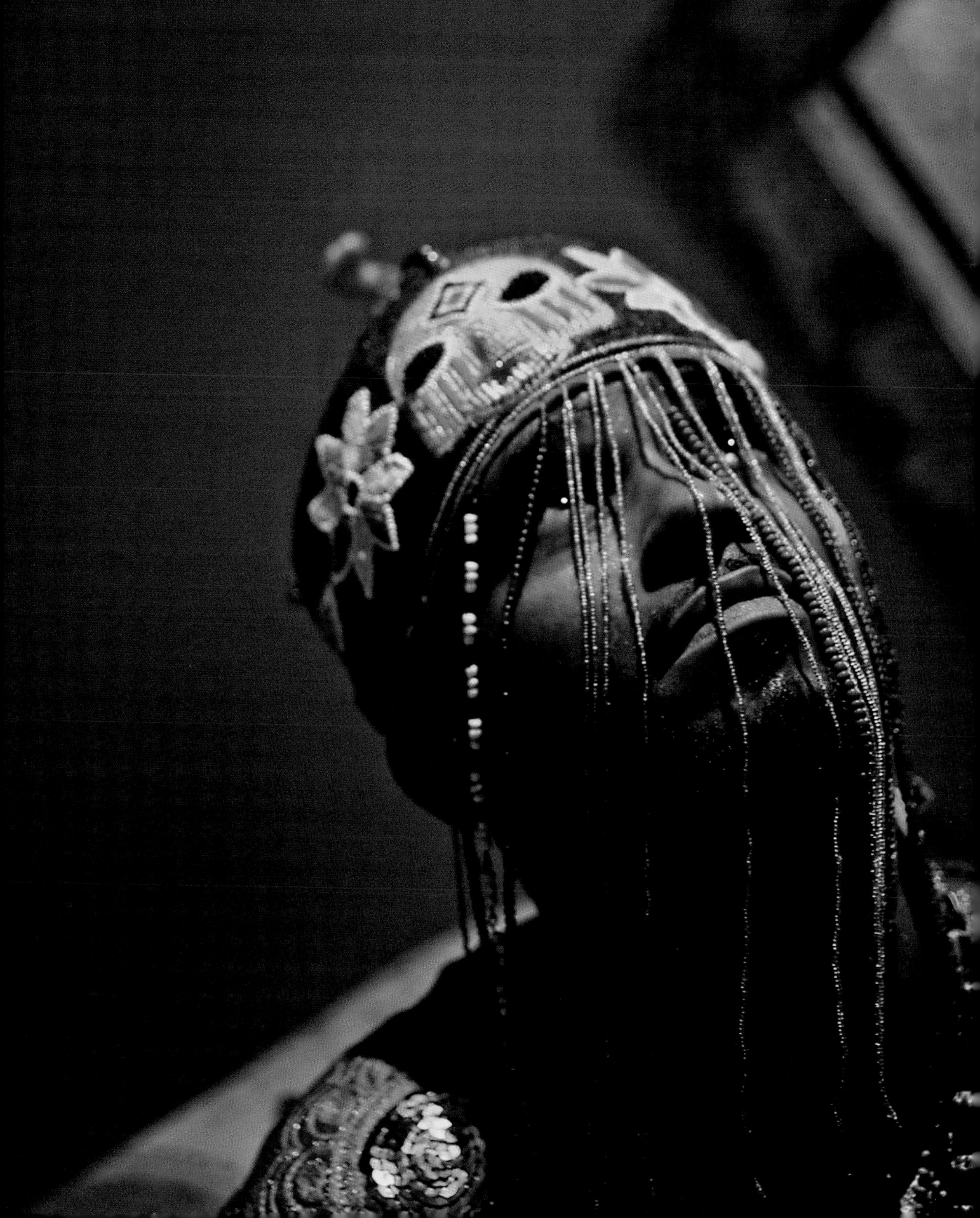

Ceremonial costume in Oyotunji African Village

ATLANTA

Plaza Fiesta in Atlanta sells Latino food, ingredients, and clothes.

Grand Indian

At 11:15 every morning amid the white stone walls of the palatial BAPS Shri Swaminarayan Mandir, men and women sit separately for a short *arti,* or ceremony of light, as Hindu monks and attendants ring bells, wave flames, and sing prayers in absolute devotion to the deities. The largest Hindu temple of its kind outside of India, the domed building was wrought in stone by hand: from the more than 34,000 pieces carved in India to the assembly of all the pieces by hundreds of workers and volunteers in the United States. From the outside, admire the delicate colors of the three types of stone: Turkish limestone, Italian marble, and Indian pink sandstone. *BAPS Shri Swaminarayan Mandir, tours and arti ceremonies available for visitors, 460 Rockbridge Rd. N.W., Lilburn, tel 678-906-2277, atlanta .baps.org*

Little Asia

"You've got strip malls with a Vietnamese pho place on one end, a Malaysian restaurant on the other, and a vegetarian Chinese place between them," says Grant Goggans, co-founder of Atlanta-based food blog "Marie, Let's Eat!", of Atlanta's Buford Highway. Cruise the continent on this 6-mile stretch of road, where the ethnic eateries are emblazoned with bold neon signage in a dozen different languages. Goggans recommends Man Chun Hong for something extra spicy. "We've been there three times and I've had the Shan City Chicken each time. It's amazing." He also suggests the Szechuan cumin-spiced lamb at Gu's Bistro, and the crispy Chong Ching Chicken at tucked-away Northern China Eatery. *Man Chun Hong Chinese Restaurant, 5953 Buford Hwy. N.E., tel 770-454-5640; Gu's Bistro, 5750 Buford Hwy. N.E., Doraville, Ga., tel 770-451-8118, gusbistro.com; Northern China Eatery, 5141 Buford Hwy N.E., tel 770-458-2282*

Shopping Mall Fiesta

On any given day, you

When I need Indian ingredients, I go to Decatur. There's a huge shopping complex there for all things Indian: travel agencies, gold jewelers, Bollywood video stores. All my spices come from Patel Brothers and Cherians, across the street from one another. Patel Brothers caters to northern Indian ingredients, and Cherians is a huge grocery store for southern Indian cooking. The flavors of the north and the south of India are so different. Even the pickles are different! Patel Brothers has a tiny pickle bar with green mango pickles, but in the south we have a lot of pickled fish like the kind at Cherians, especially during monsoon season. Next door there are at least ten Indian restaurants and a halal butcher, Georgia Halal Meat, which also happens to serve the best tandoori chicken.

ASHA GOMEZ
Chef and owner of Atlanta's Indian patisserie, Spice to Table

may run into a mariachi music–filled Latino festival (September's Mexican Independence Day, May's Cinco de Mayo) outside the abandoned shopping mall turned pulsating piece of Mexico that is Plaza Fiesta. If you can, bypass the bustle to hit the main attraction: a food court bursting with neon signs touting tortas, churros, tacos, and more. Try the black bean gorditas with *crema* sauce at Tropical Corner, or, for those with big appetites, share the torta Cubano at Puras Torta, a cholesterol-busting, Mexican-style pork-and-chorizo sandwich topped with an egg. "Plaza Fiesta can be a little overwhelming for the uninitiated but if you are friendly and humble and [make] even the worst attempts at the language, you'll do just fine," says Emily Allred, a local blogger who covers Buford Highway's diverse eateries.
Plaza Fiesta, 4166 Buford Hwy., tel 404-982-9138, plazafiesta.net

Taste of the Caribbean
Smoky flavors and steel band rhythms punctuate the scene of Atlanta's Caribbean Jerk Festival, an annual event held in Panthersville Stadium to celebrate the culture of the city's sizeable Jamaican and island population. The raison d'être is the jerk meats—there's even a Top Jerk Chef competition—but the live reggae and calypso bands give the festivities their irresistible beat. Don't leave without trying the jelly coconut, made from fermented coconut water, and a plateful or two of spicy jerk chicken and Jamaican oxtail. Inside, fierce games of dominoes unfold to a sound track of vehement *clak clak clak.*
Panthersville Stadium, 2817 Clifton Springs Rd., tel 678-760-8543, Decatur, Ga., atlantajerkfestival.com

Savory Slav
Come for the meats and the message at a simple, Eastern European outpost, Bosnian Neretva restaurant and market. At this modest refuge for former Yugoslavia immigrants, you'll find a model of a beloved bridge destroyed in the Bosnian War in 1993. The menu on the restaurant side of the market favors beef: sausages like *crevapcici* and *sudzukice* served alongside a slew of condiments like piquant, red *ajvar.*
Neretva Euro Grill & Market, 2359 Windy Hill Rd. S.E., Suite 200, Marietta, Ga., tel 770-226-0300

BAPS Shri Swaminarayan Mandir, a Hindu stone temple in Atlanta

A "conquistador" overlooks Matanzas Bay in St. Augustine's Colonial Quarter.

ST. AUGUSTINE, FLORIDA
SPANISH DAYS

It's August 28, 1565, Feast Day of St. Augustine. A gallant Spaniard by the name of Don Pedro Menéndez de Avilés has just arrived off the coast of Florida. He rows to shore with an entourage of 600 soldiers and settlers. Upon arriving, he calls the land St. Augustine. Since then, St. Augustine passed from Spanish to British rule before finally becoming the oldest permanent European settlement of the continental United States.

JOINING IN: Nothing oozes Spanish culture like a great bottle of Rioja, so plan your visit around the annual summer Spanish Wine Festival. The lowbrow highlight of the event is the Batalla de Vino, where "soldiers" in white shirts arm themselves with squirt guns of red wine and show no mercy! Or borrow a puffy shirt from a participant and catch a historical reenactment, when the Spanish sites come to life. Historian and reenactor Chad Light calls the annual restaging of the British-Spanish face-off, Drake's Raid, the "best 16th-century battle reenactment in the United States."

WHAT TO SEE: Start at Ponce de Leon's Fountain of Youth Archaeological Park that comprises the original settlement. The imposing scale of the 17th-century Spanish fort, Castillo de San Marcos, echoes the violence that plagued colonial St. Augustine. At the Colonial Quarter, take a shooting lesson from the musket-wielding reenactors who patrol the settlement.

■ *Essentials:* Spanish Wine Festival, spanishwinefestival.com; Drake's Raid, historic-florida-militia.org; Fountain of Youth Archaeological Park, 11 Magnolia Avenue St., fountainofyouthflorida.com; Castillo de San Marcos, 1 S. Castillo Dr., nps.gov/casa; Colonial Quarter, 33 St. George St., colonialquarter.com

DIGGING DEEPER

Think Plymouth Rock is the cradle of America? Think again. Juan Ponce de León landed in Florida in 1513. Don Pedro Menéndez de Avilés founded St. Augustine in 1565—42 years before Jamestown, 55 years before Plymouth Rock.

CUBAN QUARTER

Step deep into the heart of Cuba in Ybor City, once booming with cigar factories.

IN THE KNOW: Today, at least a dozen cigar shops still cluster around Seventh Avenue, Ybor City's main commercial hub. Though many of the redbrick factories now hold restaurants, discos, and other hot spots, King Corona Cigars gives a taste of bygone days with cases of hand-rolled smokes and traditional guayabera, short-sleeved, button-down shirts. As a tribute to its Cuban tobacconist roots, the city even hosts its own annual Ybor City Cigar Heritage Party, which features music, silent auctions, and, you guessed it, lots and lots of cigar puffing. For more historical context about the rise and fall of the cigar industry, visit the Ybor City Museum State Park, which includes a restored *casita* or typical cigar worker dwelling.

WHERE TO EAT: But what's Cuban culture without a Cuban sandwich? Ybor takes its *cubanos* seriously, so much so that it has been named the official sandwich of Tampa. Ybor Bunker grills up one of the city's best, made with sliced *capicola* for a spicy kick—grilled mounds of pork goodness are celebrated with religious

INSIGHT · Smokes and Mirrors

A Cuban cigar's creds lie in the box. To sniff out a fake from an authentic *Habanos*, start with the box. The stamps and markings will reveal its true provenance. Look on the top for two seals: one in the upper right corner, the other, a holographic Cuban warranty reissued in 2010, on the left. Then turn it over. The bottom is also a patchwork of Cuban-made protection: Look for the words "Habanos S.A.," "Hecho En Cuba," or "Totalmente a Mano" (handmade). A misspelling or typo screams counterfeit Cuban.

zeal at the annual Cuban Sandwich Festival in Ybor's Centennial Park.

■ *Essentials:* King Corona Cigars, 1523 E. 7th Ave., king coronacigars.com; Cigar Heritage Party, ybormuseum.org; Ybor City Museum State Park, 1818 9th Ave., ybormuseum.org; Ybor Bunker, 1907 19th St. N., tel 813-247-6964, yborbunker .com; Cuban Sandwich Festival, thecubansandwichfestival.com

Ybor City, Tampa's lively Cuban neighborhood

JAPANESE GARDENS

An oasis in a town of beachy bars and T-shirt huts since 1977, the carefully designed pebble paths and bridges of Delray Beach's Morikami Museum and Japanese Gardens invite quiet meditation. Advance through six thoughtfully arranged and historically distinct gardens inspired by the greatest horticulturists of the East. By the end of the tour, you'll have walked through 11 centuries of Japanese garden design, influenced by the politics and persuasions of each era. A visit to the gardens inspired local author Virginia Aronson to write a young readers' biography of George Morikami, the gardens' founder: "You steep in the history and culture and forget that you are in modern-day South Florida."

WHAT TO SEE: In the Shinden Garden from the ancient Heian period, zigzag bridges span pools of water, inviting an appreciation for nature. Earth meets "Sky" and "Heaven" in the Paradise Garden, designed for strolling and the contemplation of Amida Nyorai, the Buddha who presides over the Pure Land, or Paradise. Inspired by a famous temple in Kyoto, the Early Rock Garden incorporates cascades of rock to suggest a waterfall, much like the sweeping brushstrokes of Chinese landscape paintings. In the Karesansui Late Rock Garden, just a few carefully selected rocks take center stage on beds of raked gravel. This may be the most recognizable garden style in Morikami due to its popularity in Zen Buddhist temples. Finally, arrive at the Modern Romantic garden of the late 19th and early 20th centuries where the Western influence on Japanese garden

MORE · Japanese Oases

Missouri Botanical Garden, St. Louis, Missouri: Springtime is best at the Missouri Botanical Garden for its abundant Japanese cherry blossoms. *4344 Shaw Blvd., St. Louis, Mo., tel 314-577-5100, missouribotanicalgarden.org*

Japanese Garden, Portland, Oregon: The traditional gardens and bonsai exhibits are so impressive that they've inspired at least one copycat, Rockford, Illinois's Anderson Japanese Gardens. *611 S.W. Kingston Ave., Portland, Ore., tel 503-223-1321, japanesegarden.com*

Montreal Botanical Garden, Quebec: In the Chinese Garden of the Montreal Botanical Garden, study the art form of *penjing* (similar to Japanese bonsai). *4101 rue Sherbrooke Est, Montreal, Que., tel 514-872-1400, espace pourlavie.ca/en/botanical-garden*

design is apparent in the neat arrangements of plants.

After exploring the garden's sizeable collection of immaculate bonsais, you may wish to try it out for yourself. Morikami offers five-week beginner and intermediate courses in the art of bonsai.

■ *Essentials:* Morikami Museum and Japanese Gardens, 4000 Morikami Park Rd., Delray Beach, Fla., tel 561-495-0233, morikami.org

The tranquil Morikami Japanese Gardens, Delray Beach

Traditional Asian tea ceremony

TEA CEREMONIES

Indulge in the soothing yin-yang of a simple—and often quite elaborate—cup.

■ **Morikami Museum**
Lovely women draped in traditional kimonos float through the *Seishin-an* (teahouse) during the *sado*, the traditional Japanese tea ceremony at Delray, Florida's Morikami Museum. With harmony (*wa*), reverence (*kei*), purity (*sei*), and tranquillity (*jaku*), they prepare and pour the tea. The elaborate theater fosters a sense of patience, a virtue rewarded at the end of the ceremony with a sip of green tea and a sweet treat.
4000 Morikami Park Rd., Delray Beach, Fla., tel 561-495-0233, open third Sat. Oct.-June, morikami.org

■ **Dobra Tea**
At Dobra Tea in Asheville, North Carolina, pillows lay strewn around low tables and Turkish rugs, and the tea menu is the size of an encyclopedia. Craving something sweet? Ring the little bell on your table and order the Moroccan Tuareg. Your server will regale you with the tea culture of North Africa's Tuareg tribe as he pours your sweet mint tea the traditional way, in a long thin stream into little glasses. Ignited by a secret society of tea drinkers in communist Czechoslovakia, the Dobra Tea collective now claims six Bohemian outposts in the United States.
78 N. Lexington Ave., Asheville, N.C., tel 828-575-2424, dobrateanc.com

■ **Japanese Tea Garden**
Gather around the *irori*—a rustic family-style table—and watch as your hostess turns a chartreuse powder known as *matcha* into potable green tea. At San Francisco's Japanese Tea Garden in Golden Gate Park, tea ceremonies take place in the heart of the teahouse, surrounded in spring by pink cherry blossoms. After the ceremony, linger over pretty plates of mochi ice cream and fortune cookies, the house specialty.
75 Hagiwara Tea Garden Dr., San Francisco, Calif., tel 415-752-1171, japanese teagardensf.com

■ **Tao of Tea**
Ceramic teakettles perch on reclaimed wood shelves, and a little waterfall trickles in the background, setting a cozy atmosphere for tea drinking at Portland, Oregon's Tao of Tea Leaf Room. This tea parlor is one of three Tao of Tea spaces in Portland, which includes a tasting room next door and a Ming dynasty-style teahouse nestled in the Lan Su Chinese Garden where informal Chinese tea ceremonies are held.
239 N.W. Everett St., Portland, Ore., tel 503-224-8455, taooftea.com

■ **Camellia Teas**
Tea connaisseuse Rebecca Cragg prefers the term "tea gathering" to "tea ceremony" for her demonstrations at Camellia Teas, a bastion of Japanese culture in Ottawa, Ontario. A gathering begins with a history of *chanoyu*, the ancient custom of making powdered tea in Japan, followed by a tea sampling in a tatami setting. Word to the wise, sipping in silence is considered most traditional.
Mooney's Bay area (address provided upon confirmation of appt.), tel 613-739-4649, by appt. only, camelliateas.net

GREEK SPONGE CAPITAL

Once natural sponges were discovered in the 19th century off the coast of Tarpon Springs, it wasn't long before the Greek sponge divers arrived. With the divers' tradition of sponging passed down from generation to generation on islands like Kalymnos, Halki, and Symi, Florida quickly became the sponge capital of the world. Since then, a Greek community has sprouted around sponge diving. "They are why everyone else is here," says Tarpon Springs photographer Beeba Christopoulos Lekkas, whose work documents the culture of her hometown. "It is the sponge industry that brought Greek culture to Tarpon Springs, not vice versa."

IN THE KNOW: The best way to get a sense of sponge diving's history is to simply ask a diver. Stroll along the sponge docks of the fishing village past piles of old-fashioned equipment and take some time to chat up divers and shop owners along the way. At Spongeorama, shop for a natural exfoliator among what's billed as one of the world's largest natural sea sponge selections. The shop is connected to the Spongeorama Museum, which extols the history of Greek sponge diving heritage of Tarpon Springs.

INSIGHT · Deep Dive

To really dive deep on sponging history, take a cruise with St. Nicholas Boat Line. On board, a retired diver with years of experience will explain the sponging industry and a diver will demonstrate the proper, age-old techniques for harvesting sponges in his diver's outfit. His bulbous-headed suit would suggest he walked off the set of *20,000 Leagues Under the Sea.*

JOINING IN: On the first Saturday of the month, allow yourself to be whisked away to Greece during Nights in the Islands, a free event that brings traditional folk music like *nisiotika* to the streets of Tarpon for dancing and Greek dining beneath the stars.

■ *Essentials:* For information about Tarpon Springs, go to spongedocks.net; Spongeorama, 510 Dodecanese Blvd., tel 727-943-2164, spongeorama.com

Dancing in the streets on a Night in the Islands, Tarpon Springs

"Tarpon Springs is this quaint town with a touch of Old Florida and a lot of Greek culture." —Beeba Christopoulos Lekkas, Tarpon Springs photographer

A sponge harvest on the docks of Tarpon Springs

MIAMI

Mexican Aztec costumes in Miami's Calle Ocho Carnaval

Tropical Jungleland
Tucked behind the orderly suburban cul-de-sacs of Coral Gables lies a riotous jungle of exotic flora known as the Kampong gardens. The name comes from the Malay term for "village," and in this case, the village is a thriving, extended family of plants from Southeast Asia, Latin America, and the Caribbean, soaking up Miami's balmy weather for all it's worth. The garden dates back to the great botanist and explorer David Fairchild who sought to surround his home with plants from his expeditions. Let the fragrant West Indian lilac intoxicate you, the 50-ton baobab tree dwarf you, and the whole experience transport you to the jungles of Java. For an afternoon of South Pacific colonial chic (at a price), don your batik best for the Bali Ha'i garden party full of kaftans and cocktails, held annually in April. *The Kampong, 4013 S. Douglas Rd., tel 305-442-7169, ntbg.org/gardens/kampong.php*

Euro Glitz
A weather-beaten stone statue of Leda gazes past you lustily, a concupiscent swan in hand. She and her fellow statues at Vizcaya Museum and Gardens, along the just-dilapidated-enough walls and fountains, evoke a salt-corroded Mediterranean palace. Just when you thought you might be in France or Italy, a fat green iguana creeps onto the scene, reminding you you're still in southern Florida. But even better—where else can you find such an uninhibited display of opulence with such wacky wildlife? The mansion of millionaire industrialist James Deering was built as an ode to his favorite European architectural styles while also considering the subtropical climate. In accordance with that vision, many rooms of his mansion feature frescoed ceilings and rococo details. Originally open to the sky, the heart of the mansion is now protected from the elements by a glass roof. *Vizcaya Museum and Gardens, 3251 S. Miami Ave.,*

My family emigrated from Cuba in 1961 and moved to Miami. My grandparents lived in the Little Havana neighborhood for 40-plus years and never really learned a lick of English. My grandmother typically cooked a large lunch for us, but there are a few Cuban restaurants that were staples, including La Carreta. All of the males on my Dad's side (myself included) went to a school in Miami called Belen Jesuit, an all-boys school that started in Havana in 1854 and moved to Miami after Castro took power. The majority of the students, teachers, and faculty are Cuban American. The biggest change I've seen to the neighborhood is the influx of other Latin cultures—mostly Central Americans like Nicaraguans and Salvadorians. But for the most part, the Cuban presence dominates.

KRISTIAN SEDENO
Miami-born CPA

Working the cigar press, El Titan de Bronze factory in Miami's Little Havana

The waterfront Vizcaya Museum, Miami

tel 305-250-9133, vizcaya
.org

Cubano Feast

If you do only one thing on your visit to Miami, it should be to eat Cuban food. This unique blend of Afro-Caribbean flavors with a predilection for fresh, subtropical island flavors and slow-roasted meats is the calling card of the Little Havana neighborhood. Warm up your palate with a quintessential *cubano* sandwich—roasted pork, ham, tangy pickles, Swiss cheese, and mustard melded together in the embrace of crusty Cuban bread (the cubanos are particularly tasty at El Exquisito Restaurant). To fully explore the canon of Cuban cuisine, dive into the holy trinity of sides: rice, black beans, and plantains. For main

dishes you'd be remiss not to sample *léchon asado*, juicy, slow-roasted pork that yields with the slightest touch of a fork. The version at Catharsis Restaurant and Lounge is cooked for four hours and served with a guava mojito sauce.

Afterward, pull up a stool at any one of the myriad coffee shops along Calle Ocho for a quick swig of high-octane *cafesito*, brewed the traditional way—straight into sugar—or if that's too strong, a *cortadito* (with milk), or savor a creamy banana *batido* (milk shake) with a shot of coffee stirred in for extra oomph.
El Exquisito Restaurant, 1510 S.W. 8th St., tel 305-643-0227, elexquisito miami.com; Catharsis, 1644 S.W. 8th St., tel 305-479-2746, catharsis restaurant.com

Bathe Like a Russian

Does the thought of clambering into a hot sauna on a sweltering Miami day make you, well, sweat? Think of it as a cultural immersion into a quintessential Russian pastime. In the traditional Russian *banya* room at Miami's Russian & Turkish Baths, the Floridian edition of New York City's famous 19th-century bathhouse, plop down on a bench and bask in the intense heat radiating from a 15-ton, rock-walled furnace. Relief comes from a bucket of ice water dumped over your head. For a peculiar stimulation, pick up a *venik* (a bundle of oak leaves) and whack yourself with it (or ask a friend to do the honors). This ancient ritual is said to open pores, exfoliate

The Main Neighborhoods

Little Havana
Roughly 14 blocks north of Calle Ocho between N.W. 12th and 27th Avenues
BEST BET: Calle Ocho, the street and biggest block party in the land

Russian Riviera
Wealthy expats and a sprinkling of Russian delis along Collins Avenue in Sunny Isles
BEST BET: *Manti* dumplings stuffed with lamb at upscale Uzbek restaurant Chayhana Oasis

Little Managua
Nicaraguan community in the Sweetwater suburb of Miami
BEST BET: Carne asada and fried cheese at a *fritanga*, a home-style Nicaraguan cafeteria

La Petite Haïti
Biscayne Boulevard to the east, I-95 to the west, 84th Street to the north, and 34th to the south
BEST BETS: Perusing art installations at the Little Haiti Cultural Center, and shopping for Haitian arts and crafts in the Caribbean Marketplace

skin, and improve blood circulation.
Russian & Turkish Baths, 5445 Collins Ave., Miami Beach, tel 305-867-8313, open 12 p.m.–12 a.m. daily, russianandturkishbaths .com

Late Night Nicaragua

When the bars let out, the entire city seems to flock to carnivalesque Yambo in Sweetwater (aka Little Managua) for late night Nicaraguan grub. Though open 24/7, the eye-popping color scheme and vaquero-themed decor are most inviting in the wee hours of the night. The whole restaurant seems to spin in another country, in another time. An oft photographed carousel horse is the highlight of the visual, exploding with knickknacks and memorabilia hanging from every possible surface (including a somber portrait of former Nicaraguan president Anastasio Somoza DeBayle). Gut-busting portions at wallet-friendly prices are the name of the game here, where six bucks will score you enough juicy carne asada, sweet fried plantains, rice, and beans for two people with room for leftovers. Brush off your Spanish and order from the takeout window, then grab a seat at the outdoor mosaic-tiled tables. Fried food reigns supreme at this *fritanga* (typical Nicaraguan home-style eatery), so go ahead and indulge with a plate of *empanadas de maduro* (crackly deep-fried plantains stuffed with melted cheese) or a fried whole snapper, eyeballs and all. If you're craving a touch more heat, scoop a ladle of hot sauce from the great wooden bowl in the center of your table.
Yambo Restaurant, 1643 S.W. 1st St., tel 305-649-0203, open 24 hours a day

Spanish Monastic Marvel

If this Spanish monastery feels like the real deal, that's because it is. The 12th-century Monastery of St. Bernard de Clairvaux housed monks in northern Spain for nearly 700 years before it was shuttered for political reasons and retooled as a granary. In 1925, publishing magnate and serial real estate collector William Randolph Hearst bought the place and had the stones dissembled, packed in over 11,000 crates, and shipped to the United States.

Handcrafted treasures by Haitian artists in Miami's Libreri Mapou

Equine competitors at the Miami Beach Polo World Cup

Hearst's ensuing financial troubles prevented him from restoring the monastery to its original glory, and after his death the pieces were purchased by two entrepreneurs who sought to transform the head-scratching jumble of crates into a tourist attraction. Today, the Church of St. Bernard de Clairvaux is home to an active Episcopal congregation, offering services in both English and Spanish. *Ancient Spanish Monastery, 16711 W. Dixie Hwy., North Miami Beach, tel 305-945-1461, spanishmonastery .com*

Haitian Cocktail
Just north of the glittering fashion houses of the design district lies an evocative neighborhood where the sounds of Francophone rap mingle with Creole conversation. Considerably less touristy than Little Havana, La Petite Haïti offers an authentic glimpse into the cultural heart of the Haitian diaspora in Miami. Like Cuban food, Haiti has its fried plantains, but the heat is seriously cranked up on its version of *banana pesée*. Try the *griot*, fried pork in sour orange sauce, at local favorite Chez Le Bebe, or attempt

a breakfast of goat head stew on Saturday mornings. For something a tad more mystical, delve into the realm of voodoo at a local *botánica*, a sort of herbal and spiritual pharmacy. Pick up a little flask of libidinous *parfum* (Cupid's little helper) or seek out the sage counsel of a resident *vodouisant* for more serious ailments. Vierge Miracle & St. Philippe on Second Avenue is a perennial favorite. For a little shopping, head over to Libreri Mapou where owner Jan Mapou stocks his bookstore with Haitian Creole and Francophone publications. Browse beyond the bookshelves

and you'll find a treasure trove of Haitian finds: handcrafted jewelry, paintings, and other works by Haitian artists, all for sale. On the third Friday of the month, writhe, wiggle, and shake to the beats of *kreyol* jazz and *konpa*—Haitian merengue—in the plaza in front of Little Haiti's Cultural Center. The event, known as Big Night in Little Haiti, has spawned a monthly block party with local studios and businesses flinging open their doors well into the evening. *Chez Le Bebe, 114 N.E. 54th St., tel 305-751-7639; Vierge Miracle & St. Philippe, 5910 N.E.*

2nd Ave.; Libreri Mapou, 5919 N.E. 2nd Ave., tel 305-757-9922, librerimapou .com; Little Haiti Cultural Center, 212 N.E. 59 Terrace, tel 305-960-2969, little haiticulturalcenter.com

Old World Kitsch
It's a touch brassy, but Espanola Way's peach-colored facades and bougainvillea-bursting windows are just too darn charming. Modeled after cobbled villages of Spain and France, today the Historic Village of Espanola also oozes a distinctly bohemian spirit. Stroll along the palm-dotted sidewalks scoping out the boutiques and galleries, or sip rosé beneath the twinkle of white Christmas lights at one of the many European and Latin restaurants along the street. *Espanola Way, Miami Beach, myespanolaway .com*

Sport of Kings on the Beach
With foam at the bit and muscles rippling beneath taut shiny coats, the polo ponies charge seaside, down Miami Beach, spraying clumps of sand in their wake. Teams of riders in pristine white jodhpurs goad them on, hoping to be the first to score. A player close to the ball swoops his mallet high into the air, ready to strike. The crowd of hats gasps as the wooden sledgehammer comes pummeling down on the ball with precision. His pony doesn't bat an eyelash.

The sport of polo dates at least as far back as ancient Persia and has since spread out around the world, staking a particular stronghold in the pampas of Argentina. At the Miami Beach Polo World Cup, catch a glimpse of the sport's poster child, Argentine national Nacho Figueras (you may recognize him from his sultry Ralph Lauren ad campaigns), whose team routinely dominates the polo circuit. Still, this oceanfront event is no glam Hamptons polo scene. "Since the event is held on a public beach, spectators include both polo fans and the beach crowd in their bikinis," says Abigail Frye, who runs a traditional polo club with her husband in Virginia. "It feels like a constant beach party with an exotic edge." *On South Beach, between 21st and 22nd Sts., behind the Setai Hotel, miami polo.com*

Walking Map *Little Havana*

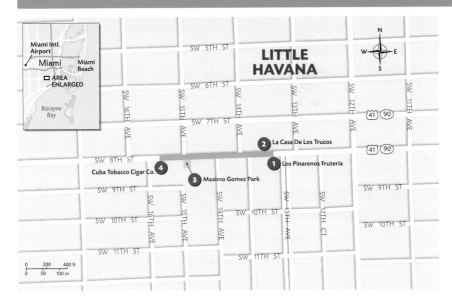

Let the scent of crusty Cuban bread and hand-rolled cigars lead the way through Little Havana.

1 | Begin your westward walk with a jolt of sugary caffeine at one of Little Havana's oldest and best walk-up coffee counters, the café cum fruit stand **Los Pinarenos Fruteria** (*1334 S.W. 8th St., tel 305-285-1135*).

2 | Across the street, provision up for Carnaval or Halloween at the storied **La Casa De Los Trucos** costume shop, which arrived from Cuba in the 1920s (*1343 S.W. 8th St., tel 305-858-5029, crazy forcostumes.com*).

3 | Hear that tiny clack-clacking? That's the sound of old-timers playing serious dominoes at nearby **Maximo Gomez Park,** aka Domino Park (*801 S.W. 15th Ave., miamigov.com/parks*).

4 | If their cigar puffing inspires you, pick up some hand-rolled smokes of your own at **Cuba Tobacco Cigar Co.** (*1528 S.W. 8th St., tel 305-649-2717, cuba tobaccocigarco.com*).

Camp Fasola, Henagar's weeklong immersion in Sacred Harp singing

HENAGAR, ALABAMA
SACRED HARP SINGING

Nothing prepares you for your first Sacred Harp singing. If you're asked to lead "a lesson"—which you inevitably will be—you must stand in the center of the "hollow square" created by treble, alto, tenor, and bass singers seated on each side, all facing you to form the square. The singing starts, the voices rising until all four sections are equally powerful and you are engulfed in a sea of song. If the surge of endorphins moves you to tears, don't fret. Your fellow singers have seen it all before.

IN THE KNOW: For many, Sacred Harp is a religious experience, historically tied to the church music of the British Isles. Much of the a cappella music comes from the poetry of 18th-century English hymns and, in the 19th century, from the songs of the American South.

Lately there has been a surge in enthusiasm for Sacred Harp. "Its been spreading like wildfire in the last 20 years," says David Ivey, chairman of Camp Fasola (get it? *fa-so-la?*), which offers weeklong immersions in Sacred Harp singing and culture in where? Alabama. "It's even back in England, where it all started," Ivey says.

WHERE TO GO: Liberty Baptist Church in Henagar, Alabama, never lost its way in its devotion to singing. All are welcome to the weekend singings, regardless of religious affiliation or ability to hold a tune. You can listen too, but that's not nearly as much fun.

■ *Essentials:* Camp Fasola, campfasola.org; Liberty Baptist Church, Henagar, Ala., fasola.org

"With a strong group of singers, you'd be amazed by the volume."
—DAVID IVEY, DIRECTOR OF SACRED HARP SINGING, CAMP FASOLA

CHINESE GROCERIES

"So many people see Mississippi and the delta in particular as black and white," says oral historian Amy Evans of the Southern Foodways Alliance, which chronicles the culture of the American South. "But it's so much more than that." In fact, the delta has a rich history of Chinese immigrants who came to America in the late 19th century seeking greener pastures. Instead, they found grueling work as cotton pickers on plantations in the Reconstruction South. As cotton became less profitable and the plantations began to retract, these Chinese laborers saw an opportunity to branch out and go their own way. If one echo remains today, it is the Chinese grocer, once ubiquitous in Mississippi. "There were in those days 50 Chinese stores in town," historian Shelby Foote once noted of his childhood growing up in Greenville.

WHERE TO GO: Today, only a few of the proper grocery stores remain (though there are plenty of small-town convenience stores run by Chinese families), and those that do have exercised exceptional vigor to stay afloat. At Wong's Foodland in Clarksdale, that energy came from new ownership in the form of Tony and Monica Li, who emigrated from Hong Kong. They bought Wong's in 1995

INSIGHT · Hoover Sauce

Word of mouth is the only advertisement fueling the cult following of Hoover Lee's "Hoover Sauce," a proprietary blend of soy sauce and other ingredients, like a southern barbecue sauce with an Asian kick. Food aficionados have touted its many wonders, but you'll have to head to Mississippi to score a bottle: You can get it only from Hoover's own general store, Lee Hong Company in Louise. *1294 Main St., tel 662-836-5131.*

from the original owners and have kept it largely the same. Walking into Wong's is like walking into a 1950s grocery. (Filmmakers behind *The Help* must have agreed since they used it in the 2011 movie.)

■ *Essentials:* For more information on Mississippi Delta Chinese grocery stores, go to mississippideltachinese.webs.com; Wong's Foodland, 520 Anderson Blvd., Clarksdale, Miss., tel 662-624-4539

Lee Hong Company in Louise, Mississippi, purveyor of "Hoover Sauce"

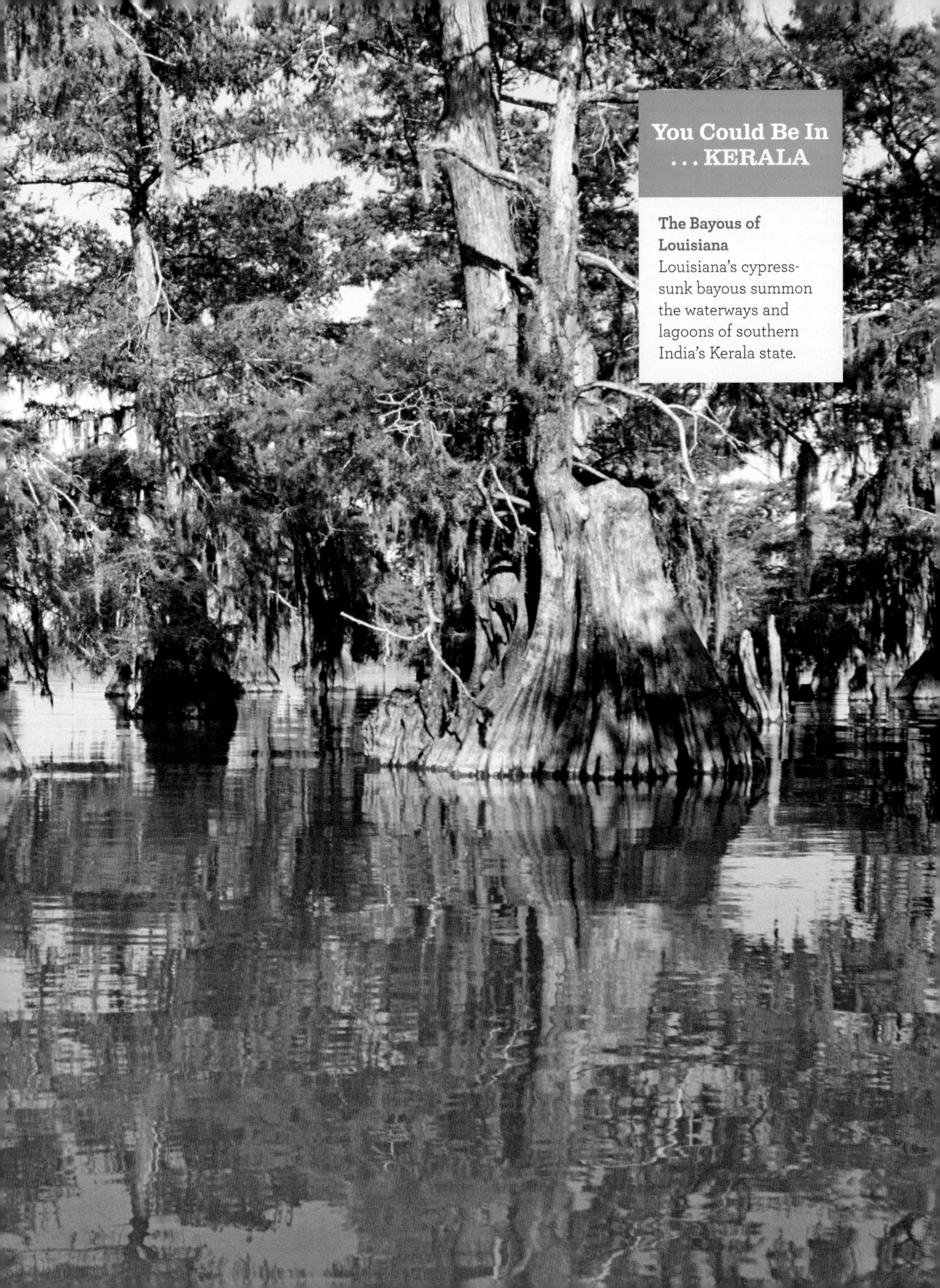

You Could Be In . . . KERALA

The Bayous of Louisiana
Louisiana's cypress-sunk bayous summon the waterways and lagoons of southern India's Kerala state.

FRENCH CAJUN COUNTRY

Acadians who landed in Louisiana in the fallout of the French and Indian War must have thought they were hallucinating from the heat. They had traded Canadian snowdrifts for steamy temps and snappy alligators. But they quickly adapted, bending their language and cooking into a new identity: Cajun, a corruption of Acadian.

WHAT TO EAT: Boudins, the Cajun sausages made from pork, rice, onions, herbs, and spices and served hot, are as easy to find in Southwest Louisiana as hot dog stands are in New York. The annual Boudin Cook-Off at Parc Sans Souci in Lafayette pits the best Cajun meat makers against one another. But for a true survey of Louisiana's favorite pork product, take a stab at the Cajun Boudin Trail, a loose collection of boudin purveyors and restaurants in and around Lafayette.

Don't just stop at boudin though, go ahead and fill up on crackling, jerky, pork sandwiches—you're in Cajun country now, and you're living high on the hog.

JOINING IN: The joyful sounds of zydeco, *fais do-do* (pronounced dough-dough), and all that jittery, Francophone, accordion-propelled music can be heard throughout the region, but it's on particular display during the annual Cajun Award and Festival in Lafayette, the so-called Grammys of Cajun music. Live music abounds during the

INSIGHT · Party 24/7

Cajun culture is festival culture. Period. Almost every day of the year is some celebration in the region, be it for rice, or crawfish, or frogs—all important ingredients, mind you, in Cajun cooking. The Festivals Acadiens et Créoles in Lafayette began as a humble music festival and has grown into a three-day, family-friendly fest of Francophone Louisiana culture that's heavy on the crawfish, catfish, and étouffée. *festivalsacadiens.com*

three-day party. "Basic Cajun music was just an accordion, a fiddle, and a triangle, then [the musicians] kept adding instruments," says Irene Reed of the Cajun Music Hall of Fame and Museum in Eunice, where visitors can listen to recordings of Cajun tunes.

■ *Essentials:* For more information on where to find boudin sausage, go to cajunboudintrail.com; Le Cajun Award and Festival, cajunfrenchmusic.org

Colorful Louisiana crawfish boil

"[For Mardi Gras] in New Orleans they have pretty floats, but here in the country they still ride on horseback."
—IRENE REED OF THE CAJUN MUSIC HALL OF FAME

Creole musician Geno
Delafose at the annual
Festivals Acadiens et
Créoles, Lafayette

VIETNAMESE HAVEN

I f New Orleans is like a great potluck party, then the Vietnamese brought the French bread. Fleeing war-torn Vietnam, refugees began arriving in New Orleans East in 1975. From their former French colonial homelands, the refugees brought recipes for perfectly crusty French bread, to be sliced and filled with Asian ingredients like salty grilled pork and bright slaws.

WHERE TO EAT: People come from all over New Orleans for the fresh bread and *bánh mì* (cousin to the po'boy) at Dong Phuong Bakery. The umami-packed beef pho is a major selling point as well.

WHEN TO GO: The best time to see the community let loose is during Vietnamese New Year, when firecrackers sizzle below and fireworks explode above.

Folk music and dragon dances entertain visitors at the free Tet Festival, but the real reason to go is the cornucopia of Vietnamese cuisine: bánh mì, pho, and an abundance of fresh fish hauled in from local fishermen and shrimpers. For the rest of the year, count on the weekly Vietnamese Farmers Market for your foodie fix. You've got to get up early; the whole show is over by 9 a.m., but your effort will be rewarded with the bounty of Southeast Asia: lemongrass, papayas, and chilies from over 20 vendors.

■ *Essentials:* Dong Phuong Bakery, 14207 Chef Menteur Hwy., tel 504-254-0296, dpbanhmi.com; Vietnamese Farmers Market, 14401 Alcee Fortier Blvd., Sat. 6 a.m.–9 a.m.

Watering herbs in New Orleans's Vietnamese neighborhood known as Versailles

"I go to the Dong Phuong Bakery for the pâté chaud, *which are like meat pies. I'd eat them anytime of day."* —ALEX TRAN, MANAGER OF DONG PHUONG BAKERY

You'll cook up Creole dishes at New Orleans's Langlois Culinary Crossroads.

FOREIGN COOKING CLASSES

Master the art of global cuisine in the comfort of an expert's kitchen.

■ Langlois

At New Orleans's Langlois Culinary Crossroads, learn to chop, stir, and taste your way through the region's famous Cajun and Creole dishes, like bouillabaisse and pecan pralines, and then dig into a feast of your own creation. The cooking and your meal will end on a sweet note—perhaps a crêpe suzette—and plenty of chicory coffee. *langloisnola.com*

■ International Culinary Center

Twice a year, Japanese chef extraordinaire Hiroko Shimbo offers a course in the Essentials of Japanese Cuisine at New York City's International Culinary Center, highlighting everything from trendy Japanese soul food like ramen to the art of sushi and sashimi, and, of course, the perfect sticky rice. If you're looking to dig even deeper, Shimbo also leads culinary tours of her native Japan. *internationalculinary center.com*

■ Julie Sahni Indian Cooking

Home cook, author, and food historian Julie Sahni invites up to three students at a time into her Brooklyn, New York, apartment for intensive classes in the wildly diverse cuisine of her native India. Explore regional flavors and staple ingredients like ghee, and master dishes like Punjabi chicken tikka. Sahni will also lead you on a provisioning trip through an Indian supermarket in Queens. Come with a notepad and a big appetite. *juliesahni.com*

■ Le Cordon Bleu

Thanks to a certain Julia Child, Le Cordon Bleu is the world's most famous culinary school for those seeking to cook *á la tradition française*. The original school in Paris now includes over a dozen satellite programs in North America for both professionals and home cooks. An Ottawa campus offers short courses in subjects ranging from *confiseries* (candies) to canapés. "It's simply a higher level than the chat-and-cook classes you might take from your local food market," says journalist and former short course student Micheline Maynard. "You're working with the same chef instructors who train chefs." *lcbottawa.com*

■ Fairburn Farmstay Culinary Retreat

Cooking classes at Canada's Fairburn Farmstay and Guesthouse on Vancouver Island favor Italian flavors. The dairy farm is the first in Canada to have its own herd of water buffalo, a crucial element for making mozzarella and *burrata*. Learn to make Italian classics like a variety of hand-rolled pastas and sauces, sourcing as many ingredients locally as possible, and meet the local farmers and winemakers who supply them. Spend the night in a 19th-century farmhouse turned B&B, and wake up early to watch the milking of the water buffalo before tucking into a breakfast of farm-fresh eggs, sausages, and muffins made with seasonal fruits. *fairburnfarm.bc.ca*

FRENCH QUARTER

Cast-iron railings skirt the balconies, and window boxes spill over with green vines, inching down toward the horse-drawn carriages below as they clip-clop their way down the street. New Orleans's French Quarter lives up to its French moniker as le Vieux Carré, or "the old quarter," with a palpably Old World charm.

WHERE TO GO: Don't bother waiting for the hostess at Café Du Monde; just do as the French: Sit at any open table and order messy, pillowy, sugar-dusted beignets. As you sip your café au lait, gaze across Decatur Street to the top of Jackson Square: The stately Cathedral-Basilica of St. Louis, King of France dominates the view. Most commonly known as St. Louis Cathedral, it claims to be the oldest Catholic cathedral in continual use in the United States. Note the Spanish colonial style, its post-1788 fire iteration from the original French facade.

WHEN TO GO: During Bastille Day (July 14), the Vieux Carré grins with a charming brand of French kitsch, right down to the *petits chiens* sporting berets in the French Dog Contest on Dutch Alley. "The basset hound in formal brocade was just hysterical," says Louisiana SPCA president Jackie Shreves of the 2014 "best dressed" winner. "The owner dressed up too! Like he was going to French court, in full stocking and waistcoat, *in July!*" At night live music and street vendors take over a block of Ponce de

INSIGHT · Cocktails

Cocktails are to New Orleans as wine is to Paris, each libation basting its city with joie de vivre. The famous French Quarter restaurant Arnaud's was actually started by a French wine salesman named Arnaud Cazenave nearly a century ago. Inside, sip French 75s at the eponymous bar, named after the classic French champagne concoction. Get the spins at Hotel Monteleone's revolving Carousel Bar and order the house invention: a Vieux Carré, a sort of New Orleanian Manhattan.

Leon Street for the Faubourg St. John Merchants Association block party. On January 6, the Krewe de Jeanne d'Arc throws a medieval parade in honor of its favorite saint's birthday. A designated young "Maid Joan" parades on horseback through the French Quarter, bringing king cake for all. Pack your best chain mail and join the fun!

■ **Essentials:** Café Du Monde, 800 Decatur St., tel 504-525-4544, cafedumonde.com; Bastille Day in the French Quarter, bastilledaynola.com; Joan of Arc Parade, joanofarcparade.org

The bustling, historic French Quarter of New Orleans

St. Louis Cathedral in New Orleans is dedicated to King Louis IX of France.

CHAPTER 3

HEARTLAND

Dutch dancers in
Holland, Michigan,
at Tulip Time Festival

CINCINNATI, OHIO
OVER-THE-RHINE

A single Cincinnati neighborhood once dominated the American beer industry—or rather, its German breweries did. German immigrants who crossed the Miami and Erie Canal to get to work earned the area the nickname "Over-the-Rhine" (OTR). Today, with the nation's largest collection of 19th-century Italianate architecture, the OTR Historic District feels far more Old World than New World. "The neighborhood still looks German, and the Music Hall there is so European it barely has a passport," says Katie Laur, former neighborhood resident and host of Ohio WNKU public radio's "Music from the Hills of Home."

WHERE TO DRINK (AND EAT): Enjoy a pint and twisted pretzel at the new Rhinegeist and historic Christian Moerlein brewery taprooms. Weekends, grab a hot, pulled-pork sandwich from vendor Eli's BBQ at Findlay Market on Essen Strasse, and, May to October, pair it with a handcrafted Moerlein ale at the OTR Biergarten at Findlay Market.

JOINING IN: No other festival celebrates OTR's German-American brewing tradition like Bockfest, held the first weekend in March. The festivities include plenty of potent bock beer, plus live music and lagering cellar tours. "When I ran Bockfest, German Americans would

INSIGHT · German Kentucky

Cincinnati's German heritage extends across the Ohio River into northern Kentucky. Covington, Kentucky's historic MainStrasse Village, a restored 19th-century German neighborhood with cobblestone walkways, hosts three annual German festivals: Maifest (May), Goettafest (June), and Oktoberfest (September). The most authentically Cincinnati German of the three just may be Goettafest, a celebration of *goetta*, a regional favorite German breakfast sausage made from a slow-cooked blend of pork, beef, onions, spices, and steel-cut oats. *goettafest.com*

come back, tell me stories about all the buildings, and cry because they loved the place so much," Laur says.

■ *Essentials:* OTR Historic District, otrfoundation.org; Rhinegeist, 1910 Elm St., tel 513-381-1367, rhinegeist.com; Christian Moerlein Brewing Company, 1621 Moore St., tel 513-771-0690, christianmoerlein.com; Findlay Market, 1801 Race St., tel 513-665-4839, findlaymarket.org; Bockfest, bockfest.com

A goat towing a keg ushers in Cincinnati's German Bockfest.

"Over-the-Rhine is like the Ellis Island of Cincinnati."

—KATIE LAUR, BLUEGRASS MUSICIAN AND ONETIME OVER-THE-RHINE RESIDENT

Cleveland-style
polka—even
the accordions
are upbeat.

POLKA

Grab a homegrown beer, a partner, and kick up your heels.

■ **Stompin' and Schnitzel**
Stop in any Friday night at Sterle's, a favorite Cleveland, Ohio, hangout of the late Frankie Yankovic, native son aka America's Polka King, to hear live music from the Polka Pirates. "People have come here for generations to celebrate," says Pirates banjo player Duffy O'Neil. "It's like being at a family party." This is the place to roll back the clock to 1950s Cleveland, when Slovenian polka music was born in the city's dance halls. Be sure to order some Slovenian comfort food (Slovenian sausage and sauerkraut, wiener schnitzel, chicken *paprikash*) for the full flashback.
Sterle's Country House, 1401 E. 55th St., Cleveland, Ohio, tel 216-881-4181, sterlescountryhouse.com

■ **BYO Accordion**
The plastic "PBR" sign hanging off the front of Kochanski's in Milwaukee, Wisconsin, sends off a serious dive bar vibe, but don't let that scare you away. Here, polka roots run deep, and Polish and German beers flow freely. It seems most of the neighborhood turns out every Wednesday night for open mic polka night. Anyone with an accordion or concertina (a squeeze box with buttonlike keys) can strut their stuff.
Kochanski's Concertina Beer Hall, 1920 S. 37th St., Milwaukee, Wis., tel 414-837-6552, beer-hall.com

■ **Wild and "Dangerous"**
Every Friday and Saturday night, the World's Most Dangerous Polka Band takes the postage stamp–size stage at Nye's in Minneapolis, Minnesota, kicking since 1950. "The dance floor is packed, and it doesn't matter if you know how to polka," says trumpeter Joe Hayden. "Last week, we had a 92-year-old with a walker dancing on her birthday."
Nye's Polonaise Room, 112 E. Hennepin Ave., Minneapolis, Minn., tel 612-379-2021, nyespolonaise.com

■ **Lone Star Polka**
Czech red, white, and blue are everywhere you look, and thousands of costumed (or not) couples are dancing in the streets of Ennis, Texas. You'll fit right in if you grab a partner because you'll be surrounded by 50,000 fellow revelers at the Lone Star State's National Polka Festival. With street dances, parades, and three Texas-size dance halls brimming with polka pride and partying, it's a full-on Bohemian blowout that's billed as America's biggest polka party.
National Polka Festival, nationalpolkafestival.com

■ **Polka Party**
One Friday night monthly, two irresistible forces combine at Penn Brewery's open Bierhalle, in the mid-19th-century E&O Brewery Building in Pittsburgh, Pennsylvania's historic Deutschtown (North Side) neighborhood: great beer—the microbrewery is known for its flagship Penn Pilsner and Penn Dark craft beers—and raucous polka music by Autobahn, a traveling western Pennsylvania German/Bavarian band known for its high-energy, Slovenia-style polkas and lederhosen-clad musicians. Call early to try to reserve a dining table (two-hour limit) near the band.
Penn Brewery, 800 Vinial St., Pittsburgh, Pa., tel 412-237-9400, pennbrew.com

Fiddling is center stage at the Irish Festival in Dublin.

DUBLIN, OHIO
IRISH ATTITUDE

A wee bit of Irish myth may be woven into the story behind the naming of Dublin, Ohio. According to local legend, an Irishman named John Shields was hired in 1810 to help survey lots for a new town on the banks of the Scioto River. When the landowner invited him to name the town, he looked to the surrounding green rolling hills and was reminded of home—Dublin, Ireland.

WHAT TO SEE: The Historic Dublin district is Emerald Isle central: Shamrock logos signify "Irish-approved" businesses such as the Brazenhead pub (serving Guinness and authentic Irish fish and chips), and strolling bagpipers and Irish step dance performances (and lessons) are part of free Jig Thursday held the first Thursday of every month.

JOINING IN: The first weekend in August, Dublin hosts what's billed as the world's second largest Irish festival (Milwaukee's is bigger). On tap: hundreds of musicians, singers, and dancers on seven stages, plus genealogy programs, adult beverage tastings, and Celtic sports. "Arrive the night before the festival opens to join the Dub Crawl," says Clay Rose, festival co-chair. "Festival musicians play in the pubs and on the plaza, the shops stay open late, and there's a 5K run." And if the luck of the Irish is with you, snag an outdoor table along the route at the Dublin Village Tavern, home of the corned beef–filled Irish Egg Roll.

■ *Essentials:* Historic Dublin, historicdublin.org; Dublin Irish Festival, dublinirishfestival.org; Brazenhead pub, 56 N. High St., tel 614-792-3738, hdrestaurants.com/brazen head; Dublin Village Tavern, 27 S. High St., tel 614-766-6250, thedublinvillagetavern.com

"Dublin [Ohio] is a little slice of Ireland. We celebrate everything Irish, value each other, and want people to feel welcome."

—CLAY ROSE, DUBLIN IRISH FESTIVAL COMMITTEE CO-CHAIR

DEARBORN, MICHIGAN
MIDEAST MECCA

Grab a bite in the heart of Dearborn, Michigan, and you're more likely to find falafel than fries. Welcome to the epicenter of Arab culture not just in the Midwest, but also in America, with the country's highest concentration of Arab Americans. Among the diverse community: residents from Lebanon, Iraq, Egypt, and Syria.

WHERE TO EAT: The city's main commercial drag, Warren Avenue, is studded with Arab bakeries, restaurants, and shops. Hashem's Nuts and Coffee sells hand-blended Middle Eastern spices, fresh-roasted Turkish coffee and nuts, and fresh *markouk*, a traditional Lebanese flatbread. For something different, Sheeba Restaurant on Dix Avenue "serves mostly Yemeni dishes, which is unique compared to most of the restaurants in Dearborn that serve Levantine [mostly Lebanese] cuisine," says Isra El-beshir, a curator at Dearborn's Arab American National Museum. "I love the tenderness of the lamb stew they use for their *aseed* [dumpling]."

And you shouldn't leave town without visiting Shatila Bakery on Warren Avenue, renowned for its delectable Middle Eastern sweets—chances are good that you'll leave with a tray of the pistachio baklava.

WHAT TO SEE: The size of seven football fields, Shia Muslim Islamic Center of America is the largest mosque in North America. This impressive spectacle of Islamic architecture offers tours to the public weekly. The one-of-a-kind Arab American National Museum showcases Arab contributions to the United States, and artifacts, including Indy race car champ Bobby Rahal's red racing suit and helmet.

■ *Essentials:* Hashem's Nuts and Coffee, 13041 W. Warren Ave., tel 313-581-3212, hashems.com; Sheeba Restaurant, 10327 Dix Ave., tel 313-841-9900, sheebarestaurant.com; Shatila Bakery, 14300 W. Warren Ave., tel 313-934-1520; Islamic Center of America, 19500 Ford Rd., tel 313-593-0000, icofa.com; Arab American National Museum, 13624 Michigan Ave., tel 313-582-2266, arabamericanmuseum.org

Islamic Center of America, Dearborn

DIGGING DEEPER

Not all of Dearborn's and metropolitan Detroit's Middle Eastern population is Arab. Dearborn has an Armenian population that practices Christianity, and Detroit is home to a large number of Iraqi Christians who identify themselves as Chaldean rather than Arab.

HOLLAND, MICHIGAN
DUTCH PRIDE

Squint and you'll think it's Holland. Of course it is—Holland, Michigan—but the working windmill on the horizon surrounded by tulips along glistening waters exudes a very Vermeeresque vibe. It all started back in 1847, with the arrival of 60 Dutch Calvinists who saw something close to home here on the banks of western Lake Macatawa.

WHAT TO SEE: Windmill Island Gardens hits the traditional Holland trifecta: windmill, tulips, and canals. April to October, climb to the top of the nation's only authentic, working Dutch windmill, built in the Netherlands in 1761, brought to Michigan in 1964, and restored in 2014. Buy a two- or three-pound bag, four recipes included.

JOINING IN: Dutch pride and six million tulips bloom during the Tulip Time Festival held the first week in May. Bring a blanket to catch the *klompen* (wooden shoe) action of Volksparade, complete with traditional "street scrubbing" by broom-pushing locals dressed in authentic Dutch folk dress, and Kinderparade, starring more than 7,000 costumed schoolkids. "Only in Holland, Michigan, can I don my own historic Dutch garb, scrub the streets with hundreds of other costumed folk, and speak rusty Dutch with neighbors and co-workers," says horticulturist

INSIGHT · Disappearing Dialects

Holland began as a Dutch-speaking "kolonie," and the town's geographical and cultural separation from other communities helped the original settlers and their offspring maintain their native language. Although English has been the official language since the mid-20th century, some descendants of the 19th-century immigrants speak Dutch in antiquated dialects rarely spoken in the Netherlands today. Linguists have visited Holland and surrounding Dutch-American communities in western Michigan to record, preserve, and analyze these disappearing dialects.

Sara Simmons, great-great-granddaughter of Holland founder Albertus C. van Raalte. She helps plant 100,000 bulbs at Windmill Island Gardens each fall.

■ *Essentials:* holland.org; Windmill Island Gardens, 1 Lincoln Ave., tel 616-355-1030, windmillisland.org; Tulip Time Festival, tuliptime.com

Street scrubbing opens the Volksparade in Holland, Michigan.

"When I walk through Holland I get a warm and fuzzy feeling. All those Dutch names make me think of my homeland."

—DUTCH IMMIGRANT AND TOWN CRIER JOHN KARSTEN

Tulips create a vivid tapestry at Windmill Island Gardens, Holland, Michigan.

DETROIT

Learn the art of *pisanki*, or egg decorating, at Detroit, Michigan's Polish Art Center.

Polish Pope Stop

Even if you're not Catholic or Polish, attending a Polish Mass at St. Florian Roman Catholic Church will transport you to the days when the Detroit suburb of Hamtramck was largely a Polish Catholic community. It's not hard to imagine when Polish Pope John Paul II stood on the altar to deliver Mass among the glittering stained-glass altar windows depicting other famous Polish saints. Stop into the Polish Art Center to peruse Polish pottery and folk art, and ask owners Raymond and Jean Bittner about attending a class in *pisanki* (Polish egg decorating). Buy homemade pierogies and kielbasa at Srodek's Deli, and make sure you have a *paczki*

(filled Polish pastry) or *nalesniki* (Polish crepe) at one of Hamtramck's Polish eateries before you go. "The nalesniki is delicious at Polonia Restaurant," Bittner says. "They put chocolate on theirs."
St. Florian Roman Catholic Church, 2626 Poland St., Hamtramck, Mich., tel 313-871-2778, stflorianparish.org; Polish Art Center, 9539 Joseph Campau St., Hamtramck, Mich., tel 888-619-9771, polartcenter .com; Srodek's Deli, 9601 Joseph Campau Ave., Hamtramck, Mich., tel 313-871-8080, srodek.com; Polonia Restaurant, 2934 Yemans St., Hamtramck, Mich., tel 313-873-8432

Belgian Games

Grab a Belgian beer, order some mussels, and wait your turn to play a round

of old-fashioned feather bowling at Detroit's Cadieux Café. It's the only place left in the United States (or practically anywhere, for that matter) where you can play the almost extinct Belgian sport. The challenge: rolling what looks like a large round of cheese down a concave court and hitting a feather. "The original owners started a feather bowling league in 1933," says Paul Misuraca, whose family has run the café since the '60s. "The league still plays regularly today." The public can play too, and even though feather bowling is rarely played in Belgium anymore, it's very popular here so make a reservation.
Cadieux Café, 4300 Cadieux Rd., tel 313-882-8560, cadieuxcafe.com

These days, Hamtramck is more diverse, but the scents of the neighborhood can take you back to the days when it was 80 percent Polish, and Polish was spoken on the streets. There were many bakeries in town when I was a child and even a major baking company, Metropolitan Baking Co. It's still there today and you can still smell the wonderful aroma of freshly baked bread. Growing up, I lived just a block away from the Kowalski Sausage Co., and when they smoked meats, the spicy aroma would blanket the area. You can still experience that from time to time at Srodek's market. You can buy butter lamb there to place in your Easter basket to be blessed on Holy Saturday before Easter Sunday. That's a long-standing tradition, which people still honor today.

GREG KOWALSKI
Lifelong resident and local historian

Irish Corktown

Down a pint Irish-style at Detroit's Irish American Club, where you'll rub shoulders with the city's very active Gaelic League. The surrounding historic Corktown neighborhood immerses you in a microcosm of the city's Irish roots. Start a tour on Sixth Street to find a restored, 19th-century row house (1420 6th St.) once home to the laborers who helped build the city. Then stroll down Leverette Street to see the federal-style detached houses and row houses that Irish immigrants built in the mid-1840s. A block north on Church Street are Victorian houses with Queen Anne and Italianate details built later in the century, signaling the neighborhood's gradual ascent in affluence. *Gaelic League and Irish-American Club, 2068 Michigan Ave., tel 313-964-8700, gaelicleagueofdetroit.org*

The Best of Mexicantown

You have dining options aplenty in Mexicantown, but start your visit on West Vernor Highway at Taqueria El Rey. It's a gritty hole-in-the-wall place, but this family-run eatery serves up authentic Mexican food (its chicken dishes are particularly excellent). Then head east to La Jalisciense on Bagley Avenue for fresh tortillas made from corn cooked and mill-ground on site every day. "If you want to create your own Mexican fiesta, this is the place," writes journalist Martina Guzmán in *Hour Detroit Magazine.* Then stop in at La Gloria Bakery for some fresh churros. On your way around, keep an eye out for public art including the brilliant Chicano murals and artwork that breathe vibrancy into this busy Latino hub. Take a postprandial rest in Clark Park, where the whimsical mosaic tile benches by Latino artist Mary Luevanos make you feel right at home—somewhere in Mexico. *Taqueria El Rey, 4730 W. Vernor Hwy., tel 313-357-3094, taqueria-elrey .com; La Jalisciense Tortilla Factory, 2650 Bagley Ave., tel 313-237-0008, tortillamundo .com; La Gloria Bakery, 3345 Bagley Ave., tel 313-842-5722*

Greek on the Avenue

Historic Greektown, settled by Detroit's first known Greek immigrant in 1860, is described by the National Park Service as "one of the last surviving Victorian-era commercial streetscapes in downtown Detroit." Get a table at Pegasus Tavernas to experience the spectacle of—and then consume—Saganaki "Opa," a flaming, gooey Greek *kasseri* cheese drizzled with brandy and delivered to your table ablaze amid spirited shouts of *"Opa!" Greektown, nps.gov/nr/ travel/detroit/d12.htm; Pegasus Tavernas, 558 Monroe St., tel 313-964-6800, pegasustavernas.com*

Greek Independence Day Parade, Detroit

OLDENBURG, INDIANA
OLD WORLD GERMAN

Just look at the skyline and you'll see how this tiny rural town got its nickname, the "Village of Spires." The church steeples and spires recall north German villages, and even street names are posted in German as well as English. Oldenburg's 150-year-old German Catholic heritage still defines it.

WHAT TO SEE: Walk down Haupt Strasse (Main Street) and crane your neck at the handsome religious buildings of the Immaculate Conception Convent and Holy Family Church. Then head down brick-paved Perlen Strasse (Pearl Street) to see some of the town's historic stone and brick buildings, most more than a century old. Note the fire hydrants as you wander the town—they are whimsically painted to resemble German figures in traditional garb and lederhosen. Finish up by washing down some Indiana fried chicken with a German ale at the Brau Haus on Water Street.

ON THE FARM: Return to Oldenburg's earliest days as a German Catholic settlement by visiting Michaela Farm, just outside town. In the 19th century, the Sisters of St. Francis, newly arrived from Europe, farmed the land for subsistence living to feed the convent. Today, sisters still raise livestock, chickens, and produce—but as a community farming renewal effort. The impressive early 20th-century

INSIGHT · Sacred Living

Known as the Castle on the Hill, the Romanesque-style Immaculate Conception Convent began as a humble log cabin. Sister Theresa Hackelmeier arrived in Oldenburg from Vienna, Austria, at age 24, in 1851. She founded both the convent and parochial school for the village's German-speaking children. Sister Theresa died only nine years later, but by then the convent had grown into a religious congregation that's still very active in and around Oldenburg.

barn was built from bricks fired in an Oldenburg brickyard *(now closed)* started by a German immigrant in the 1850s. "We raise our own cattle and chickens, so you'll find grass-fed beef and eggs downstairs," Sister Peg Maher says. "Produce is upstairs, and it changes by the week!"

■ *Essentials:* Brau Haus, 22170 Water St., tel 812-934-4840, oldenburgbrauhaus.com; Michaela Farm, 3127 Indiana 229, Batesville, Ind., tel 812-933-0661, oldenburgfranciscans.org

Skyline of the "Village of Spires," Oldenburg

"Oldenburg is only about 12 blocks, but they're lined with European-style architecture more than a century old." —SUE SIEFERT, GRADUATE OF OLDENBURG ACADEMY

German flags at Freudenfest, Oldenburg, Indiana's salute to its German roots

GERMAN FESTIVALS

Celebrate the New World's Bavarian roots with plenty of small-town spirit.

■ Freudenfest

Small-town Oldenburg, a pocket of Old World German in rural Indiana, goes all out every July. "Our entire town of 700 gets caught up in Freudenfest," says area resident Sue Seifert. Freudenfest is held along the brick-paved Perlen Strasse (Pearl Street) and celebrates all things German—meaning plenty of beer, a beer hall with live music and dancing, even the occasional homemade pie (as in sauerkraut pie, plus plenty of bratwursts, Reuben sandwiches, and even sauerkraut balls). On tap for nondrinkers: stein-holding and stein-sliding contests, along with living-history reenactors and walking tours of the countryside. *freudenfest.com*

■ Maifest

Come witness a tradition in the Deep South that's more than a century old: girls in brightly colored, old-fashioned German dresses and ribbons dancing around a festively decorated *maipole* (maypole) to greet the arrival of spring. Celebrate winter's end in Brenham, Texas, with an Old World German accent at Maifest, an annual street party that's been around since 1881. The old-fashioned festivities feature a Kinder Village, antique carousel, and even a German polka church service. Stick around for the big reveal: the coronation of Maifest royalty, elected from the area's youth. *maifest.org*

■ Oktoberfest

"There are usually two things always available at Mount Angel's Oktoberfest: a place to dance the schottische and a bratwurst straight from the grill," writes *The Oregonian*'s Molly Harbarger. It's not hard to imagine you're in the hills of western Europe, instead of the western United States, come October in this small Oregon town. A *biergarten,* polka music, Bavarian dancing, soft pretzels, traditional crafts—Mount Angel's late September festival has all you could want from a Bavarian-themed Oktoberfest, except maybe the Alps. But the town's roots are authentic—German pioneers settled it in the late 19th century—and the town's architecture, culture, and Glockenspiel clock tower reflect that. Mount Angel's pastoral setting even evokes scenic rural Bavaria. *oktoberfest.org*

■ Spargelfest

Asparagus soup? Asparagus crepes? Asparagus cake garnish? If there's a way to prepare asparagus, you'll probably encounter it at Spargelfest in Saskatchewan's Regina. The April festival marks the beginning of the brief asparagus-growing season in Germany, and because the vegetable is rarely eaten out of season, the window to savor it is small. A four-course meal starring asparagus kicks off the season. *saskgermancouncil.org*

■ Christkindlmarkt

The former German settlement of Lovettsville, Virginia, stages Christkindlmarkt, a traditional German Christmas market for two days in December. Imbibe homemade *glühwein* (German mulled wine), stock up on holiday treats like *lebkuchen* cookies amid the sounds German-Austrian carolers. *Loudoun Valley German Society, lovettsvillegame club.org*

AROUND THE WORLD IN
CHICAGO

Chinese New Year Parade, Chicago

German Immersion
Wander the North Side's Lincoln Square and you may think you've left the Windy City for the old hills of Germany. "Stop in old-timey Merz Apothecary, lunch at Chicago Brauhaus for traditional German fare and music, and then have a beer on the rooftop beer and wine garden at Gene's Sausage Shop & Delicatessen," says Lisa Lubin, Chicago food writer and TV producer. "Take a break and sit on a bench at Giddings Plaza, and you'll almost feel as if you are in Europe."

This is the neighborhood where German immigrant Oscar Mayer launched his sausage business, a story told at the DANK Haus German American Cultural Center museum's permanent "Lost German Chicago" exhibit. Today, Lincoln Square remains the city's German cultural core. And it throws its share of festivals to prove it: Plan a visit during late May's Maifest or September's Von Steuben Parade and German American Festival to hear the brass bands, dance the polka, and get your fill of authentic German brats and beer. Dress for the occasion by taking a pre-fest lederhosen and dirndls shopping trip to International Fashions by Ingrid, one of several German-themed Lincoln Square shops.
Merz Apothecary, 4716 N. Lincoln Ave., tel 773-989-0900, merzapothecary .com; Chicago Brauhaus, 4732 N. Lincoln Ave., tel 773-784-4444, *chicagobrauhaus.com; Gene's Sausage Shop & Delicatessen, 4750 N. Lincoln Ave., tel 773-728-7243, genessausageshop .com; DANK Haus German American Cultural Center, 4740 N. Western Ave., tel 773-561-9181, (closed Jan.) dankhaus.com; Maifest, mayfestchicago.com; Von Steuben Parade and German American Festival, germanday.com; International Fashions by Ingrid, 4714 N. Lincoln Ave., 773-878-8382, fashionsbyingrid.com*

Pierogi Pride
Eat, pray, and party in Polish in Chicago, where an estimated 743,000 people of Polish descent form the largest Polish population outside of Poland. For the full flavor of Chicago-style

In the late 1800s, my paternal great-grandmother was one of the Polish immigrants who helped found St. John Cantius Church in West Town. My grandmother was baptized and married at St. John there, and grew up in the Polish neighborhood around the church. She even met my grandpa at a church dance. I was raised in another part of Chicago, but my parents would take my brothers and me to St. John's on special Sundays. I always knew that I wanted my first apartment to be here. Now, I only live a mile and a half from St. John's (and steps away from one of the city's old Polish taverns, Innertown Pub). I meet my family for Mass at the church on Sunday, and my grandma still sees her friends there. The neighborhood and St. John's aren't exclusively Polish anymore, but the sense of community endures.

MARIA LAJEWSKI
Manager, Center for Financial Services Innovation

The Taste of
Polonia Festival in
Copernicus Center,
Chicago

The South Side Irish Parade, Chicago—go green or go home

Polish, target Labor Day weekend for the Taste of Polonia festival, a four-day polka-pierogi-Polish pride party in Jefferson Park (named for Polish scientist and father of modern astronomy Nicolaus Copernicus).

For a tamer but authentic experience, head to Polish Village, centered along Milwaukee Avenue in Avondale. Polish-language Mass is said twice daily on weekdays and four times on Sunday at St. Wenceslaus Church and St. Hyacinth Basilica. Polish also is the language—and, of course, food—of choice at several Milwaukee Avenue businesses including Kurowski's Sausage Shop and Rich's Bakery. You may want to stock up: The Old World deli up front, bakery in back is known as much for its rye bread,

paczkis (filled pastries), and *kapusniak* (cabbage soup) as for the dozen or so different kinds of fresh Eastern European sausages ground daily. *Taste of Polonia, top chicago.org; Kurowski's Sausage Shop, 2976 N. Milwaukee Ave., tel 773-645-1692*

Destination Vietnam With a Twist
You'd expect to find steaming bowls of authentic pho in the hole-in-the-wall Vietnamese restaurants lining Argyle Street—Pho 777 (try the Pho Tai Bo Vien, sliced beef and meatballs) and Nha Hang Viet Nam (which serves up free vanilla ice cream topped with crushed peanuts for dessert) are two of the best. What may be surprising is that Chinese Americans flock to Little Vietnam for the authentic

Cantonese Peking duck prepared by the Cheng family at Sun Wah BBQ, just around the corner from Argyle on North Broadway. "Nothing reminds me more of my early childhood in Hong Kong than Peking duck, and Sun Wah does one of the best I've had in the U.S.," says Chicago resident and Hong Kong native Eric Lam, who makes a monthly Peking duck pilgrimage to Sun Wah. The golden-brown ducks hanging unceremoniously from hooks in the front window are meticulously carved tableside by the chef who—along with the servers—banters with regulars in Cantonese. "The whole experience rarely is seen away from the streets of Beijing and Hong Kong," adds Lam. *Pho 777, 1065 W. Argyle St., tel 773-561-9909; Nha Hang*

The Main Neighborhoods

Lincoln Square
German enterprises on Lincoln Avenue from Lawrence to Montrose
BEST BET: Chicago Brauhaus for cuisine, beer, and music

Avondale
Polish enclave in northwest Chicago
BEST BET: The sausage shops on Milwaukee Avenue

Little Vietnam
Around Argyle Red Line stop, Uptown
BEST BET: Tank Noodle is tops for pho.

Greektown
West of The Loop on Halsted between Van Buren and Madison
BEST BET: Taste of Greece festival

Pilsen Neighborhood
Chicago's near South Side, bordered by the Chicago River, 16th and Damen
BEST BET: All the outdoor murals

Andersonville
Swedish food, drink, and history on Clark
BEST BET: The very Swedish Midsommarfest and St. Lucia celebrations

Viet Nam, 1032 W. Argyle St., tel 773-878 8895; Sun Wah BBQ, 5039 N. Broadway, tel 773-769-1254, closed Thurs., sunwahbbq.com

Greek Holdout
A highway runs through it, but a small Chicago neighborhood (about four blocks) boasts a big Greek presence. (The three-lane Circle Interchange demolished much of the city's once thriving Greek neighborhood in the 1960s.) Stop in the family-owned restaurants and bakeries along Halsted Street to savor a short (one street) but wonderfully sweet and savory culinary tour of Greece. Start with a grilled octopus lunch at Greek Islands restaurant. For dessert, pick up a *loukoumades* (honey puffs, cinnamon, nuts, and sesame seeds) or *galaktoboureko* (lemon custard with light orange blossom syrup) pastry at Artopolis before touring the National Hellenic Museum. Finish up the with classic *mezethes* (Greek-style tapas) repast—accompanied by a glass of Santorini *assyrtiko* white wine and Chicago skyline views— on the rooftop veranda (open Memorial Day to Labor Day) of Pegasus Restaurant and Taverna. *Greek Islands, 200 S. Halsted St., tel 312-782-9855, greekislands.net; Artopolis Bakery & Cafe, 306. S. Halsted St., tel 312-559-9000, artopolischicago.com; National Hellenic Museum, 333 S. Halsted St., tel 312-655-1234, nationalhellenicmuseum.org; Pegasus Restaurant and Taverna, 130 S. Halsted St., tel 312-226-3377, pegasuschicago.com*

Brilliant Latino
The grayest, coldest days may well be the best for appreciating Chicago's always-hot Pilsen neighborhood, ablaze with Latino colors and tastes. The color-saturated murals covering the exterior of Casa Aztlan, one of the Pilsen's oldest community organizations, are considered a masterwork of the Chicano art movement. Although Pilsen is predominantly Mexican-American and taquerias are ubiquitous, one of the best of the mom-and-pop places is Pupuseria El Excelente, an El Salvadoran place specializing in

Walking Map *Ukrainian Village*

2 | Head to **Shokolad Pastry & Café** for *frikadelky* (meatball soup), *holubtsi* (stuffed cabbage), and other beloved Ukrainian *baba* (grandma) dishes (*2524 W. Chicago Ave., tel 773-276-6402, shokolad pastryandcafe.com*).

3 | **Old Lviv**'s babushka-cooked comfort food buffet is all you can eat, and there's no extra charge for the Ukrainian/Russian conversations (*2228 W. Chicago Ave., tel 773-772-7250*).

4 | Over 400 *pysanky* (Ukrainian Easter eggs) are on display at the **Ukrainian National Museum** (*2249 W. Superior St., tel 312-421-8020, ukrainian nationalmuseum.org*).

Named for the immigrants who began settling here in the early 1900s, trendy Ukrainian Village remains the place to taste old country cuisine (potato pancakes and pierogies) and hear a variety of Slavic languages.

1 | The Ukrainian vibe gets amped up on Sundays when worshippers flock to the three Ukrainian-language Masses at **St. Nicholas Ukrainian Catholic Cathedral** (*835 N. Oakley Blvd., tel 773-489-7572, stnicholaschicago.org*).

pupusas, similar to Mexican gorditas, but stuffed with cheese and beans or pork before they are cooked. "I love listening—and watching—the lady in the kitchen smack the masa [dough] for the pupusas [tortillas] between her hands," says Lupe de la Torre, a Chicago native and frequent lunch customer whose extended family lives in Pilsen. "It reminds me of when my grandmother made fresh masa tortillas and gorditas."
Casa Aztlan, 1831 S. Racine Ave.; Pupuseria El Excelente, 1758 W. 18th St., tel 773-978-8270

Irish to the Core
In a city with a hard-core Irish history (no fewer than nine mayors claim Irish ancestry, not to mention hometown boy Michael Flatley of "Lord of the Dance" fame), you'll find the biggest single dose of Emerald Isle culture at the Irish American Heritage Center, in Irving Park. Complete with everything from an impressive 500-piece collection of famed Irish Belleek porcelain to an Irish pub, the center features live music every weekend. It also stages Chicago's two biggest Irish parties— July's Irish Fest (more than 100 Irish singers, dancers, and musicians on five stages) and a post-parade St. Patrick's Day bash in March. The latter spans three days and includes a family-friendly party, Irish music, and a traditional Irish element lacking at most American St. Patrick's Day celebrations— Catholic Mass.
Irish American Heritage Center, 4626 N. Knox Ave., tel 773-282-7035, irish-american.org

Swedish Find
The Nordic piece of Andersonville, now home to lots of Latinos and LGBT Chicagoans, may not be its most obvious part anymore, but it's the sweetest. The Swedish Bakery, an Andersonville landmark since the late 1920s, opens at 6:30 a.m. six days a week *(closed Sun.)*. If you show up much later than that on a Saturday, you'll likely end up waiting in a long line (be sure to take a numbered ticket). But you'll appreciate the extra time to mull the overwhelming array of Swedish pastries and European sweets, including traditional Toska Tarts (little glazed almond cakes) and marzipan slices.
Swedish Bakery, 5348 N. Clark St., tel 773-561-8919, swedishbakery .com

24/7 Mexican Fiesta
Walk down 26th Street through Little Village and you're likely to inhale the sizzling scents of Mexico that always fill these city streets: fresh-made churros, *chicharrones* (pork rinds), and hot tamales. Food trucks and vendors peddle chili-spiked sweets, and, in summer, *raspas* (sugary Mexican snow cones), sold from pushcarts packed with a rainbow of plastic pump-top bottles filled with flavored syrups like *guayaba* (guava), *rompope* (Mexican eggnog), and *durazno* (peach).

Check out simple El Nopal for *empanadas de camote* (sweet potato turnovers) and its selection of *pan dulce* (sweet bread); Western wear stores selling bolo ties and boots; and small grocery stores where you can buy dried chilies, adobo, chorizo, and every other ingredient needed to cook the real thing at home. Colorful, cafeteria-style El Milagro is known for its variety, huge portions, and house-made tortillas; it even sells its own famed chips.
Little Village, chicago neighborhoods.cc; El Nopal, 3648 W. 26th St., tel 773-762-9204; El Milagro, 3050 W. 26th St., tel 773-579-6120, el-milagro.com

A mural in Pilsen, Chicago's Latin Quarter

Pierogies, derived from time-honored Eastern European recipes

PIEROGIES

Try the beloved dumplings where they're loaded with care (among other things).

■ **Staropolska**

Step inside and enter a 19th-century Silesian hunting lodge: wood-beam ceilings, tile floors, dark, comfy booths, and a blazing fire in the hearth in cold weather. The pierogies at Chicago's Staropolska are just as authentic—like your *babcia* (grandmother) used to make, or would have made if she were Polish. There's an assortment of the stuffed dumplings to choose from, including the "Ruskie" (potato and cheese), sauerkraut, or blueberry. Add a Zywiec draft, and listen to the Logan Square old-timers chat up the servers in Polish. *3030 N. Milwaukee Ave., Chicago, Ill., tel 773-342-0779, staropolska restaurant.com*

■ **Prairie Cottage Perogies**

To sample the most authentic of pierogies at Prairie Cottage Perogies in Langley, British Columbia, go for the basic boiled, cottage cheese–filled version, says owner Judy Hrynenko. "You'll have to fly to Lviv or Kyiv for a more authentic pierogi," she says confidently. For Hrynenko, it's personal: The *pryohy* (pierogi) recipe was handed down from her Ukrainian *baba* (great-grandmother). Baba's simple recipes (flour, salt, and warm water dough, with traditional fillings like cheese, potato, fruit, bacon, and sauerkraut) are handmade fresh daily by a crew of pierogi ladies in the back. Loaded (potato/cheese/onion/bacon) is the customer favorite. Hrynenko's personal choice is sour cherry. In summer, blackberry pierogi is the way to go. "They are to die for," Hrynenko says. "The seeds are very hard, but it's worth a cracked tooth." *20771 Langley Bypass, Langley, B.C., tel 604-533-9354, prairiecottage perogies.com*

■ **Lomzynianka**

Eat authentic Polish pierogies at Lomzynianka in Brooklyn, New York's Greenpoint neighborhood, known as "Little Poland." The interior of the mom-and-pop restaurant screams '70s basement rec room—drop ceilings, lots of wallpaper, faux flowers, and a deer trophy mounted on the wall. But the pierogies (try the sauerkraut and mushrooms) taste straight from a Polish kitchen. *646 Manhattan Ave., Brooklyn, N.Y., tel 718-389-9439, lomzynianka.com*

■ **Homemade Pirogi**

Mike Dutch and his crew have been turning out 18 different kinds of home-cooked pierogies six days a week *(closed Sun.)* since 1986. His Clifton, N.J., hole-in-the-wall shop is strictly takeout ($5.50 and up per dozen). If you can't make it to Clifton by noon, give Dutch a call before making the drive. When the day's batch is gone, that's it. Everything's made from scratch: unbromated flour and fresh eggs for the dough, and fresh filling ingredients prepped on-site. "Making pierogies is an art form," says Dutch, who suggests trying one of his most artistic creations: Broccoli & Spinach Royale made with broccoli, spinach, ricotta cheese, mozzarella, and fresh-grated Parmesan. *1295 Main Ave., Clifton, N.J., tel 973-340-0340, homemadepirogi.com*

BRIDGEVIEW, ILLINOIS
LITTLE PALESTINE

Wearing a kaffiyeh head scarf and leather holster, a waiter pours complimentary, cardamom-infused coffee at Al Bawadi, a former Arby's turned Arab food destination on busy Harlem Avenue in Bridgeview, a Chicago-adjacent suburb sometimes called Little Palestine. Here, families of eight and ten crowd around tables brimming with baba ghanoush, olives, and spiced pita chips, platters of charcoal-grilled lamb, beef kebabs, and chicken, all accompanied by abundant rice, flatbread, and hummus.

IN THE KNOW: Palestinians began emigrating here after Chicago's 1893 World's Fair, a global lure for businessmen and traders, though most came much later, after the creation of Israel. Bridgeview, the clear center of Chicago's Muslim Arab community, is home to the area's first mosque, a source of pride even for non-Muslim Arabs. "What's neat about Bridgeview is you can drive through and actually see Arab words and Arab names," says Ray Hanania, a Palestinian-American media consultant who offers private tours of Chicago's Arab neighborhoods. "The funny thing is we want to see ourselves reflected in daily life, and it's depressing if we don't."

WHERE TO GO: Though Bridgeview is perhaps best known as the home of the Chicago Fire, a Major League Soccer team that plays at Toyota Park, its Arab restaurants like Al Bawadi, and the modest take-out joint The Best Shawerma

INSIGHT • Arabs of All Kinds

Religion distinguishes the southwest suburb of Bridgeview, the focal point for Muslim immigrants, while Christian Arabs historically settled on Chicago's northwest side in a more concentrated neighborhood known as Little Arabia. In nearby Rogers Park, services are still held in Arabic at St. Elias Christian Church. Chicago's Arab community has grown with the more recent arrival of thousands of Assyrians after the Gulf War brought shortages of food and medicine. *St. Elias Christian Church, steliaschicago.org*

in neighboring Burbank, draw aficionados of Middle Eastern food from around Chicagoland. And every year in mid-May, Palestinians celebrate their heritage at Nakba Day, showcasing copies of important Palestinian landmarks such as Al Aqsa mosque and Dome of the Rock, *dabke* performances, and fresh falafel and shawarma sandwiches.

■ *Essentials:* Al Bawadi, 7216 W. 87th St., tel 708-599-1999; The Best Shawerma, 6934 W. 79th St., Burbank, tel 708-233-9220; Nakba Day, ampalestine.org/nakba

Bridgeview's Al Bawadi Grill serves up authentic Arabic dishes.

Celebrating
Nakba Day in
Bridgeview

You Could Be In ... MEXICO

Colinsville, Illinois
You'll see earth architecture like the Mesoamerican mounds of La Venta, Mexico, at Illinois's Cahokia Mounds.

MILWAUKEE

At Milwaukee's blockbuster Irish Fest

Polka Fling

On Sunday mornings, in the post-Mass hours before noon, families file into Polonez, a banquet hall and dining room that stages a substantial brunch buffet, sound tracked by an accordionist. Long tables groan with ham, Polish potato salad, *bigos* (aka hunter's stew), pierogies, and the house-famed Polonez cheesecake, all based on recipes chef George Burzynski learned from his grandmother in Poland. On Saturday evenings, a similar spread fuels dancers twirling to "Polka King" Jeff Winard. "It's in the suburbs but it's still Milwaukee's best Polish restaurant," says Susan Mikos, president of Milwaukee's Polish Heritage Alliance. "Try to catch it when they have music."

Polonez Restaurant, 4016 S. Packard Ave., St. Francis, tel 414-482-0080, polonez restaurant.com

Manga Bene

The scent of simmering marinara sauce mingles with the spices of homemade sausages at Glorioso's Italian Market, a favorite for authentic Italian foods and family spirit. "The deli alone is worth the trip," says Jen Ede, editor in chief of *Edible Milwaukee*. "Don't miss the Milwaukee Muffaletta." Glorioso's is an anchor in the traditionally Italian Brady Street district, also home to Peter Sciortino's Bakery. Sample the area via a walking tour of the district with Historic Milwaukee on summer Saturdays. *Glorioso's Italian Market, 1011 E. Brady St.,*

tel 414-272-0540, gloriosos .com; Peter Sciortino's Bakery, 1101 E. Brady St., tel 414-272-4623, petersciortinosbakery .com; Historic Milwaukee, tel 414-277-7795, historicmilwaukee.org

Eirinn on the Lake

Whether you like your Irish St. Paddy's Day wild (another Guinness?) or Book of Kells reverent (Sunday Mass), Milwaukee Irish Fest, the nation's largest Irish festival, delivers on all expectations. And exceeds them, with red hair and freckles contests, poetry readings, hurling demonstrations, and even meet-and-greets with Irish setters. Held over four days each August at Henry W. Maier Festival Park on the lakefront, what started as a grand

Dome of the
19th-century Basilica
of St. Josaphat in
Milwaukee

party—and remains one of Milwaukee's top revels—has expanded into a dedicated center for teaching and music preservation; its Ward Irish Music Archives compiles over 40,000 sound recordings. *Sláinte! Milwaukee Irish Fest, irishfest.com*

Gemütlichkeit on Third
The Friday-night free beer program (be there at 6 p.m.) is enough to pack the Bavarian-channeling Old German Beer Hall downtown. But it also happens to be fish fry night, a beloved Wisconsin tradition accompanied by an oompah band of lederhosen-clad men. Long wooden tables and benches replicate Munich's most famous beer hall, Hofbräuhaus,

and proudly taps its Hofbrau in substantial steins to wash down local Usinger's sausages made across the street. At the off-site Estabrook Beer Garden, open in summer, BYO stein (or rent one) and picnic. *Old German Beer Hall, 1009 N. Old World 3rd St. and Estabrook Beer Garden, 4600 Estabrook Dr., tel 414-226-2728, oldgermanbeerhall.com*

Chinese Floats
Under a blue July sky, teams of 20 paddlers, encouraged by a syncopating drummer on the bow of long, narrow canoes painted in dragon scales, churn their way across Veterans Park Lagoon. The Milwaukee Chinese Community Center first brought the race, with its 2,000-year

history, to town in 2013 as a showcase for the culture. It immediately drew teams both from within and outside of the community for a day of Chinese dragon pageantry (plus games, dancing, and folk music), on and off the water. *Chinese Dragon Boat Festival, milwaukee dragonboatfest.org*

Olde English Christmas and Cream
After his humanitarian conversion, the home of Ebenezer Scrooge might well look like the Schuster Mansion each December, trimmed in boughs and holly and warmly staffed by Victorian-clad innkeepers Rick and Laura Sue Mosier. Dubbed the Red Castle when it was built in 1891

by tobacco king George J. Schuster, the antique-filled B&B conjures not just holidays of yore, but also traditions that go way back. In addition to a tree, the couple trims a three-foot wreath that was the central decoration in homes before trees across middle Europe. Over scones and clotted cream at afternoon teas held throughout December, Laura Sue explains the significance. "Everything you put on it had a reason," she says. "Holly was for your health, mistletoe was for fertility, and boughs for good luck." *Schuster Mansion, 3209 W. Wells St., tel 414-342-3210, schustermansion.com*

Midwestern Mercado
Piles of nopales cactus and tomatillos flank the produce aisles, kids pull on their mothers' arms begging for animal-shaped piñatas hanging overhead, and locally made tortillas arrive warm at Nuevo Mercado El Rey, a sensory trip to Mexico in the Clarke Square neighborhood. The market anchors Latino-centric Cesar Chavez Drive, home to Mexican baker-ies, taquerias, and soccer shops. Come for the color, stay for the flavor: The supermarket houses its own grill, serving every-thing from *chilaquiles* to tacos. *Nuevo Mercado El Rey, 916 S. Cesar E. Chavez Dr., tel 414-643-1640, elrey foods.com*

Milwaukee's Festa Italiana parade

Pendarvis Historic Site preserves Mineral Point's Cornish history.

MINERAL POINT, WISCONSIN
CORNISH HERITAGE

Relive the boomtown heyday of little Mineral Point, when enterprising Cornish miners from England's Cornwall region flocked here in quest of lead and zinc. Mining came and went, but the community has worked hard to preserve the Celtic village as it stood almost two centuries ago.

JOINING IN: The town mines its Cornish roots every year for a concurrent pair of celebrations, Cornish Festival and Taste of Mineral Point. The Celtic-flavored fare includes five days of hurling, tours, Cornish folk singers, scones, and raisin-studded pastries called figgyhobbin. While you're in town, stop by Shake Rag Alley, which occupies several former mining-era homes across the street from the original Cornish mine. At one time larger than Chicago, Mineral Point prides itself on its arts legacy, embodied by its restored 1915 Opera House, which goes as far back as its mining days. Potters, sculptors, painters, and other artists have embraced the town's Cornish spirit and made downtown a draw. "Arts really brought this town back to life," says Megan O'Connell, Shake Rag Alley executive director. "The personalities of the people here are more than half of what makes the place so special."

WHERE TO STAY: Fans of history and architecture meet in Mineral Point, where visitors can explore the Cornish-built Pendarvis, a series of preserved homes and outbuildings. Book an overnight stay in one of several historic limestone renovations from Brewery Creek Inn or Cothren House.

■ *Essentials:* Mineral Point, mineralpoint.com; Cornish Festival, cornishfest.org; Shake Rag Alley, 18 Shake Rag St., tel 608-987-3292, shakeragalley.com; Mineral Point Opera House, 139 High St., tel 608-987-3501, mpoh.org; Pendarvis Historic Site, 114 Shake Rag St., tel 608-987-2122, pendarvis.wisconsin history.org; Brewery Creek Inn, 23 Commerce St., tel 608-987-3298; Cothren House, 320 Tower St., tel 608-987-1522, cothrenhouse.com

DIGGING DEEPER

Shake Rag Alley faces Merry Christmas Mine Hill, now a 43-acre preserve of thigh-high prairie grasses. Local legend has it miners' wives would shake rags to call their husbands home for dinner, though "Shake Rag" also connoted a poor residential area.

St. Joan of Arc Chapel, Marquette University, Milwaukee

EUROPEAN LANDMARKS

Walk, worship, picnic, and escape among these grand imports.

■ **St. Joan of Arc Chapel**
Before battle, it is said, Joan of Arc prayed in the chapel near Lyon, France, and kissed the stone on which she stood, leaving it forever colder than others. Now, this stone and the medieval chapel that houses it are in Milwaukee—seemingly another miracle, this time of American ambition. Reconstructed stone by stone, St. Joan of Arc Chapel holds Mass during the academic year and offers complimentary tours by appointment. *1250 W. Wisconsin Ave., tel 414-288-6873, Milwaukee, Wis., marquette.edu*

■ **The Cloisters Museum**
The echo of footsteps rings out from vaulted colonnades, but otherwise silence prevails—a hush intuitively induced in the Cloisters, a medieval European fortress of five ancient abbeys reconstructed in Manhattan's northern Fort Tryon Park. The museum houses illuminated manuscripts, lustrous stained glass, intricate tapestries, and ornate sculptures, and doubles as a center for solace in the otherwise teeming city. *99 Margaret Corbin Dr., New York, N.Y., tel 212-923-3700, metmuseum.org*

■ **Cotswold Cottage**
Enjoy an unmistakably British caddy of finger sandwiches and scones with clotted cream amid the lush English garden encircling Dearborn, Michigan's 17th-century Cotswold Cottage. Moved from Chedworth in England's Cotswolds, the limestone cottage now resides amid the Henry Ford Museum's time-tripping Greenfield Village as southern Michigan's most transporting summer tea garden. *20900 Oakwood Blvd., Dearborn, Mich., tel 313-982-6001, thehenryford.org*

■ **Church of St. Mary**
This stark and airy, white-stone church in Fulton, Missouri, marks a piece of Anglophile heaven. It was here in 1946, on the small campus of Westminster College, that British Prime Minister Winston Churchill made his legendary speech declaring, "An Iron Curtain has descended across the Continent," signaling the start of the Cold War. In 1964, a grateful school alighted on an ambitious commemoration: It imported and rebuilt the remains of a treasured British church designed by famed 17th-century British architect Christopher Wren that was all but destroyed during the London Blitz of World War II. In 1992, ex-Russian President Mikhail Gorbachev sealed the college's place in history in a speech there declaring the Cold War was over. *501 Westminster Ave., Fulton, Mo., tel 573-592-5369, nationalchurchill museum.org*

■ **Agecroft Hall**
Sunken gardens, hedges shaped into an Elizabethan knot, a great, wood-paneled hall—you are forgiven for confusing your *Downton Abbey* and *Henry VIII* fantasies at Richmond, Virginia's Agecroft Hall. The 15th-century Tudor estate, sold in 1925 in Lancashire, England, was reconstructed near the banks of the James River. *4305 Sulgrave Rd., Richmond, Va., tel 804-353-4241, agecrofthall.com*

NORWEGIAN CHARMS

Pot bellies and long noses protruding, the smiling trolls of Mount Horeb, Wisconsin, extend a quirky welcome to visitors. According to Norwegian lore, the trolls appear frightening, a countenance that masks their naivety and good nature. Today, they serve as pranking ambassadors to this tidy town, once three-quarters Norwegian.

IN THE KNOW: After the owners of a Scandinavian gift shop on Main Street put trolls in their front yard in 1976, "Truck drivers would drive by and get on their radios and say, 'I saw your sister on the side of the road,' and it caught on," says Melissa Theisen, executive director of the Mount Horeb Chamber of Commerce. The trolls' popularity grew among visitors along with the troll population, and the road became known as the Trollway.

WHAT TO EAT: July's Kaffe Stue meal offers everything from *varme pølse* (*lefse*-wrapped hot dogs) to blueberry *bondepike* (parfaits), while the spread at Host Frokost, an October breakfast, includes *rullepølse* (headcheese) and flat Norwegian pancakes. "A lot of our heritage goes toward food," says George Sievers, past president of Sons of Norway, who has the wooden compass his great-great-grandfather used to navigate to southern Wisconsin. "Food is a natural gathering place." Century-old Schubert's, a bakery and diner, still makes Norwegian lefse flatbread and rosettes daily. And locals still rush to Open House Imports to buy Sølje jewelry from Norway to celebrate a

MORE · Norwegian Celebrations

Fyr Bal Festival: A bonfire followed by sunset fireworks over Ephraim's Eagle Harbor highlight this Door County fest (pronounced fear-ball) celebrating Midsummer's Eve. *ephraim-doorcounty.com*

Midsummer Fest: It's an all-day party every June at Westby's Norskedalen Nature & Heritage Center's Midsummer Fest. The day kicks off with a pancake breakfast and continues with wood-carving shows and Norwegian dances. *norskedalen.org*

Syttende Mai: Everyone's Norwegian for Stoughton's festival celebrating Norway's Constitution Day. Festivities include a 10-mile "ugly troll" run. Held the closest weekend to May 17. *stoughtonwi.com/syttendemai.shtml* (See also "The Best Syttende Mai Festivals" on p. 127.)

confirmation or a wedding, as well as Norwegian candy, hand-painted Dala horses, and, of course, trolls.

■ *Essentials:* Mount Horeb, 300 E. Main St., tel 608-437-5924, trollway.com; Sons of Norway, vennelag513.com; Schubert's, 128 E. Main St., tel 608-437-3393, schubertsrestaurant.com; Open House Imports, 308 E. Main St., tel 608-437-5468, openhouseimports.com

Mount Horeb's trolls reflect its Norwegian heritage.

SWISS TOWN

Bright red geraniums in wooden flower boxes front peak-roofed buildings designed to bear piles of snow come winter. Painted fiberglass cows loiter under street signs scripted in Swiss German, while the real things—Swiss browns and Holsteins—graze in the rolling pastures outside of town. It's not Switzerland, but New Glarus comes close. "What we don't have that's Swiss is the mountains all over," says Esther Zgraggen, a Swiss-born, New Glarus resident who owns Esther's European Imports. This is Wisconsin's so-called "driftless" (never glaciated) region of undulating hills and dipping valleys, where farming is fertile and cheese is choice. "I can totally see why the Swiss immigrated to this area because of the hills," she says.

WHAT TO SEE: In a Bernese-style home, peruse Swiss wood carvings, paintings, and antiques at the Chalet of the Golden Fleece Museum donated by the late Edwin Barlow, founder of the popular Wilhelm Tell Drama festival. Fourteen authentic dwellings staffed by costumed interpreters conjure pioneer life at the Swiss Historical Village. Shop Esther's European Imports for a cowbell or Swiss raclette set.

JOINING IN: Each June, the Heidi Festival stages the Johanna Spyri classic, including live goats on stage, while the Wilhelm Tell Festival showcases the story of the Swiss

INSIGHT · Stinky Cheese

The original 135 Swiss colonists from Canton of Glarus arrived in 1845 and carved the region into small dairy farms. In 1868, the first area cheese factory opened, producing Limburger, the pungent European cheese that became a lunch favorite of local laborers. Farmers made Emmentaler and cheddar too, but Green County, home of New Glarus, became famous for the stinky stuff. "You can still come and have a Limburger sandwich here, if you can stand it," says resident Esther Zgraggen.

archer in September. If you yen for the Swiss sounds of yodeling and alpenhorns, Zgraggen recommends Swiss Volksfest, held the first Sunday in August.

■ *Essentials:* New Glarus, swisstown.com; Chalet of the Golden Fleece Museum, 618 2nd St., tel 608-527-2614; Swiss Historical Village & Museum, 612 7th Ave., tel 608-527-2317, swisshistoricalvillage.org; Esther's European Imports, 102 5th Ave., tel 608-527-2417, shopswiss.com

Pastoral landscape of New Glarus

"We have a festival nearly every weekend. It's worth coming here to experience what small-town Swiss hospitality is."
—BETH ZURBUCHEN, PRESIDENT OF THE SWISS CENTER OF NORTH AMERICA

Dancers at the
Wilhelm Tell
Festival, New Glarus

Even the washrooms are art at Sheboygan's John Michael Kohler Arts Center.

SHEBOYGAN, WISCONSIN
GERMAN HERITAGE

Sheboygan touts its German roots proudly and often, starting with its nickname, "The Wurst City in the World." The city's famed bratwurst sausages—produced, grilled, and consumed here by the tons every year—are the enduring, savory symbol of this lakefront community.

WHAT TO EAT: Sample some of the best brats at Al & Al's Steinhaus, which also features German-style music and one of the best Oktoberfests around. To stock up, Miesfeld's Meat Market sells 30 different varieties of brats.

IN THE KNOW: Working-class German immigrants already had discovered Sheboygan when Austrian-born John Michael Kohler showed up in 1873 and built what would become a backbone of American Midwest industry, the plumbing titan Kohler Co. In 1899, he founded nearby Kohler village, one of the country's first planned communities. Sculptures scattered around Kohler village are as much a part of its heritage as its brats. Kohler (the man) "felt everyone should be exposed to art and have experience with it," says Angela Miller, archivist at Kohler. Every year, the company invites artists to use the company foundry and ceramic shops. Sheboygan's John Michael Kohler Arts Center frequently displays their works.

■ *Essentials:* Al & Al's Steinhaus, 1502 S. 12th St., tel 920-452-5530, alnals.com; Miesfeld's Meat Market, 4811 Venture Dr., tel 920 565-6328, miesfelds.com; John Michael Kohler Arts Center, 608 New York Ave., tel 920-458-6144, jmkac.org

DIGGING DEEPER

Kohler village's coffered-ceilinged, vintage 1918 American Club, built to house German immigrants who couldn't afford their own homes, is now a luxury golf resort steeped in history. Its Wisconsin Room dining room, once a workers' cafeteria, features an Arts and Crafts mural.

SCANDINAVIAN FISH BOILS

A roaring fire and a boiling pot of water cooking up the day's catch always accompanied the hard work of survival—catching, cleaning, and sorting fish on the windswept shores of this Wisconsin peninsula. So goes the legend of the Scandinavian settlers in Wisconsin's Door County. The fish boil spread to local homes and churches. "It became the Door County answer to the backyard barbecue," says Andy Coulson, owner of the White Gull Inn in Fish Creek, famous for its fish boils. "It was something local people did because someone in your family was in commercial fishing or you fished for yourself."

WHERE TO GO: Today, diners gather around an outdoor wood fire at the White Gull Inn and the Viking Grill in Ellison Bay, cameras ready, watching heavy iron pots come to a boil. Once the red potatoes and whitefish are added, the "boiler," or chef, squirts extra kerosene on the fire. Flames explode into the sky, the pot overflows, and smoke engulfs the bonfire in a theatrical, predinner tradition known as the "boil over." "Fish boils became popular because of local ingredients even before the local ingredient movement," Coulson says.

BEYOND BOILS: Door County's love of food and fire doesn't end at fish boils. Goats graze the sod roof above

INSIGHT · Locavore Door

The natural bounty of Door County, which includes its cherry orchards (and pies), was already the envy of the Old World when the Scandinavians arrived. Seventeenth-century French fur trader Pierre-Esprit Radisson hailed Wisconsin's Door County as "a kingdom so delicious." The whitefish Scandinavian settlers caught for their fish boils are now sustainably harvested from Lake Michigan. At one time, the area was also home to potato and cabbage farms that supplied the sides of boiled potatoes and coleslaw.

Al Johnson's Swedish Restaurant and Butik in Sister Bay, which serves generous Swedish pancakes and meatball sandwiches.

■ *Essentials:* White Gull Inn, 4225 Main St., tel 888-364-9542, Fish Creek, Wis., whitegullinn.com; Viking Grill, 12029 Hwy. 42, Ellison Bay, Wis., tel 920-854-2998, thevikinggrill.com; Al Johnson's Swedish Restaurant, 10698 N. Bay Shore Dr., Sister Bay, Wis., tel 920-854-2626, aljohnsons.com

A Scandinavian fish boil at White Gull Inn in Door County

AROUND THE WORLD IN
MINNEAPOLIS

Traditional African dance at the Midtown Global Market, Minneapolis

My Neighborhood

SWEDISH MINNESOTA

Minneapolis Institute of Art/Global
Check out the undulating van Gogh olive grove, riotous Delacroix, and especially haunting Francis Bacon dating from 19th-century Europe. Or perhaps your taste runs more to the ancients. The Minneapolis Institute of Art presents 80,000 items reflecting 17 cultures spanning of 40,000 years over its eight sprawling acres. Get a sense of place before you go by heading to the Institute's website to see then-and-now maps. And there's more: The high-tech interactive African collection offers a special experience.
Minneapolis Institute of Art, 2400 3rd Ave. S., tel 612-870-3000, new *.artsmia.org*

Scandinavian Smörgasbord
Cases crammed with sausages, salami, and all sizes of cured meats opposite shelves of Norwegian Henning figurines and brightly painted Swedish wooden toys—these are among the pickings at Ingebretsen's, a cornucopia of Scandinavian clothing, books, music, crafts, home furnishings, needlework, Viking kitsch, kitchen tools, jewelry, and food. Maybe you can walk away from the Viking helmets, but it is tough to leave this Nordic emporium without at least some lingonberry preserves

and Swedish pancake mix. With its homey storefront and simple, pale-wood furniture in the window, this invitingly old-fashioned bastion of all things Scandinavian has underscored the city's heritage since 1921.
Ingebretsen's, 1601 E. Lake St., tel 800-279-9333, ingebretsens.com

World Music
Rhythmic Peruvian electric guitars and drums, West African a cappella harmonies, and pulsating Cambodian psychedelic pop are among the global tunes showcased at the Cedar, as it's known. Enjoy a relatively small venue—fewer than 500 seats—in a redone 1940s music theater. Fulfilling

My Neighborhood
SWEDISH MINNESOTA

It's easy to "be Swedish" in Minnesota, and that's a good thing for me and my family—we emigrated to the United States in 1962. From the American Swedish Institute—ground zero for all with ties to or interest in historic and contemporary Scandinavia—to Swedish-Lutheran-founded colleges; from Midsommar, Svenskarnas Dag, and Santa Lucia celebrations to lutefisk dinners aplenty; from Swedish-language and handicraft classes to Ingebretsen's (a local food market) to FIKA, with all its modern takes on favorite Swedish dishes; from Swede Hollow (where early immigrants lived) to contemporary art exhibits, movie screenings, and films, there are plentiful ways to connect with Sweden past and present. All of this and more binds me to my roots and allows me to carry forward my Swedishness and share it with others.

CAROLE ARWIDSON
Swedish-born Minneapolis resident

Exquisite woodwork at the American Swedish Institute's Turnblad Mansion in Minneapolis

its mission to promote intercultural appreciation and understanding through the presentation of global music, the Cedar Cultural Center stages more than 200 shows a year.
Cedar Cultural Center, 416 Cedar Ave. S., tel 612-338-2674, thecedar.org

Swedish Eats and Crafts
Learn how to make gravlax yourself. Or how about constructing a box out of birch bark, also very traditionally Swedish? These are the sorts of workshops offered by the American Sweden Institute, which displays artifacts and artwork by leading Swedish artists. In addition to gravlax, the award-winning café in the lobby, FIKA (from the Swedish word *fika,* which means a daily coffee-and-pastry break), offers mother county–inspired comfort foods such as beet soup, open-faced sandwiches on rye, braised beef, juniper-spiced meatballs, cardamom rolls, and, yes, pastries. Nordic design—both classic and modern—in a variety of permutations—from jewelry to household items—is what you'll find in the ASI museum shop.
America Sweden Institute, 2600 Park Ave. S., tel 612-871-4907, asimn.org

Salsa While You Shop
Free live weekend entertainment provided by performers from around the world is the icing on the cake at this marketplace where shoppers show up for food, crafts, and useful objects from many corners of the planet. Cooking lessons (learn how to create great examples of ethnic food tastes) and salsa dancing (every other Sunday morning) add even more spice to this bustling, beloved destination. An annual global music festival in July features dancing as well as vocal and instrumental sets performed on two outdoor and one indoor stage.
Midtown Global Market, 920 E. Lake St., tel 612-872-4041, midtownglobalmarket.org

Provocative, Peaceful Japanese
What started out as a "lab" to see which annual and perennial plants could survive Minnesota winters (no small feat) has become a lush example of flora survival. But another main attraction is its bittersweet link to Japan. In addition to Asia-influenced plantings along the Lyndale Park Peace Garden's lower edge are two "peace" stones from Hiroshima and Nagasaki, and a *yatsu-hashi* (crooked path) bridge designed to keep evil spirits at bay. A bronze sculpture, "The Spirit of Peace," features words of peace in 23 languages on its base.
Lyndale Park Peace Garden, Lyndale Park, 4124 Roseway Rd., tel 612-230-6400, minneapolisparks.org

British Tea and Games
Apart from the sausage-wrapped fried Scotch eggs and daily afternoon tea, the real draw of Brit's Pub is the swath of green the size of a baseball diamond—on the roof. Come in the early evening to nab an outdoor table with a view—of the quite civilized and very British action: lawn bowling (also known as bowls). On summer weekends, anyone can play; just be aware that in this bocce-like game, the ball is supposed to be gently tossed, not thrown.
1110 Nicollet Ave., tel 612-332-3908, britspub.com

Asian influence in Lyndale Park Peace Garden, Minneapolis

The Syttende Mai
Youth Parade,
Stoughton,
Wisconsin

SYTTENDE MAI FESTIVALS

Party on: Join in and celebrate May's Norwegian Constitution Day.

■ Lutefisk Fest
Maybe you have a taste for lutefisk (dried cod soaked in lye), but that doesn't mean you'll necessarily want to belly up for a lutefisk-eating contest. (Don't feel badly; even Norwegians like to joke about this native comestible.) To just about everyone's taste at the three-day Syttende Mai (meaning "May 17" in Norwegian and pronounced soot-n-d-MY) celebration in Spring Grove, Minnesota, is the Viking ship, replete with Vikings who parade down Main Street. Also on tap: carnival rides, classic car show, stay-on-a-sheep-for-eight-seconds competition, art auction, and lots of food. *sgsyttendemai.org*

■ Cross-Cultural Happening
One of the world's largest Syttende Mai celebrations takes place in Stoughton,

Wisconsin, over three days, marrying the traditions of Norway with those of Wisconsin. The Stoughton Norwegian Dancers perform several times during the celebration, and the events roster overflows with crafts, boat races, face painting, cheese tasting, food, music, chain saw carving, bingo, theatrical performances, and more. *stoughtonwi.com/ syttendemai*

■ Get Rowdy With Rømmergrøt
The Syttende Mai festivities in Westby, Wisconsin—a three-day affair—include a kiddie tractor pull, traditional Norwegian tunes, a contest to see who can consume the most *rømmergrøt* (a rich cream pudding), lots of music, raffles, a bike race for kids, craft demonstrations, a Syttende Mai princess

banquet and coronation, and, yes, a troll hunt. *westbysyttendemai.com*

■ Downtown Struttin' and Singing
A children's parade at the Vesterheim Norwegian-American Museum kicks off the Syttende Mai festivities in Decorah, Iowa. Also on the program is a performance by Decorah's Nordic Dancers and an opportunity for everyone to show off fancy footwork accompanied by the Foot-Notes, an old-time Nordic band. *vesterheim.org*

■ Go Nordic in the Northwest
There's plenty of Norwegian pride to go around in Seattle, Washington's Ballard neighborhood, home of both the Nordic Heritage Museum and the Leif Erikson Lodge. The celebration comes complete

with Vikings, accordion players, crafts for kids at the museum, and, of course, a big, big parade with marching bands that ends with yet more merrymaking and music in Bergen Place Park. *Ballard, myballard.com; Nordic Heritage Museum and the Leif Erikson Lodge, 2245 N.W. 57th St., Seattle, Wash., tel 206-783-1274, nordicmuseum.org, leif eriksonlodge.com*

■ Honorary Norwegians Welcome
The Norwegian Club of Montreal (Norkseklubben) in Canada, whose ranks include folks of Norwegian descent as well as "honorary Norwegians" (if you appreciate Norwegian culture and traditions, you're in), marks the holiday with a night of eating, toasting, singing, and dancing. *norskeklubben.ca*

FINNISH SAUNA

Let's get real, as in "authentic": A Finnish sauna is made of wood and heated by fire-baked rocks. When the Finnish first showed up in these remote, wooded communities, they brought the real deal with them: simple, very hot (somewhere between 170°F and 230°F), lighting moodily low, and, above all, silence reigning supreme. The "sow-na," as the Finnish say it, is still around if you look hard enough.

IN THE KNOW: "Taking a sauna" is not a once-in-a-while luxury for native Finns. It's an intrinsic part of the fiber of their culture. The numbers tell the story: In Finland, there are more than five million Finns and two million saunas. That comes down to approximately one sauna per family. Location? Preferably at the water's edge.

JOINING IN: Sit there serenely, trying to clear your mind, soaking up the heat, and sweating until you just cannot take it anymore. Next on the agenda: a jump into the lake to switch things up and cool you down. (Never mind if there's a paper-thin sheet of ice on the water.) Experience this slice of Helsinki on the North Shore of Lake Superior, at cozy Larsmont Cottages, where a Finnish sauna is just the thing after a day of hiking and, weather permitting, biking and canoeing. Come nightfall, there's heat of another sort, that which radiates from a bonfire and is just the

MORE · Finnish Saunas

Palmquist Farm, Brantwood, Wisconsin: A cozy reading room invites relaxation inside the wood-fired Finnish sauna, perfect after a day of bald eagle spotting, biking through the forest, and fishing. *River Rd., tel 715-564-2558, palmquistfarm.com*

Kangas Sauna, Thunder Bay, Ontario, Canada: A public bathhouse with 18 private, boiling-hot saunas, each with its own changing room and showers. And you can stop by for a pancake breakfast first. *379 Oliver Rd., tel 807-344-6761, kangassauna.ca*

Nurture Through Nature, Denmark, Maine: Relax in a Finnish sauna at this eco-retreat bordered by more than 1,300 acres of Nature Conservancy woodlands. Take your escapist choice: a basic solar-powered cabin with porch or a yurt. *77 Warren Rd., tel 855-207-7387, ntnretreats.com*

right temperature for toasting marshmallows, crafting s'mores, and thinking about the next day's sauna.

■ *Essentials:* Larsmont Cottages, 596 Larsmont Way, Two Harbors, Minn., tel 866-687-5634, larsmontcottages.com

Bonfire at the Larsmont Cottages, Two Harbors, Minnesota

Nature Through Nurture Retreat Center, Denmark, Maine

FROGTOWN

Relatively undiscovered, St. Paul's Frogtown is a historic neighborhood settled in the mid-19th century by European immigrants. Remaining true to its melting pot roots, Frogtown has residents who come largely from Mexico (Cinco de Mayo is jubilantly celebrated here), Africa, Asia, and—most notably—also include the Hmong, an Asian ethnic group from the mountainous regions of China, Thailand, Vietnam, and Laos whose Twin Cities population is the largest outside Southeast Asia (53,000).

WHERE TO GO: A stroll along University Avenue takes you past a fusion of restaurants celebrating this neighborhood's global flair. Ngon Vietnamese Bistro and Trieu Chau are local favorites. And in warmer months a bustling farmers market showcasing Southeast Asian specialties sets up here, offering a taste of the exotic (look for edible amaranth plants and spiky melons with glow-pink insides) and common (pho, bubble tea, stuffed chicken wings). For a bit of background on who's behind much of this tantalizing food, stop by the Hmong Cultural Center.

IN THE KNOW: It may or may not have anything to do with the French, depending on whom you believe. Some say the Frogtown appellation started as an anti-French settler slur. The other interpretation is a little swampy: The Bohemian-German immigrants who settled here some 150 years ago found that they were sharing their new turf with a slew of . . . frogs.

■ *Essentials:* Ngon Vietnamese Bistro, 799 University Ave., tel 651-222-3301, ngonbistro.com; Trieu Chau, 500 W. University Ave., tel 651-222-6148; Hmongtown Marketplace Farmers Market, 217 Como Ave., tel 651-487-3700, hmongtownmarketplace.com; Hmong Cultural Center, 375 University Ave. W., tel 651-917-9937, hmongcc.org

New Year's dress fitting at Frogtown's Hmong Marketplace

"Frogtown is liberally dotted with small, family-owned Asian restaurants." —CATHERINE FLYNN, ST. PAUL RESIDENT

The Houby Days Festival in Cedar Rapids celebrates Czech and Slovak culture.

CEDAR RAPIDS, IOWA
CZECH VILLAGE

Sporting a colorful embroidered dress with a flower garland ringing her head, Iowa's Miss Czech-Slovak offers the queen's slow wave from her pickup-towed float. It's St. Joseph's Day in March, aka the Czech St. Patrick's Day, and the turnout, despite the perennially nippy weather, is impressive. "There is an identity here," says Gail Naughton, president and CEO of the Cedar Rapids, Iowa, National Czech & Slovak Museum & Library. "People are very proud of it. Flags fly."

JOINING IN: In addition to St. Joseph's Day, Czech and Slovak pride shine during annual festivals devoted to spring mushrooms (Houby Days Festival), beer in fall (Czechtoberfest), and Christmas ornaments in December (Old World Christmas Market). But it's a part of everyday life too. "Because there was a heritage of struggle, it has really made people closer to that history," Naughton says. The strength of the town's Czech roots was on display when three sitting presidents—Bill Clinton, Vaclav Havel (Czech Republic), and Michal Kovac (Slovakia)—attended the opening of the museum.

WHAT TO EAT: Among the thriving businesses in the three-block-long strip known as Czech Village, follow your nose to the jam-filled *koláče* pastries and rye bread at Sykora Bakery. And toss back a pint of Živá Voda beer,

INSIGHT · Midwestern Melting Pot

Czech and Slovak workers originally settled Czech Village and the larger New Bohemia neighborhoods, together about 40 recently revitalized blocks, a success story but not the only one in multicultural Cedar Rapids. New Bohemia is also home to the African American Museum of Iowa. And the city hosts the 12-acre Muslim National Cemetery established in 1948, long after immigrants from today's Syria and Lebanon began arriving in the late 20th century.

named for the healing water of Czech fairy tales, at boutique Lion Bridge Brewing Company.

■ *Essentials:* National Czech & Slovak Museum & Library, 1400 Inspiration Pl. S.W., tel 319-362-8500, ncsml.org; Houby Days Festival, cedar-rapids.com; Czechtoberfest, czechtober .com; Old World Christmas Market, ncsml.org; Czech Village, czechvillagecedarrapids.com; Sykora Bakery, 73 16th Ave., tel 319-364-5271, sykorabakery.com; Lion Bridge Brewing Company, 59 16th Ave. S.W., tel 319-200-4460, lionbridgebrewing.com

DUTCH VILLAGE

A slowly revolving windmill, fields of tulips, and canal houses with Amsterdam-style peaked roofs—Pella's landmarks suggest a check of the GPS. Central Iowa this is, where the custom-designed Klokkenspel, with eight four-foot mechanical figures and 147 bell chimes, performs regularly throughout the day.

IN THE KNOW: In 1847, some 800 Dutch immigrants seeking religious freedom followed Amsterdam-born Hendrik Pieter Scholte to Pella, or City of Refuge. Today, a vital economy—Pella is home to the eponymous window company, Vermeer equipment manufacturer, and Central College—helps the lively town of just 10,000 maintain its heritage.

WHAT TO SEE: The canal-spanning Molengracht drawbridge looks lifted out of a van Gogh painting. The country's tallest working windmill, the Vermeer Mill landmarks the 20-building Pella Historical Village, preserving a historic church, bakery, and the boyhood home of Western legend Wyatt Earp. On the town square, the home of Pella founder Scholte exhibits period antiques and paintings.

WHAT TO EAT: Indulge your sweet tooth at one of Pella's traditional Dutch bakeries, including Vander Ploeg Bakery, specialist in "Dutch letters," S-shaped pastry filled with almond paste. Try Jaarsma Bakery on the town square for treats including *speculaas* (Dutch spice cookies) and *boter koek* (almond butter cake). Stay at the Cheesemaker's Inn at Frisian Farms, where the innkeepers make aged Gouda cheese in small batches.

■ *Essentials:* Pella Historical Village, 507 Franklin St., tel 641-620-9463, pellahistorical.org; Scholte House, 507 Franklin St., tel 641-628-3684; Vander Ploeg Bakery, 711 Franklin St., tel 641-628-2293, pellabakery.com; Jaarsma Bakery, 727 Franklin St., tel 641-628-2940, jaarsmabakery.com; The Cheesemaker's Inn, 420 Idaho Dr., tel 641-628-1448, cheesemakersinn.com

The Klompen (wooden shoe) Maker float, Pella's Tulip Time Parade

DIGGING DEEPER

Though the 124-foot Vermeer Mill looks like an authentic 1850s-era gristmill, it was actually built in 2002 by Dutch craftsmen. But the wind-powered mill is authentic in the most essential regard: It grinds wheat into flour, sold in the gift shop.

Pella's Vermeer Mill is a working Dutch-style grain mill.

NORWEGIAN HERITAGE

If someone wants to pull your leg in Decorah, Iowa, they'll tell you they like lutefisk—that smelly Norwegian staple of whitefish treated in lye—especially if you slather it in butter. Families in the northern Iowa community, many of whom have been here since the 1850s, apply a healthy sense of humor to their traditions, and rib the gullible in the process.

JOINING IN: Each July, Nordic Fest showcases the town's well-traveled Nordic Dancers made up of children who audition at age three and, if they make the cut, stay on through high school. The festival also features a juried competition in wood carving, weaving, and other crafts, all taught at the town's impressive Vesterheim Norwegian-American Museum, the largest museum devoted to one ethnic group. "We're much more than a museum," says tour guide David Amdahl of the 24,000-object museum.

Also be sure to explore the ground's dozen Norwegian-style buildings, mostly built in the mid-19th century.

IN THE KNOW: In addition to providing genealogy classes, Vesterheim proudly offers classes in making traditional foods such as *lefse* and Christmas cookies; Norwegian rosemaling, a form of decorative painting; and *nalbinding*, a kind of crochet technique. On a regular basis visitors can take home Norwegian candy, plus painted Dala horse figurines, Viking motif jewelry, and lutefisk cookbooks from Vanberia International Gifts just a few blocks from the museum.

■ *Essentials:* Nordic Fest, nordicfest.com; Vesterheim Norwegian-American Museum, 502 W. Water St., tel 563-382-9681, vesterheim.org; Vanberia International Gifts, 217 W. Water St., tel 563-382-4892, vanberiadecorah.com

The Vikings take a breather at Decorah's Nordic Fest.

"He said he didn't realize there was a place that could be as Norwegian as we are here." —Museum guide David Amdahl, quoting a visitor

John D. McGurk's Irish Pub, St. Louis, Missouri

IRISH PUBS

Enjoy a pint (or more) along with some neighborhood bluster and brogue.

■ John D. McGurk's
Few of the pubs in Dublin's touristy Temple Bar even match the authentic vibe of McGurk's in St. Louis, Missouri: worn, wood floors; high-backed wood booths; a maze of mismatched rooms; and live Celtic music, including acts straight from the Auld Sod, seven nights a week. Some 16 beers are on tap and about 45 in bottles. Barkeeps are schooled in the art of the perfect pour: the tilt, the settle, and the temperature, 42 to 45°F. *1200 Russell Blvd., St. Louis, Mo., tel 314-776-8309, mcgurks.com*

■ Clancy's Tavern and Whiskey House
It helps if you're an Irish whisky drinker (the bar stocks more than 25), but don't let that stop you from popping inside this Knoxville, Tennessee, Irish mainstay. Custom woodworker Art Clancy designed and installed the gleaming wood interiors, which look as authentically Irish as the four Clancy brothers. Younger brother Danny is a co-owner, and an extended Clancy clan helps keep the place humming. *602 S. Gay St., Knoxville, Tenn., tel 865-219-1266, clancystavernknoxville.com*

■ Fifth Province Pub at the Irish American Heritage Center
Families are a fixture in Ireland's village pubs, so it only seems appropriate that this most Irish of bars in Chicago, Illinois, is tucked inside a former elementary school. The local Irish-American stonemasons, woodworkers, and other craftsmen who built the space wanted to create a homey place for Irish expats and Irish Americans (and those who wish they were) to share news and celebrate special occasions. There's live music on weekends and a full menu (including curry fries, Shepherd's Pie, and Irish Country Stew). *4626 N. Knox Ave., Chicago, Ill., tel 773-282-7035, irish-american.org*

■ Johnnie Fox's Irish Snug
Johnnie Fox's in Vancouver, British Columbia, skips the main pub part and goes straight to the intimate "snug," traditional clandestine rooms where pub patrons (parish priests, illicit couples) could sip a pint away from prying eyes. Plan a midafternoon visit (before the after-work crowd arrives) for the authentic Irish pub trifecta: muffled conversations in the back booths, curry chips (homemade fries and Jasmine rice smothered in curry sauce), and a Crown Float (Magners Cider and Guinness). *1033 Granville St., Vancouver, B.C., tel 604-685-4946, johnniefox.ca*

■ The Burren
At the Burren in Somerville, Massachusetts, the owners are traditional Irish musicians, a few of the bartenders' thick brogues are indecipherable, and the atmospherics are blue-collar comfy. Most nights the traditional Celtic harmonies and fiddling you hear are performed by actual Irishmen (past acts include Bono, the Chieftains, and Altan). Meet some Irish expats at the Monday (twice monthly) dancing lessons and sessions. Says patron and documentary film producer Jess Barnthouse, "Some people think the waiters are rude, but they're actually just Irish." *247 Elm St., Somerville, Mass., tel 617-776-6896, burren.com*

RHINELAND ON THE MISSOURI

W hen German immigrants, frustrated by Philadelphia conservatism, settled on the scenic bluffs of the Missouri River here almost 200 years ago, Hermann immediately became a Rhineland stand-in. Wine, more than beer, was the name of the game. The German flair still prospers, with Bavarian-style buildings, a wurst festival, a Maifest, and, of course Oktoberfest.

WHAT TO DO: Sitting in the heart of Missouri's so-called Rhineland, or Weinstrasse, Hermann's nine wineries link the area to its German past. In the heart of town, Stone Hill Winery, with its pastoral rolling-hill views, is housed in a building that dates from 1869. A tour and tasting starts at $2.50.

WHAT TO EAT: It's not just bottles that bear the Hermann-German heritage. For many residents here, a real meal means one thing: lots of sausage. "More people make sausage here than any place I know of," explains Mike Sloan, a sausage-making vet who opened Hermann Wurst Haus in 2011. He now makes sure the number of sausage makers is growing by hosting summer soup-to-nuts (actually fermenting to casing) beginners' classes—something visitors can time a stay to do.

INSIGHT · Bike the "Rhineland"

Explore the region's picturesque hills and bluffs along the Katy Trail, a 240-mile rail-to-trail project along the Missouri River, the longest in the United States, that passes right by Hermann. Heartier visitors can pedal winery to winery, exploring other picturesque small towns along the way. Or opt for a makeshift picnic on a woodsy spot just outside town.

JOINING IN: To get an extra dose of oompah into your itinerary, time a visit for one of the local festivals, particularly March's Wurstfest for sausage (third weekend in March), Maifest (third weekend of May), or Oktoberfest (every weekend in October).

■ *Essentials:* hermannmo.com; Stone Hill Winery, 1110 Stone Hill Hwy., tel 573-486-2221, stonehillwinery.com; Hermann Wurst Haus, 234 1st St., tel 573-415-8330, hermannwurst haus.com

Wurst Haus, Hermann's go-to for German sausage and bratwurst

"When our ancestors came here, they had wine in one hand, and a sausage in the other." —MIKE SLOANE, HERMANN WURST HAUS

FRENCH VALLEY PANACHE

A time-warp street scene of historic buildings beckons you to this button-cute town of 4,000 just 75 miles south of St. Louis. Named for Paris's patron saint, Missouri's oldest town passed into Spanish then American hands after the Louisiana Purchase in 1803, but the French settlers stuck around.

WHAT TO DO: As you amble around to absorb Ste. Genevieve's Francophile flair, you'll notice many buildings sporting the distinctive *poteaux sur solle* ("posts-on-a-sill") style. Perhaps the best stop is the Bolduc House, a French Creole "vertical log house" built in 1770 with a wide wraparound porch for summer shade. Nearly all the wood furnishings inside are originals, and the garden is kept up especially for Zuts (French for "heck!"), the site's squirrel mascot. The Felix Vallé House State Historic Site, showcasing a little cottage built in 1818, stages a French pastry–filled Christmas event complete with dulcimer music, candles, and presenters posing as the post–Louisiana Purchase French couple who lived there.

WHAT TO EAT: For some duck *à l'orange* and champignons in your soup, Ste. Genevieve's excellent French

INSIGHT • French Connection

The flatbed Ste. Genevieve-Modoc River Ferry connects the Ste. Genevieve area with French sites in Illinois. First built in 1720, Fort de Chartres hosts a rendezvous event in June, while Kaskaskia is home to a "Liberty Bell of the West," donated by Louis XV and rung after American independence. The five-minute trip across the Mississippi runs all year—cheaper if you're going by horse, as some residents do. *stegenmodocferry.com*

restaurant is found at the historic Inn St. Gemme Beauvais. Of course, you'll see wineries here too, along with a fair share of fleur-de-lis emblems on storefronts.

■ *Essentials:* Bolduc House Museum, 125 S. Main St., tel 573-883-3105, bolduchouse.org; Felix Vallé House State Historic Site, 198 Merchant St., mostateparks.com; Inn St. Gemme Beauvais, 78 N. Main St., tel 800-818-5744, innstgemme.com

French Heritage Festival at Felix Vallé House State Historic Site

Lindsborg celebrates the Scandinavian legend of Lucia in December.

LINDSBORG, KANSAS
SWEDEN ON THE PLAINS

Founded by Swedish immigrants after the Civil War, Lindsborg—named for three similarly named Swedes—wears its heritage openly. About one in three residents have Swedish surnames, or, as Mark Lysell, who runs the Ol Stuga ("Ale House") bar, puts it, "Look in the phone book and you'll see maybe one Miller or Jones, then about 34 Larsens."

WHAT TO SEE: Pony-size, brightly painted wooden Swedish Dala horses line the central streets. Look for the biggest one, standing sentry outside Hemslöjd, a gift shop filled with Swedish handicrafts. Afterward, visit the original Swedish Pavilion, transported here from St. Louis's World's Fair in 1904, part of a complex that champions the town's past.

A few miles north of town, Coronado Heights, marking a spot the Spanish conquistador supposedly visited in the 16th century, has a sandstone castle from the 1930s, offering big views of Lindsborg and the plains stretching beyond.

WHERE TO EAT: Lysell's Ol Stuga (which sells its kooky retro-themed Viking T-shirts by the bundle) serves a pickled herring and *bond-ost* cheese plate for $6.25. It's busy with locals (who mostly come for non-Swedish fare—and beer). You can't leave town without trying other Swedish favorites, like pancakes or meatballs. A popular Swedish restaurant, the Swedish Crown, serves them, and even dunks its barbecue sauce with lingonberries, another Swedish staple from the Old World.

■ *Essentials:* Hemslöjd, 201 N. Main St., tel 785-227-2983, hemslojd.com; Swedish Pavilion, 120 Mill St., tel 785-227-3595; Ol Stuga, 119 S. Main St., tel 785-227-8762; Swedish Crown, 121 N. Main St., tel 785-227-8422, theswedishcrown.com

DIGGING DEEPER

It wasn't until the early 20th century that Lindsborg's Swedish settlers started to speak English. According to Kansas Historical Society documents, in 1919 "children often answered . . . their parents in English, although the mother or father had used Swedish in making the inquiry."

You Could Be In . . . HUNGARY

**Prairielands of
the Dakotas**
Get lost in the Dakota
prairie and you could
almost be standing on
the steppes of the Great
Hungarian Plain.

AROUND THE WORLD IN
OMAHA

Traditional costumes and dancing at Omaha, Nebraska's Greek festival

Little Bohemia

The lifeblood of Omaha's Little Bohemia district, the Bohemian Café has been run by Czech Americans since the 1920s. It's hard to miss. South of the tracks from downtown, the sky-blue and crimson restaurant shouts fun. Inside, half-century-old paintings of Czech figures line walls, and fresh plates of plum dumplings, *svickova* (Czech sauerbraten), and *koláče* (pastries) fill the tables. You'll find Pilsner Urquell on draft too, of course. The adjoining Bohemian Girl Cocktail Lounge is on hipster radar, with (very sweet) Bohemian Shepherd Pie cocktails. "It's not just polka anymore," explains Terry Capoun, café manager.

Bohemian Café, 1406 S. 13th St., tel 402-342-9838, bohemiancafe.net

Goodness Greek!

Done up in the stark blue and white of a Greek Orthodox cathedral in Corfu, Center Street finds a surprise in this cube-like establishment across from a golf course (a couple blocks west of Gerald Ford's birth site). For more than 30 years, the family-run Greek Islands has been a beloved go-to for flaming cheese *sanganaki*, yogurt-dunked souvlaki, and weekend lamb shank dinners. *Greek Islands, 3821 Center St., tel 402-346-1528, greekislandsomaha.com*

German Feast

Modest to the eye, Gerda's—a simple one-floor place next to a gas station—makes a big mark on the Omaha palate for serious devotion to schnitzel and Reubens. The German native offers freshly baked loaves of German rye or strudels, as well as D-mark . . . Euro-friendly, that is, dinners complete with breaded pork in burgundy sauce, a glass of imported Dunkel beer on tap, and a black forest cherry torte. Try to come in mid-September, when Gerda throws her own Oktoberfest, with German bands and a lot of wurst. There will be clarinets and lederhosen. *Gerda's German Restaurant & Bakery, 5180 Leavenworth St., tel 402-553-6774, gerdas germanrestaurant.com*

South Omaha has always been diverse. But 20 years ago, there were vacant buildings along 24th Street. I remember having to have bread shipped in for Day of the Dead celebrations. Today, hardly anything's empty and there are bakeries making *rosca de reyes*, the king's bread we have for the celebrations. It's a very rich part of the city, very much alive, very unique for Omaha. Not just during festivals, but any time you can see all this hustle and bustle, people walking the sidewalks, going to groceries, or shops, or bakeries. It's a real taste of Latin America.

MAGDALENA GARCIA
Executive director, El Museo Latino

Heartland Latino

Around the corner from 24th Street in South Omaha, El Museo Latino serves as a base for area events like Cinco de Mayo, and a breathless source of classes and art exhibits on subjects like Latin American graphics and history of Omaha Latinos. Housed in a former school (then a Polish cultural center), the museum itself is a rarity. Open since 1993, it's the only Museo Latino in the Midwest, and just one of 11 in the United States. *El Museo Latino, 4701 S. 25th St., tel 402-731-1137, elmuseolatino.org*

Polka Detour

In a state where polka is alive and quite real, the best side trip may well be 40 miles west of Omaha, Wahoo's Starlite Ballroom. The wood-floor dance hall fills with couples who've been into this scene for half a century or more. A regular is the Mark Vyhlidal Orchestra, whose leader is host of the *All-Star Polka Show*, a long-time Columbus, Nebraska, radio show. Brought by Czechs in the 1850s, Omaha's polka roots persist on cornmeal-coated AM radio too— as "a kind of weekly newspaper for the older generations" per the *New York Times*. *Starlite Ballroom, 2045 Cty. Rd. K, tel 402-443-3533, starliteballroom.org*

International Omaha

South Omaha (aka "Magic City") has always been an immigrant hub, with droves of Czechs, Germans, Lithuanians, Somali, and Latin Americans settling in. The nearby stockyards are gone, but the international buzz remains. Twenty-fourth Street is lined with Spanish-speaking butchers, grocers, bakeries, and taco stands—and some colorful murals at N Street. "It's a very active streetscape, family oriented and diverse," explains Vince Furlong, who runs walking tours of the area. "It's unlike any other part of the city. Just go mosey from Avenue L to Avenue P." One place to head that's the real deal, very popular Mexican *panadería* (bakery), International Bakery, a couple blocks south of the main crawl, is a self-service maze of goodies, most for under a dollar. *South 24th Walking Tour, tel 402-709-2586, south24thomahatour .com; International Bakery, 5106 S. 24th St., tel 402-731-0988*

Celebrating Cinco de Mayo in Omaha

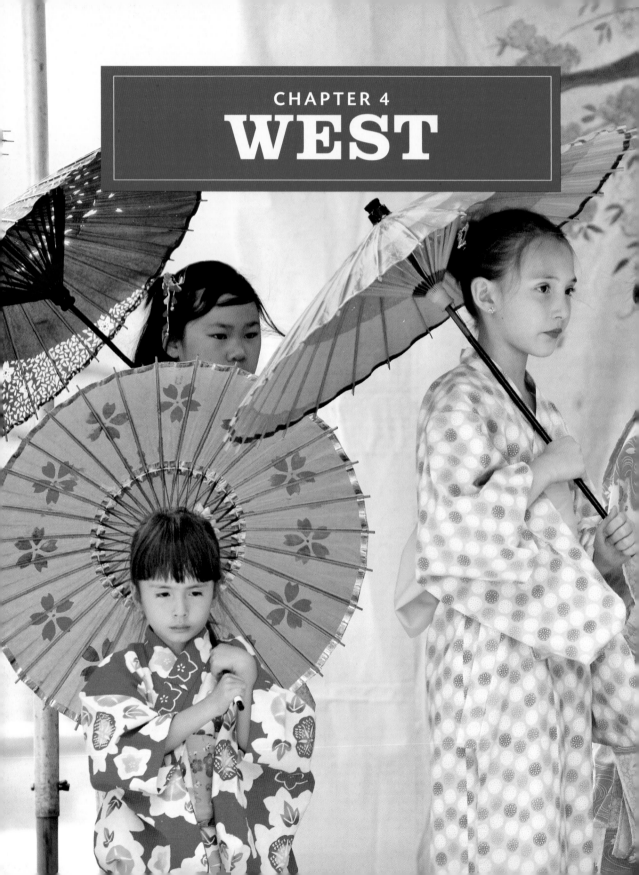

Preparing to perform a traditional Japanese children's dance at the Denver, Colorado, Cherry Blossom Festival

AROUND THE WORLD IN
HOUSTON

Cooking class at the Raindrop Turkish House in Houston

Asian Treasure

See how H-town has grown into a city with elegant, international cred at the understated Asia Society Texas Center. This newish (completed in 2012), $48.4 million building itself is worth the trip to the city's Museum District. Respected Japanese architect Yoshio Taniguchi—he redesigned New York's Museum of Modern Art—spared nothing in its sleek design. Those huge slabs of limestone? Handpicked from Germany's Black Forest. The marble underfoot? Straight from Italy. Still, you'll feel as if you're floating through a continent of Asian creativity as you browse the changing exhibits,

including painting and sculpture from leading contemporary Asian artists.
Asia Society Texas Center, 1370 Southmore Blvd., tel 713-496-9901, asiasociety.org/texas

Nostrovia!

Assemble a Slavic picnic at the Russian General Store. If you can't read the Cyrillic labels and the guy behind the counter doesn't speak much English, just take a closer look: Caviars of all kinds, smoked mackerel, Hungarian salamis, breads, and imported candies are among the Slavic selections here. Food is arranged by country of origin and extends beyond Russia to include Poland, Israel, and Armenia.

The Russian General Store, 9629 Hillcroft St., tel 713-665-1177

Indian Threads (and Treats)

Fashionistas will want to get their shop on at Gurya Rani Designer Boutique in a neighborhood sometimes called Little India (officially designated the Mahatma Gandhi District). Indian, Pakistani, and American clientele shop for traditional casual, bridal, and "party wear" ensembles in eye-popping colors and a variety of fabrics including cotton, silk, and chiffon. Some of the more elaborate stone-and-thread-embellished pieces can weigh up

This place means a lot to me because you're speaking in your native tongue, eating the kind of food you would have at home, and you are bumping into long-lost friends. It developed in the 1980s. There was a need for immigrants to come together, and one little restaurant, Raja, was the nucleus. The owner, Yogi Gahunia, would sit with you over chai, samosas, and *pakora* (fried snack food); it's still there. Since then there's been a lot of growth—grocery stores, jewelry, and clothing stores, coffee shops and restaurants that are very appealing not only to Indian and Pakistani people, but those from other communities. India Coffee House is very popular with the younger generation; everything starts over a cup of tea or coffee.

SHOBANA MURATEE
Editor, Voice of Asia

Grand lion dance at Houston's Tet Festival

to 30 pounds. (Cash customers receive a discount.). Afterward, just down the street in this "Little India" neighborhood, don't miss Raja Quality Restaurant and Sweets. Despite its modest, strip mall bearing, it's known for its fresh, traditional Indian treats, including *jalebi* (a sweet fried pretzel), sweet and syrupy doughnut-like *jamun*, and a case-ful of hard-to-resist sweet finds.
Gurya Rani Designer Boutique, 5711 Hillcroft St., tel 713-614-0325, facebook.com/ guryaranidesigner; Raja Quality Restaurant and Sweets, 5667 Hillcroft St., tel 713-782-5667

Turkish Delight
Tables of ornate necklaces and dangly copper earrings, platters of kebabs right off the grill, henna artists at the ready to decorate your extremities—along with the occasional costumed Ottoman band—gather for two days every fall at Houston's annual Turkishfest. Or year-round, follow the lead of the city's Turkish community for an Istanbul-worthy meal at the Empire Turkish Grill. Its vegetarian- and carnivore-friendly Ottoman menu starts with cold appetizers, or *mezze,* like the standout *lebni,* a soft yogurt cheese flavored with walnuts and dill. Turkish pasta with feta, butter, parsley, and rich tomato sauce is a house specialty rarely seen on menus. Cap your meal with a cup of famed Turkish coffee: finely pulverized beans and sugar that combine to yield a potent, velvety sipping experience.
Turkishfest, turkishfest houston.com; Empire Turkish Grill, 12448 Memorial Dr., tel 713-827-7475, empiretrgrill.com

Little Saigon
Foodies will want to head over to Houston's original Vietnamese enclave on Milam Street in midtown Bellaire. Mai's, one of the city's first Vietnamese restaurants, is a favorite of Vietnamese Houstonians. (To satisfy demand, it serves until 4 a.m. on weekends.) Try the crabmeat and asparagus soup and fresh lemonade. Up for karaoke? Test your mettle at Glitter Karaoke. Bellaire, a major thoroughfare, is also at the heart of the action for the city's Vietnamese population.
Mai's Restaurant, 3403 Milam St., tel 713-520-5300, maishouston.com; Glitter Karaoke, 2621 Milam St., tel 713-526-4900, glitterkaraoke.com

Mahatma Gandhi in bronze, Hermann Park, Houston

MAHATMA GANDHI
October 2, 1869 - January 30, 1948

An apostle of truth, peace and non-violence who led India to Freedom from British rule in 1947, and is hailed as the Father of the Nation

South African *potjies* lined up for competition in Trinity

TRINITY, TEXAS
SOUTH AFRICA COOK-OFF

By some estimates, at least 80,000 South African expats are living in the United States, but it's Trinity, Texas, that plays host to the one-of-a-kind U.S. Potjie Festival. (Ontario, Canada, also hosts a popular *potjie* festival in late August every year.) Though not as well known stateside as chili cook-offs or barbecue competitions, a *potjie* contest in South African circles is a heated affair. A *potjie* is a cousin of the Dutch oven, a three-legged cast-iron pot introduced in South Africa in the 17th century.

JOINING IN: Held every Labor Day weekend, the Texas Potjie Festival draws hundreds of attendees for a family-friendly weekend of camping, *sokkie* dancing (Afrikaans for "sock hop"), and team cooking competitions. Preparation begins months in advance. By Friday of the three-day weekend, the *braai* (fire) is lit and the aromas begin wafting through the grounds. The prizes are modest but the judging is rigorous; it's bragging rights that really matter when you're talking about such traditional culinary staples as *boerewors* (sausage), *biltong*, a jerky-like dried, salted meat snack, and rusks, or biscuits. For those 16 and under, there's a youth competition. Since it started in 2000, the festival has grown to include a watermelon-eating contest, tug-of-war battle, and a Sunday church service in Afrikaans. "The Potjie Festival has grown significantly over the years, with about 600 people attending it now," says organizer John Els. "It has become a type of homecoming for many, with many attendees coming from outside Texas, and sometimes even from outside the U.S.A."

■ *Essentials:* Texas Potjie Festival, texaspotjie.com

CHICANO AUTHENTICO

You can hear strolling mariachis or shop for *artesanías* (handicrafts) at "El Mercado," bustling Market Square, San Antonio's must-see hub of Latino everything. All good fun, but to explore the real heart of the city's authentic Hispanic experience, you'll need to venture just west into the city's Westside.

WHAT TO SEE: Buzzing with energy, the Guadalupe Cultural Arts Center, made up of six buildings, is a multimedia bonanza of Chicano music, art, dance, theater—you name it. It hosts an artist incubator, a museum, film festivals, plus May's Tejano Conjunto, celebrating button accordionists and a local music form that blends German and Mexican traditions. And, of course, there's food. Its newest addition: a corn garden to demonstrate how tortillas are made, from seed to the pan.

WHERE TO EAT: Another must-stop is Ray's Drive Inn, a diner-esque, 1950s survivor. The family-oriented eatery, decked in neon and nostalgia, is famous for the world's first "puffy taco" (at least by name). The doughy shell is cooked in hot oil until it bubbles into a flaky, fun shell, best when filled with *carne guisada* (stewed beef).

WHERE TO SHOP: Flamenco fans should stop by Mariachi Connection, set in a historic mansion. Women's

INSIGHT · Murals, Murals, Murals

On and off Guadalupe and Commerce Streets, you'll see more than 100 brightly painted murals covering the sides of old warehouses or brick walls of corner market stores. Together, they tell a tale of the Latino community, often with Chicano art styles that grew up in the "barrio" here five decades ago. The best way to see them is on a guided bike tour with San Anto Cultural Arts, instrumental in mapping and planning the area's artscape. *sananto.org*

dancing shoes and lace-up boots along with decorative fans may inspire even the flat-footed.

■ *Essentials:* Guadalupe Cultural Arts Center, 723 S. Brazos St., tel 210-271-3151, guadalupeculturalarts.org; Ray's Drive Inn, 822 S.W. 19th St., tel 210-432-7171, raysdriveinn.net; Mariachi Connection, 2106 W. Commerce St., tel 210-271-3655, mariachiconnection.com

The mural "La Musica de San Anto" honors San Antonio musicians.

"We are still the barrio, but now there are nice coffee shops, restaurants, and the public bikes are coming in."
—YVONNE MONTOYA, GUADALUPE CULTURAL ARTS CENTER

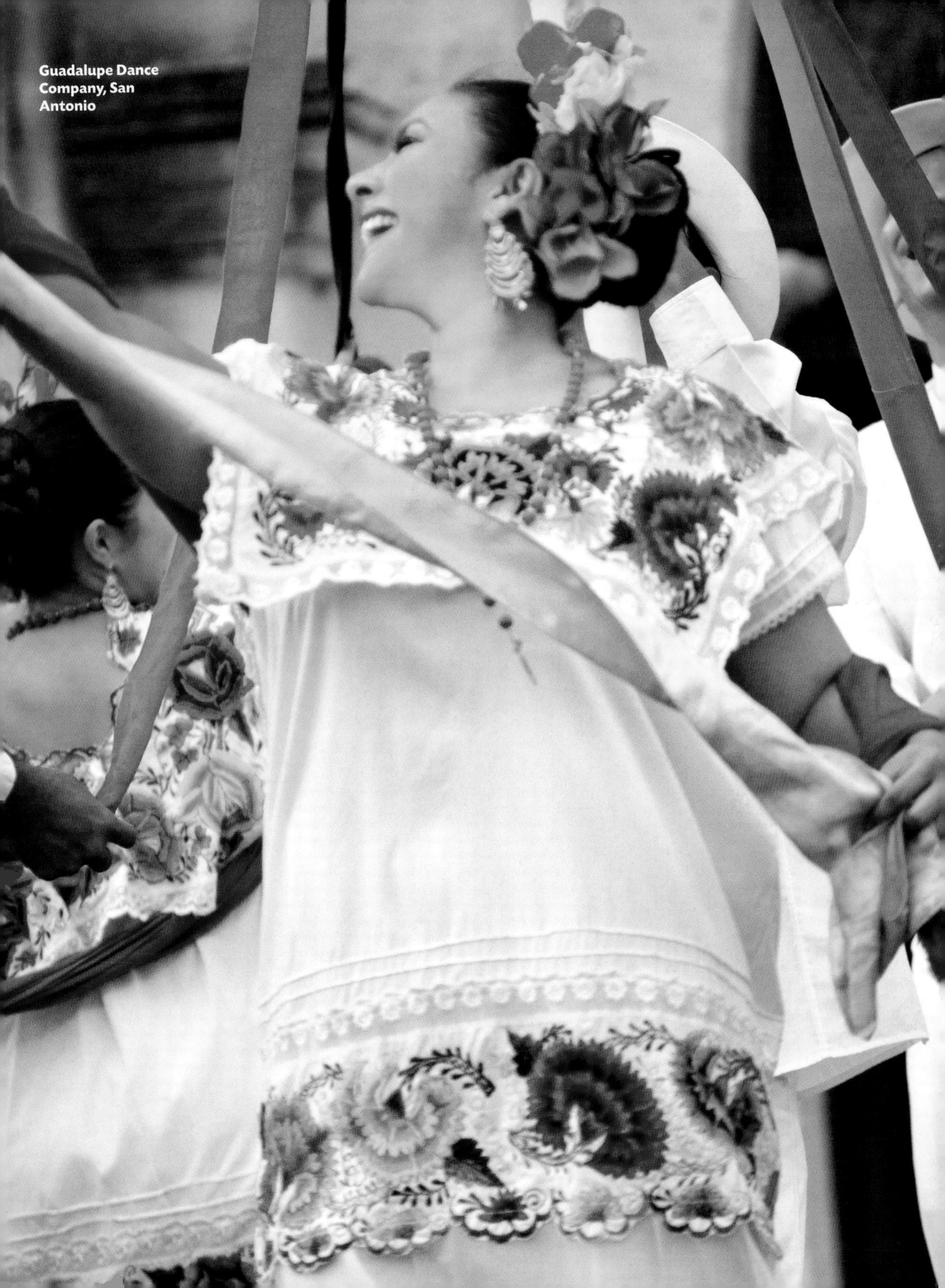

Guadalupe Dance Company, San Antonio

You Could Be In . . . KENYA

San Antonio, Texas
Zebras, giraffes, rhinos—
Natural Bridge Wildlife
Ranch is an African
safari brought to you in
the heart of Texas.

Creamy Italian
gelato at
San Antonio's
Paciugo Gelato
& Caffè

ITALIAN GELATO

Rivaling the best of Italy, these gelaterias are the ultimate sweet spots.

■ **Paciugo Gelato & Caffè**

With at least 44 locations in 16 states, including one in San Antonio, this family-run operation boasts a coast-to-coast following. Unusual offerings include black pepper olive oil and rose sangria, along with perennial favorites like *dulce de leche*.
Tel 212-654-9501. For locations, go to paciugo.com.

■ **That's Amore**

When desert temperatures soar, the smart set heads to this shop near picturesque hiking hot spot Pinnacle Peak in Scottsdale, Arizona. Artisan-crafted flavors include coconut, wild raspberry, and cinnamon.
7605 E. Pinnacle Peak Rd., Scottsdale, Ariz., tel 480-419-6280, thats amoregelato.com

■ **Fainting Goat Gelato**

In Seattle, Washington's trendy Wallingford neighborhood, this shop has a chill personality that complements its swoon-worthy scoops of pistachio and salted caramel, made with organic milk, natch.
1903 N. 45th St., Seattle, Wash., tel 206-327-9459, faintinggoatseattle .blogspot.com

■ **Gelato Bus Stop**

Travel photographer Nancy Ross praises the rich and creamy hazelnut and straight-from-Italy pistachio at this Pacific Beach gelateria in San Diego, California, that doubles as a prime beachfront, people-watching locale.
1001 Garnet Ave., San Diego, Calif., tel 619-578-3828, sdgelato.com

■ **Ono Gelato Company**

After hanging ten, try a post-surf sweet such as Big Island Coffee Crunch and Lilikoi in Lahaina, Hawaii, a locally grown passion fruit. The owners' roots stretch from Hawaii to Torino.
815 Front St., Lahaina, Hawaii, tel 808-495-0203, onogelatocompany.com

■ **Bella Gelateria**

This Vancouver, British Columbia, shop claims to be the first to use classic Italian equipment in North America; the New World results have garnered numerous awards. Among 24 flavors available daily are favorites like espresso and vanilla, along with unusual concoctions such as black sesame and *faloudah*, a rosewater and noodle combo.
1001 W. Cordova St., Vancouver, B.C., tel 604-569-1010, bellagelateria.com

■ **Morano Gelato**

Enthusiasts rave that this Hanover, New Hampshire, store is the real deal: a Sicilian gelateria that uses seasonal ingredients to craft small batches of flavors such as sweet milk and melon in a small college town almost worth the price of admission.
57 South Main St., Suite 101, Hanover, N.H., tel 603-643-4233, moranogelato hanover.com

■ **Black Dog Gelato**

Chicago, Illinois's pastry chef turned gelato maker Jessie Oloroso has built a reputation—and a following at two in-town locations—for her sweet and savory treats, which include luscious goat cheese cashew caramel and maple cayenne bacon.
859 N. Damen Ave., tel 773-235-3116, and 1955 W. Belmont Ave., Chicago, Ill., tel 773-348-7935, blackdogchicago.com

GERMAN ROOTS

For a good decade of the 19th century, much of Germany dreamed of Texas. Or rather a "New Germany" based in Texas. The center of all that sprung from 1845, when Prince Carl founded New Braunfels (then left for Germany when his fiancée refused to follow). What survives, and thrives, is one of the country's most historic German-American communities—and famed for its Schlitterbahn, a German-themed water park.

WHERE TO EAT: Empty bellies find themselves filled fast in New Braunfels, often with a uniquely German-Texan taste. Start at Naegelin's, Texas's oldest bakery, which sticks with its original lineup of molasses cookies, pecan-filled pretzels, and strudels.

JOINING IN: Hope you like sausage. "The first German immigrants had to find new ways to spice their sausage, with what they could find locally," says Rocky Tays of New Braunfels Smokehouse, and *opa* (grandfather) of November's ten-day Wurstfest. A good place to go for German-style schnitzel (topped in jalapeno gravy, if you choose) is the *biergarten* at Friesenhaus, which hosts real-deal German oompah music most weekends.

WHAT TO SEE: There are plenty of physical reminders of German roots too. The Sophienburg Museum has several built by German craftsmen. And you can stay in a unique one at the atmospheric Prince Solms Inn, around since

INSIGHT · Hot Stuff

Texas chili owes its kick to German immigrant William Gebhardt, who set up shop in New Braunfels and developed a taste, when in season, for Mexican chili peppers. He grew tired of waiting for chili season, so used a meat grinder to create (and can) chili powder. See the blessed spot—it was just behind a historic bar now called the Phoenix Saloon—then try the sirloin chili doused, of course, in Gebhardt's masterpiece. *193 W. San Antonio St., tel 830-643-1400, thephoenixsaloon.com*

1898. Go for its Joseph Klein Haus, a one-time German immigrant's cobbler shop, now a cozy cottage on a leafy side street.

■ *Essentials:* nbtexas.org; Naegelin's Bakery, 129 S. Seguin Ave., tel 830-625-5722, naegelins.com; Friesenhaus, 148 S. Castell Ave., tel 830-625-1040, friesenhausnb.com; Sophienburg Museum, 401 W. Coll St., tel 830-629-1572, sophienburg.com; Prince Solms Inn, 295 E. San Antonio St., tel 830-625-9169, princesolmsinn.com

The Weihnachtsmarkt (or Christmas Market), Sophienburg Museum in New Braunfels

SPANISH SHRINE

El Santuario de Chimayo (also known as Lourdes of America) in remote Chimayo, New Mexico, is a modest adobe church with a big reputation. The shrine is legendary for its tales of miracles, legends, and mysterious healing powers. More than 300,000 pilgrims a year flock here. Visitors are also transported to the dry hills of Guatemala, where the story begins.

IN THE KNOW: El Santuario de Chimayo, one of the oldest Spanish settlements in the southwestern United States, is steeped in stories of miracles. The legend of a miraculous apparition of Christ and shrine in Guatemala was first carried here by early (18th- and early 19th-century) Catholic Spanish immigrants. A local priest is said to have seen a mysterious light emerging from the ground. When he dug to see what was there, he discovered a crucifix, which he associated with the Guatemalan legend. The church was built on the spot in 1813.

WHAT TO SEE: After passing through a small courtyard, you enter the church through carved wooden doors. *Retablos,* colorfully painted images of saints on wood or tin, and *bultos,* statues of saints, line the adobe walls. Walk through the cool, darkened passageway, ducking under a short doorway to reach a dried-up well. Many collect its

INSIGHT · Welcome Center

Considered the most important Catholic pilgrimage spot in the United States, Lourdes of America was named a National Historic Landmark in 1970. Part of its enormous draw is that everyone, not just Catholics or Christians, is welcome. People of all faiths—or no faith—speak of finding consolation and a sense of the sacred here. Although many are first-timers, for others, it's a multiple-generational family experience. Numerous visitors bring newborns or newly baptized children to Chimayo.

"holy dirt" in plastic bags or smear it on their bodies. Check out the room crowded with abandoned crutches, rosaries, before-and-after photographs, and tokens the faithful have left behind. "There are as many different experiences as there are different people," says Joanne Dupont Sandoval, secretary of the Santuario. "It's a place of peace."

■ *Essentials:* El Santuario de Chimayo, 15 Santuario Dr., tel 505-351-9961, elsantuariodechimayo.us

Praying before a likeness of the Virgin of Guadalupe, Chimayo

"People come here for healing—physical, spiritual, and psychological." —JOANNE DUPONT SANDOVAL, SECRETARY, EL SANTUARIO DE CHIMAYO

The shrine
El Santuario
de Chimayo in
Chimayo

You Could Be In . . . CAPPADOCIA

Los Alamos, New Mexico
The cliff dwellings of Bandelier National Monument in Los Alamos are a ringer for the rock houses of Cappadocia in Turkey.

Tlaquepaque Arts and Crafts Village, Sedona, Arizona

AUTHENTIC INTERNATIONAL MARKETS

Shop the world—from homemade French pâtisseries to Asian-inspired soy pudding.

■ Tlaquepaque

Beat the Southwestern heat with a stroll beneath the shade of sycamores in Tlaquepaque, an open-air artisans market in Sedona, Arizona, modeled on a traditional Mexican village. The name means "best of everything," and here you'll find the best of the region's creative offerings. Pop into any one of the 40-some galleries and visit with potters at their wheels and painters at their easels. The cobblestone alleyways and brilliant flowers sprouting from every surface only enhance the natural splendor of Sedona's polychrome vistas. *336 State Rte. 179, Sedona, Ariz., tel 928-282-4838, tlaq.com*

■ Reading Terminal Market

Seek out the Pennsylvania Dutch merchants clustered in the northwest corner of Reading Terminal Market in Philadelphia, Pennsylvania, where women in white bonnets and crisp aprons twist tendrils of dough into deeply chewy pretzels. Among the 75 food stalls, you'll also find hometown favorites like Italian cannoli (and, of course, Philly cheesesteaks) here, America's oldest continuously operated farmers market. *12th and Arch Sts., Philadelphia, Pa., tel 215-922-2317, open daily except Dutch merchants (Wed.–Sat. only), readingterminal market.org*

■ Christkindlmarket

Grab a mug of mulled wine and munch on curry wursts hot off the grill at the annual Christkindlmarket in Chicago, Illinois. An angelic Christkind adorned in robes and a golden crown spreads joy throughout the market, reminding visitors of her role in German folklore as a bearer of gifts to children. Chicago's open-air holiday village draws inspiration from Nuremberg, Germany, home of the first recorded Christmas market in 1545. *Daley Plaza between Washington, Clark, and Dearborn Sts., Chicago, Ill., tel 312-494-2175, the month leading up to Christmas, christkindlmarket.com*

■ 626 Night Market

On various summer weekends, the funky smell of stinky tofu mingles with crispy fried pig ears at L.A.'s Asian-inspired 626 Night Market. Fashioned after the pulsating night markets of Taiwan, the 626 brings together foodies and food trucks for a night of big-flavored street eats and live music. The market's popularity has spawned two others, the OC Night Market in Costa Mesa and the DTLA Night Market in downtown L.A. *285 W. Huntington Dr., Arcadia, Calif., 626night market.com*

■ Jean-Talon Market

A sprawl of *boulangeries*, pâtisseries, *fromageries*, charcuteries, and stall after stall of seasonal flowers, fruits, and vegetables comprise the European-style Marché Jean-Talon in Montreal's Little Italy. The sheer number of potato varieties at Birri Brothers will impress. In summer, head to Havres-aux-glaces to cool off with a scoop of pear and *sortilège* sorbet, made with maple syrup liqueur. *7070 Henri-Julien Ave., Montreal, Que., open spring–fall, marchespublics-mtl .com/en*

Honoring the living and the dead, All Souls Procession, in Tucson

TUCSON, ARIZONA
DAY OF THE DEAD

Part full-on street party, part spellbinding Mexican tradition, Tucson's All Souls Procession will no doubt let the spirits (of the dead) move you. The Procession is thrown every year to celebrate the holiday Día de los Muertos, also known as Day of the Dead.

JOINING IN: Participants of all ages and backgrounds, including any and all visitors, dress in garments belonging to deceased loved ones, clutch photographs, or wear white skeleton makeup or masks, while parading the streets of downtown with lanterns and marigolds. "The sacred and profane walk side by side here," says Paul Weir, technical director of both the Procession and Flam Chen, the pyrotechnics theater that organizes the event, adding, "It makes you feel like the world is a better place." The daylong event feels like a Mexican Mardi Gras with soul. Seemingly everyone in town comes out in costume for the bash. Some beat drums; others sing or chant. A 2-mile parade is buffeted by lots of food and street music.

IN THE KNOW: Consider taking a lawn chair to watch the festivities go by, maybe a post-sunset blanket, and, if you don't have a mask handy, just stop by a bar on the route: Many offer free face painting.

The gathering draws 100,000 people downtown. The procession ends at a huge urn filled with the notes and prayers to the departed from loved ones that are burned as part of the final ceremony. It all goes out in a blaze, with a big fireworks display.

■ *Essentials:* All Souls Procession, allsoulsprocession.org

DIGGING DEEPER

Every November 2, another annual fest honors the dear departed in a Terlingua, Texas, cemetery, just 25 miles from the Mexican border. Residents build a bonfire and altar, and serve potluck while musicians play. "Love is timeless," says resident Cynta de Narvaez.

AROUND THE WORLD IN
PHOENIX

Arizona Buddhist Temple, Phoenix

Desert Ireland
Rising like an Irish phoenix (pardon the pun) in the heart of this desert town, you'll find one of the more incongruous sites of the American West: a 12th-century Norman castle. Welcome to a wee bit of Ireland in Arizona. Inside the stone replica built from real Irish limestone is a hub of Irish activity. Trace your Irish roots at the McClelland Irish Library, dance a Gaelic jig at the attached Irish Cultural Center, or just check out the authentic and unlikely Irish stone cottage. *Phoenix Irish Cultural Center, 1106 N. Central Ave., open Tuesday through Saturday, 10 a.m. to 3 p.m., tel 602-258-0109, azirish.org*

Asian Supermarket
Shelves stacked with staples that may stump you (familiar with *kabocha*, Japanese pumpkin, or Jubes Nata De Coco, jelly candy?). Your first visit to the sprawling Super L Ranch Asian market may seem a little more dizzying—and more odoriferous (lots of fresh fish for sushi)—than a typical American grocery store. But Phoenix massage therapist Marissa Banh, part of a self-described "mixed-culture household"—her chef husband is half Chinese, half Vietnamese, she's half Hispanic—says not to worry. She says most employees speak English and are happy to point out their favorite items.

Super L Ranch Market, 668 N. 44th St., tel 602-225-2288, phxchinatown .com/SuperL-Deli.htm

Be Like Buddha
The smell of incense wafts through the temple as adherents chant a sutra that translates "I take refuge in the Amida Buddha." At the Arizona Buddhist Temple, open to the public and boasting a diverse membership, the short practice prior to the dharma talk (sermon) clears the mind. Once you step inside, you'll see a large urn in front of the gold-leafed altar, flanked by photographs of the Shin Buddhist sect's founder, Shinran Shonin, and Rennyo Shonin, who popularized the practice in Japan. The resonating sound of a bell helps center

The stretch along 16th Street and Roosevelt is like Little Mexico. La Michoacana makes very traditional ice cream; the *nuez*, a pecan-based ice cream, is my favorite. And you can get it served with so many toppings that are not your average 32 flavors, like fresh fruit and chilies. The fresh fruit frozen confections, called *paletas*, are also delicious. At Dulceria Pico Rico, you can buy candy, piñatas, and party supplies. It's one-stop shopping for *quinceañera* parties. The Hive is an eclectic collection of art studios, a funky vintage resale store, and a space for community events like poetry readings and children's workshops.

SILVANA SALCIDO ESPARZA

Chef/owner, Phoenix's Barrio Café, and a Calle 16 mural project founder

ARTISTAS:
SINEK
ARMANDO
SRVNT
DUROK
SENTROCK
KEISR
MES ONE
SLIM
MARTIN MORENO
CHEE
PRUE
SERPONE
DETOR
ENUF

"Los Tres Grandes"

grafftruth@yahoo.com

One of the dynamic murals along Phoenix's Calle 16

practitioners. "Buddhism is a religion to cure oneself, not others," says the Reverend Ungyo Lynn Sugiyama. The experience differs for everyone, but most find quiet reflection and a welcome calm from daily stresses. *Arizona Buddhist Temple, 4142 W. Clarendon Ave., tel 602-278-0036, services Sun. 10 a.m., azbuddhist temple.org*

Urban Japanese Zen
Though it's closed for the summer, in-the-know locals flock to the Japanese Friendship Garden as the weather moderates. Secreted smack-dab in the middle of the concrete jungle of skyscrapers that is downtown Phoenix, the garden offers a tranquil—and cool—retreat. Conceived in 1987 as a joint project between Phoenix and sister city Himeji, Japan, the serene grounds foster cultural understanding. Authentic tea ceremonies are held in a special room on some Saturdays; reserve, as they fill quickly. "The 30-minute ceremony is very precise," says Masako Takiguchi, Phoenix Sister Cities Commission Himeji committee Chair. "It's been handed down for 500 years. Your host will offer you a tea sweet [candy] before serving the green tea. It's special and kind of hard to explain; you have to experience it." Self- or docent-guided garden tours are also offered. *Japanese Friendship Garden, 1125 N. 3rd Ave., tel 602-256-3204, japanesefriendship garden.org*

Viva Latino!
An ever changing pastiche of colors and images adorn Calle 16. The murals are far more than just a beautification effort by Latino artists. They've helped spur the once rundown barrio back to life. Born out of frustration in the wake of Arizona's controversial anti-immigration measure, the artists' effort has transformed the neighborhood and helped create a vibrant destination intersection of art, cuisine, culture, and community for both visitors and residents. Walk around to photograph the witty, colorful murals and you might meet artists painting their next masterwork. *Calle 16 runs on N. 16th St. from E. Thomas Rd. to E. Roosevelt St.*

The Japanese Friendship Garden, tucked away in downtown Phoenix

Las Noches de las Luminarias in Phoenix's Desert Botanical Garden

LUMINARIAS

Light up the holidays in the Southwest with a 300-year-old Hispanic tradition.

■ **Las Noches de las Luminarias**
Phoenix's 140-acre Desert Botanical Garden shines after dark for 31 consecutive nights during the holiday season with more than 8,000 glimmering, hand-lit luminarias, votive candles in sand-filled, brown paper sacks. A cup of cider takes the chill off a desert evening as carolers serenade guests. *201 N. Galvin Pkwy., tel 480-941-1225, dbg.org/events-exhibitions*

■ **Luminaria—Arts Come to Light**
Leave it to artists to shake things up. San Antonio's luminarias come with a delightfully creative twist as dozens of local and national artists alight on downtown San Antonio and give the glowing lanterns their own creative spin. The result is a dazzling display of light that changes every year, plus live performances, music, and, of course, food that attracts 300,000 attendees to this free event. *luminariasa.org*

■ **Annual Posadas Celebration and Luminaria Lighting Festival**
Come sundown, the San Elizario Historic District in El Paso, Texas, comes aglow with 5,000 luminarias. Stick around for the second part of the show, a Mexican Christmas celebration re-creating Mary and Joseph's search for a place to stay in Bethlehem, followed by live music, a traditional Christmas star-shaped piñata ceremony, and feather headdress–festooned Matachin dancers. *sanelizariohistoricart district.com*

■ **Farolito Walk on Canyon Road**
Crowded with galleries and shops by day, Sante Fe, New Mexico's Canyon Road twinkles with thousands of *farolitos*, the Spanish word for paper lanterns, on Christmas Eve night. Participants sing as they walk the serpentine streets of the historic, adobe-walled neighborhood during this free and much loved seasonal event. *farolitowalk.com*

■ **Annual ABQ RIDE Luminaria Tour**
Albuquerque, New Mexico's half-century-old luminaria tour on Christmas Eve comes with a twist: a bus rolling through holiday-dressed neighborhoods in Old Town and beyond. According to Julia Brown with the Old Town Merchants, it takes 487 hours—nearly three months of labor—to prepare for the big night with thousands of luminarias. *cabq.gov/transit/programs-and-projects/luminaria-tour*

■ **Light Among the Ruins: Christmas Celebration**
Every December, the ancient ruins of Jemez Historic Site in Jemez, New Mexico, including the pueblo and Spanish San José de los Jemez church, glow with hundreds of luminarias. The evening program includes Native American flute music and a dance performance between bonfires; refreshments are served. *nmmonuments.org/jemez*

AROUND THE WORLD IN
DENVER

The Mexican flag is front and center on Cinco de Mayo in Denver.

My Neighborhood

GREEK TOWN

Sashimi in the Square
The rhythmic echo of Japanese *taiko* drums fills the air as those in the know seek out the beloved Spam *musubi* (grilled Spam and a block of rice, *omusubi* style) during June's Cherry Blossom Denver Festival in Sakura Square. This is the only time of year that the saffron-robed priests open the doors to their nearby TriState Denver Buddhist Temple—a chance to explore hallways filled with bonsai exhibits (and a beer garden downstairs!). Then get your salmon sashimi and nori at the nearby Pacific Mercantile Company, a fully stocked Japanese market. "I can't live without this place," says Chad Yokoo, a retail manager in Denver. "There is basically everything you can think of that you would want in a specialty Asian store."

Cherry Blossom Denver, cherryblossomdenver.org; Pacific Mercantile Company, 1925 Lawrence St., tel 303-295-0293, pacific eastwest.com

Latin Charm
Su Teatro is the nation's third oldest Chicano theater—and the first place to go to experience the history and pathos of Latino culture, particularly through its original stage productions. Try to get there on a "First Friday"—the entire arts district opens its doors with free art showings of all kinds the first Friday of every month. The belly of Denver's Hispanic population is a short drive away on the "North Side" at 59th and Federal Boulevard. *Elotes* (corn on the cob with mayonnaise and chili powder) sold by street vendors and restaurants along Hampden Boulevard are a local favorite.
Su Teatro, 721 Santa Fe Dr., tel 303-296-0219, suteatro.org

China Grove
At Celestial Bakery, in Denver's Asian district, you can try everything from fried crullers and pineapple custard buns to roasted duck and barbecue pork. For knickknacks such as origami kits and parasols, locals swear by Truong An Gifts and Beauty. "This is an awesome store for all your Asian needs!" says Daphne Tsung, an educational assistant from Denver.
Celestial Bakery, 333 S. Federal Blvd., tel 303-936-2339; Truong An Gifts and Beauty, 333 S. Federal Blvd., tel 303-936-5004, truongangifts.com

I came to Denver from Greece in 1955. When I arrived, I didn't speak a word of English. Greek Town is very special to me. It's the only official ethnic neighborhood in Denver. The city council passed a resolution in the 1990s to create the designation, and the mayor approved it. The pedestrian mall shows how proud we are of our heritage, especially with blue-and-white sidewalks, which were added in 1997. The trees are decorated with lights. There's also the smell of lamb gyros. And the bakery. I started my first restaurant [of six], the Satire Lounge, in 1962. Now I spend a lot of time at [my] Pete's Kitchen, because we stay open 24 hours. Greek Town adds a lot of tradition to the city.

PETE CONTOS
A Greek Town founder and owner of six restaurants there

Japanese
drumming by
Denver Taiko at
the city's Asian
Festival

MIDWAY, UTAH
SWISS LANDS

Cradled by the gentle foothills of the Uinta Mountains and the dramatic Wasatch Mountains, the verdant Heber Valley can appear Alpine, with wildflowers, snowcapped peaks, and even historic railways to boot. No wonder a small group of families from the highlands of Bern, Switzerland, decided to settle in the town of Midway in the mid-19th century. Today, this homestead of roughly 4,000 people proudly keeps its Swiss character alive with ranching and farming.

JOINING IN: Kay Probst, who was born in Midway in 1927 and has spent his whole life there except during his missionary and military stints, remembers when you could hear Swiss German all around town. "In fact, most of the people who came from Switzerland couldn't speak any English," he says. "They had their own one-room meeting house—which became the post office." Today, the best reminder of the town's heritage is its summer Midway Swiss Days, when about half the townspeople participate and proudly don Swiss costumes to celebrate with music by the town's Swiss choral groups (one is a children's group), handicrafts, and *bratzeli*. "Many of us have *bratzeli* makers at home," says Probst, referring to the waffle iron–like machine that makes traditional Swiss cookies. Also on the day's menu: locally made Swiss cheese.

ALPINE STAY: Those who aren't lucky enough to attend the homespun festival can check into the timbered buildings of Zermatt Resort, a Swiss-themed hotel named after a Matterhorn village, which offers Alpine-themed rooms. The hotel even has its own *bäckerei* (bakery) that bakes fresh *bratzeli*.

■ *Essentials:* Midway, gohebervalley.com; Midway Swiss Days, midwayswissdays.com; Zermatt Resort, 784 W. Resort Dr., tel 866-937-6288, zermattresort.com

DIGGING DEEPER

What's an Alpine experience without slaloming down a snowy slope? A number of world-class ski courses are easily accessible from Midway, including Canyons, one of the largest in the United States, and Deer Valley, consistently ranked among the best American ski resorts.

ICELANDIC DAY

The name of the town may derive from the two Franciscan friars from Iberia who passed through here in 1776, but Spanish Fork's claim to fame is its Icelandic roots. The first wave of 410 Icelanders, after converting to Mormonism, arrived between 1855 and 1860 and kept the unique heritage alive. Today, their descendants are sprinkled around Utah and beyond, but Spanish Fork, as the longest continuous Icelandic settlement in America, remains its cultural nucleus.

WHAT TO SEE: It's a slightly odd sight—a 20-foot lighthouse perched in the middle of landlocked Utah. "My grandfather's name is on it," says Jack Tobiasson proudly of Spanish Fork's 1938 Icelandic Monument, complete with a volcanic rock brought in from the island nation, honoring the original inhabitants. Adds Tobiasson, a member of the Icelandic Association of Utah, "It reminds me that here's a piece of a city that's dedicated specifically to my heritage." Tobiasson honors his culture by learning and performing Icelandic folk songs. "It's usually the third generation of immigrants that takes an active interest in the heritage," he says with laughter.

JOINING IN: Today, the descendants of the original settlers congregate every February for Þorrablót, a midwinter feast with shark meat, dried fish, and sheep. And for those

INSIGHT · Sharks and Sheep

The Icelandic kitchen has a tradition of making do with limited resources on the isolated island. *Hangikjöt,* smoked lamb, derives its flavor not only from its birch smoke, but also the excellent taste of the Icelandic sheep, which graze on grass and herbs in the highlands all summer long. *Skyr* is a rich and tart cross between yogurt and gelatinous soft cheese. For the adventurous, there's also *hákarl,* shark fermented for up to five months, and *svið,* boiled sheep's head. Sample eats are imported for June's Iceland Days.

who want to join in on the fun, the Icelandic Association of Utah, which dates back to 1897, celebrates Iceland's Independence Day (June 17) with a parade in Icelandic costumes and performance by a *barnakór,* or children's choir. Everyone is welcome to both events.

■ *Essentials:* Icelandic Memorial, 800 E. Canyon Rd.; Iceland Days, facebook.com/IcelandicAssociationofUtah

Young Vikings at Spanish Fork's Icelandic Festival

LAS VEGAS

Bright lights of Chinatown Plaza, Las Vegas

Since I came to live in Las Vegas from Hawaii in 1979, the Filipino population has mushroomed. Filipinos came as laborers in the hotels and casinos in the 1950s, and as time passed and acceptance grew, many came as entertainers. Today we have many executives in gaming, hundreds of professionals in medical and law practices, and thousands of entrepreneurs in small businesses. I live in the center of town. My home is in one of the oldest neighborhoods in the heart of the city, Las Vegas Country Club Estates. I love living here, where there are many Filipino establishments in a five-block area. My Filipino friends come, treating it as though they're back home as they shop, dine, *chismis* (gossip), and smell the fragrance of freshly baked *pandesal* rolls.

ROZITA VILLANUEVA LEE
Filipino American Chamber of Commerce of Greater Nevada

Buddhism and Tom Yum
On three acres of land near the Strip, Chaiya Meditation Monastery is an oasis of calm accommodating a community of ordained monks and nuns who serve Thai, Laotian, and Burmese congregants of Theravada Buddhism. (A growing Thai community has meant no fewer than six Thai temples springing up in Vegas's home, Clark County.) But you don't have to be a believer to sample the authentic fare at the monthly CMM Monthly Food Fair. This nonprofit event raises money for the monastery, so not only will you have fresh (and really inexpensive) papaya salad, mango sticky rice, and curry puffs, but you'll also gain some good karma.

Chaiya Meditation Monastery, 7925 Virtue Ct., tel 702-456-3838, chaiyacmm.org

Something About Vietnamese Mary
Venetian canals, miniature Eiffel Tower, displaced Statue of Liberty . . . the Sin City may be famous for its fake landmarks, but no other replica celebrates something as holy as the Vietnamese shrine of Our Lady of La Vang. Dedicated to a legendary 18th-century Marian appearance in southern Vietnam, this Catholic shrine re-creates the original bell tower and shrine, destroyed during the Vietnam War. The granite-tiled church doubles as a performance stage for Vietnamese cultural events. Says

Rebecca Snetselaar, Folklife Program associate for the Nevada Arts Council, "Las Vegas is not what you think it is once you get off the Strip."
Our Lady of La Vang, 4835 S. Pearl St., tel 702-821-1459

Holy City
Las Vegas boasts a lively Armenian community—and we don't mean the Kardashian clan on a night out. With over 20,000 members, the more-than-century-old group is vibrant and diverse. So it's actually not too surprising that in the middle of Sin City, you can see an authentic Armenian church. St. Garabed Armenian Apostolic Church was designed according to the age-old

traditional Armenian Apostolic design, with a floor plan in the shape of a cross, topped with a dome where the two sections come together. The prayer books inside have four translations for each passage: ancient Armenian, modern Armenian, Armenian phonetically transcribed in the Roman alphabet, and English. (Fun fact: Armenian-American Kirk Kerkorian, one of the community's most famous sons, is credited with being the "father of mega resorts," who shaped Vegas as we know it.)
St. Garabed Armenian Apostolic Church, 2054 E. Desert Inn Rd., tel 702-755-3910, stgarabedlv.org

Sated in China
Ring in the Chinese Lunar New Year with a series of pan-Asian cultural performances, like Chinese acrobatics, Japanese *taiko* drums, and Korean fan dance, thrown every year in Vegas's Chinatown. Forget the image of winding alleyways lit by red lanterns. Vegas's version is a decidedly modern variant, a series of large malls built to emulate traditional Chinese architecture. They harbor a convenient concentration of decidedly authentic Chinese restaurants. Chinese food blogger David R. Chan touts several in Chinatown Plaza, including Sam Woo BBQ. *Chinatown Plaza, lvchinatown.com; Sam Woo BBQ, 4215 Spring Mountain Rd., tel 702-368-7628*

Filipino Feast
Thanks to its sizeable Filipino community, Las Vegas is one of the best cities in the country for food from the Asian archipelago. There are countless restaurants spread across the city to satisfy the growing Filipino community.

At Café de Cebu, you can have flavorful slow-roasted pork belly, *kaldereta* tomato beef stew, or *turon*—a deep-fried banana jackfruit spring roll. The friendly owner of Baba's Tsi-bugan Restaurant serves what some locals call the area's best *halo-halo*, a whimsical dessert of shaved ice, condensed milk, jelly, and sweet beans, as well as a rotating roster of national dishes like *karekare* (oxtail stew). *Café de Cebu, 6680 W. Flamingo Rd. Ste. 12, tel 702-538-7588; Baba's Tsi-bugan Restaurant, 4588 N. Rancho Dr. Ste. 7, tel 702-396-9711*

Armenian Catholic ritual, St. Garabed Armeian Apostolic Church, Las Vegas

Traditional Basque dancers in Winnemucca

WINNEMUCCA & ELKO, NEVADA
BASQUE COUNTRY

From gold rush fever to pastoral serenity, European Basque immigrants in the 1850s quickly abandoned their dashed, strike-it-rich dreams to return to their old way of life of sheepherding. Today, the sheep may be almost gone, but northern Nevada's Basque legacy is still going strong, especially in the cities of Winnemucca and Elko.

JOINING IN: The city of Elko's Euzkaldunak Club throws a three-day National Basque Festival every July, when the Ariñak dance troupe don costumes—a red scarf and *txapela* (beret) for men and a voluminous skirt and *zapi* (head scarf) for women—to perform traditional *jota* and other dances. The town of Winnemucca—whose motto is simply "Proud of It"—also carries on its Basque past with the June festival, where locals indulge in traditional games like weight carrying and wood chopping.

WHERE TO EAT: A number of historic hotels where Basque sheepherders passed winter months have survived. The Martin Hotel in Winnemucca, built in 1898 and included on the National Register of Historic Places, continues to serve hungry travelers hearty, family-style Basque cuisine. Try the *solomo*, a boneless pork loin simmered in a sauce of garlic and pimento, or deep-fried sweetbreads, a Basque staple. At the Star Hotel in Elko,

INSIGHT · Basqueing in Mystery

Basque Euskara is a language isolate, related to no other known dialect. Its origin remains a complete mystery, the Basque people defying all odds to preserve their unique tongue surrounded by Romance language speakers. Euskara is still spoken among the descendants of Basque immigrants, and you can learn it at the University of Nevada, Reno's Center for Basque Studies, which has the largest Basque library outside of the motherland. *basque.unr.edu*

continuously Basque-owned since 1910, you can taste a typical boarder's lunch of roasted beef and signature Basque beans simmered with salt pork.

■ *Essentials:* National Basque Festival, elkobasqueclub.com; Winnemucca Basque Festival, winnemucca.nv.us; Martin Hotel, 94 W. Railroad St., Winnemucca, Nev., tel 775-623-3197, themartinhotel.com; Star Hotel, 246 Silver St., Elko, Nev., tel 775-738-9925, eatdrinkandbebasque.com

"[Basque festivals are a] great opportunity to chat with the Basque immigrants." —KATE CAMINO, BASQUE INSTRUCTOR, UNIVERSITY OF NEVADA, RENO

BOCCE BALL

In a leafy, residential pocket of eastern Sacramento, five long, white bocce courts form the unlikely epicenter of a lively community with deep Italian roots. People at the almost half-century-old East Portal Bocce Club gather most nights and weekends to play bocce, an ancient game not dissimilar to lawn bowling embraced by the Romans and brought to America by Italian immigrants—one that's taking the United States by storm. In Sacramento's case, an Italian American got the Italian ball rolling and started a bocce club in the 1970s. With team names like Scouza Me, Andiamo, and Puttanesca, the games give a playful nod to the Old World—not to mention one of its timeless simple pleasures: chitchat. East Portal Bocce Club president Lisa Dobeck says, "Neighbors play because it gives you a reason to see someone once a week; it's a way to build a social network."

WHAT TO DO: East Portal Bocce Club, Sacramento's only and one of the United States' oldest bocce clubs, no longer restricts its membership to Italians. But the fun for nonmembers comes from watching. Bocce is pretty easy to follow: Teams take turns rolling balls down the oyster shell court in an attempt to land closest to the *pallino*, a smaller ball thrown by the opening team to begin play. The club also hosts two to four weekend tournaments a year, incorporating regional clubs and drawing a larger crowd.

MORE · Pasta and Play

Campo di Bocce, Livermore and Los Gatos, California: Two modern Italian villas with traditional fare each boasts eight regulation bocce courts and a selection of 60-plus local and Italian wines. *campodibocce.com*

Vancouver Il Centro (Italian Cultural Centre), Vancouver, British Columbia: Indoor bocce accommodates up to 32 players per game year-round. A resident instructor can explain the rules. *italianculturalcentre.ca*

Palazzo di Bocce, Orion, Michigan: Try antipasto or bruschetta courtside at this stylish court where players dress to impress. *palazzodibocce.com*

American Italian Club, Phoenix, Arizona: Bocce is a popular ambassador at this cultural club. Wednesday is family spaghetti night, and everyone gets to play. *azaiclub.org*

Want to try bocce for yourself? Bring a set to the courts in East Portal's public park during nonleague play. Chances are you won't be the only one.

■ *Essentials:* East Portal Park, 1120 Rodeo Way, Sacramento, Calif., eastportalbocceclub.com (for club schedule)

Inches make a difference in bocce ball.

AROUND THE WORLD IN
SAN FRANCISCO

**The Churrigueresque-
style Mission Dolores
Basilica, San Francisco**

**Sushi, Sake, and
Stickers**
It's impossible to choose
at San Francisco's
Japantown. This is
modern Japan—concrete,
glass, and steel rather
than rice paper screens
and tatami mats. Out-
of-this-world *hamachi,
maguro,* and *tako* at Ino
Sushi: musts. Learning
how to drum the
Japanese way at Taiko
Dojo: a hoot. Making like
a Japanese teenager at
Pika Pika, a pop culture
boutique where photo
booths produce stickers
emblazoned with your
own image: whimsical.
And selecting a bottle
at True Sake: a tad
daunting. The *nihonshu*
(sake) store stocks
more than 250 different
varieties of the rice wine.
*Japantown, sfjapantown
.org; Ino Sushi, 22 Peace*

*Plaza #510, tel 415-922-
3121; Pika Pika, 1581
Webster St. #185, tel 415-
673-7898, pikapikasf.com;
True Sake, 560 Hayes St.,
tel 415-355-9555, truesake
.com*

Hot Java and Joltin' Joe
Follow your nose to one
of the Italian bakeries,
bars, or cafés on and
around Columbus
Avenue and Broadway
in North Beach. At Caffe
Trieste, munch Italian
pastries, sip the city's
best espresso, and listen
to live opera tunes
performed by members
of the Giotta family at
this same location since
the 1950s. More than a
century on, North Beach
retains its Italian dolce
vita, especially when
it comes to food and
drink. "San Francisco
attracted populations

from particular places
in Italy—Genoa, Lucca,
and Sicily," says Audrey
Tomaselli, a North Beach
resident who spent ten
years collecting stories
for an oral history project
on the area's Italians.
"Even though they came
from different parts
of Italy, this became a
very cohesive Italian
neighborhood." She
recommends the thin-
crust pizza and pesto
pasta at Baonecci
Ristorante, run by a
recent immigrant family
from Lucca. While you're
in the neighborhood,
grab a tree-shaded bench
in Washington Square
Park and stare up at the
whitewashed Sts. Peter
and Paul Church, where
a local Italian-American
kid by the name of Joe
DiMaggio snapped
wedding photos with

I have great memo-
ries of growing up
in the Tenderloin,
surrounded by
so many cultures
and customs. A
lot of my good
friends were Chi-
nese, Vietnamese,
Filipino, Latino, and
black. Chinese New
Year was always a
big holiday because
of the large Chinese
population. The
parade, one of San
Francisco's biggest
events, was just a
short walk from
where we lived. My
mother is Catholic,
so I have a lot of
memories going to
St. Boniface Catho-
lic Church. Even
though I grew up
in the Tenderloin
in a time when
there was very bad
crack cocaine and
heroin drug activ-
ity and different
gangs from differ-
ent backgrounds, I
never got involved
in any of it because
of the strong sup-
port and closeness
of my family. When
I think back, I
remember all the
good times.

MARIO SANCHEZ
*Mural artist and travel
industry professional*

Lanterns in the
Chinese New Year
Parade, San Francisco

Back of the house, Chinatown's Imperial Palace Restaurant, San Francisco

bride Marilyn Monroe and where Joltin' Joe later had his funeral. *Caffe Trieste, 601 Vallejo St., tel 415-392-6739, caffetrieste.com; Baonecci Ristorante, 516 Green St., tel 415-989-1806, caffebaonecci .com; Saints Peter and Paul Church, 666 Filbert St., tel 415-421-0809, sspeterpaulsf.org/church*

Sounds of Africa
A rapid rhythm of drumbeats emerges from the open doors of a brightly colored shop front in San Francisco's Mission District, accompanied by the culinary scents that are both enticing and exotic. The place is called Bissap Baobab, a Senegalese restaurant that doubles as a community center and cultural venue for thousands of French-speaking African

émigrés who live in the Bay Area. Tantalize your taste buds with traditional West African dishes like *dibi* (grilled lamb served with fried plantains, salad, rice, and a tangy *yassa* sauce), *somone* (breaded and fried mashed potatoes with tamarind sauce), or *mafe* chicken with a curry peanut sauce. Come Wednesday for weekly *timba* drumming sessions, or Friday and Saturday for Paris-Dakar dance parties. Got an itch to practice your French? Once a month, Bissap Baobab hosts Francophile socials. Other events to look out for are African film screenings, live telecasts of African soccer matches, poetry and book readings, and community action events like a recent "Bring Back Our Girls" information session

on the kidnapped Nigerian schoolgirls.

For a one-of-a-kind African immersion, head to the Museum of the African Diaspora. Next to the Museum of Modern Art in the trendy SOMA (South of Market) district, the museum is one of the few collections anywhere on the planet dedicated to the migration of Africans to the United States, Caribbean, South America, and elsewhere. Browse permanent exhibits on the origins of the diaspora, culinary traditions, African ritual and ceremony, the music of the diaspora, and slavery passages both old (the Middle Passage across the Atlantic) and modern (Sudan). Watch a multimedia presentation in the Freedom Theater that spans several hundred years of freedom

fighters from Toussaint to Mandela. Catch one of the regular public programs—lectures, workshops, movies, book signings, symposiums—on Africa and the diaspora. And come away with a much greater understanding of how Africa has influenced the rest of the world and other global cultures. *Bissap Baobab, 3372 19th St., tel 415-643-3558, bissapbaobab .com; Museum of the African Diaspora, 685 Mission St., tel 415-977-0754, closed Mon.–Tues., moadsf.org*

Shamrock Sports
Long before the 49ers played football at Kezar, Candlestick, or Levi's Stadium in Santa Clara, the city was besotted with other brawny ball games: Gaelic football and hurling. Ireland's ancient sports sailed through the Golden Gate with Irish immigrants. "They have been playing Gaelic football and hurling in the Bay Area for over 100 years," says Mike Nash of San Francisco's Gaelic Athletic Association. Nash says the best place to catch a game is Páirc na nGael (Gaelic Park) on Treasure Island in the middle of the bay, where the GAA maintains a clubhouse with an Irish-style bar and 12 acres of manicured fields. Those who want to learn Irish-style football or hurling should contact the

GAA or one of 17 Gaelic athletic clubs in the Bay Area. "Good eye to hand coordination and the ability to catch the ball in the air are all necessary skills for mastering Gaelic football," Nash says. Hurling, on the other hand, is sort of like hitting a baseball with an ice hockey stick while charging down a soccer field. *Gaelic Athletic*

Association Clubhouse, Building 33, 401 13th St., Treasure Island, tel 415-398-2092, sanfranciscogaa.com

Take a Chance on Swedes
Explore the Swedenborgian Church in Pacific Heights and discover how 18th-century Swedish inventor and theologian Emanuel Swedenborg

left his mark on San Francisco, without ever visiting the city. An early proponent of blending science and Christianity, he preached that mankind should revere the "divine in nature" long before East Bay resident John Muir advocated a similar philosophy. Built in 1895, the structure flaunts a hybrid architecture that blends Old and

New World styles, a facade of arches and red brick that would not look out of place on a California mission, and a warm, rustic interior straight out of the Swedish woods. The church is still run by the local branch of the Swedenborgian Church of North America, which more than 200 years after his death continues to espouse a philosophy

Walking Map *Chinatown*

5 | Backtrack two blocks and turn left onto Waverly Place to the **Tin How Temple,** the oldest Chinese temple in the United States (*125 Waverly Pl.*).

6 | Wander to Jackson and back to Grant and **Ten Ren Tea Company** to sample one of the 50 tea varieties (*949 Grant Ave., tel 415-362-0656, tenren .com*).

7 | If something stronger is in order, stroll farther down Grant for Chinese mai tais at **Li Po Cocktail Lounge,** a distinguished dive since 1937 (*916 Grant Ave., tel 415-982-0072, lipolounge.com*).

8 | Dinner or lunch is just a few steps away at another venerable institution, the **Empress of China,** with its roof garden and skyline views (*838 Grant Ave., tel 415-434-1345, empressofchinasf.com*).

Explore California's oldest Asian enclave on foot.

1 | Hop off the cable car at California and Grant, and walk north through **Dragon's Gate** along Grant Avenue and into the heart of Chinatown.

2 | Up ahead on the left is the **Chinatown Kite**

Shop and its zany flying machines (*717 Grant Ave., tel 415-989-5182, china townkite.com*).

3 | Cross the street to munch a lotus golden yolk moon cake at **Eastern Bakery** before ambling on (*720 Grant Ave., tel 415-982-5157, eastern bakery.com*).

4 | Turn left onto Clay Street and hoof it up the hill to the **Chinese Historical Society of America Museum.** Inside the old YWCA building, photographs and artifacts document the lives of Chinese immigrants (*965 Clay St., tel 415-391-1188, chsa.org*).

Cappuccino, pastries, and focaccia at San Francisco's Mara's Italian Pastries

that "encourages inquiry, respect for differences, and acceptance of other traditions of life and religion"—in many respects an ideal creed for counterculture San Francisco.
Swedenborgian Church of San Francisco, 2107 Lyon St., tel 415-346-6466, sfswedenborgian.org

Spanish Mission
Immerse yourself in early California, when Spanish missions stole the show. Founded in 1776, just five days before America's birthday, San Francisco de Asís doubles as the oldest building in San Francisco and the oldest original California mission building that's still fully intact. (It's now called Mission Dolores by just about everyone after a creek that was once there.) After more than a couple of

centuries, you'll find the place still bustles with activity. It anchors the city's largest Hispanic neighborhood. Attend a Spanish-language Mass in the old mission or the adjacent basilica, and be on the lookout for colorful *quinceañeras* ceremonies often held on the mission grounds. Take a docent tour of the mission buildings and cemetery, which contains the graves of many early San Franciscans like Governor Luis Antonio Argüello. If the cemetery feels especially creepy, it may be a flashback. It features prominently in Alfred Hitchcock's classic 1958 movie *Vertigo*. Visit the mission gardens, planted with native trees, shrubs, and flowers and an Ohlone Indian ethnobotanic garden with examples of Native American

plants and artifacts. And explore the surrounding neighborhood—the hip Mission District— which has expanded in recent decades from its longtime Mexican-American base into a population that includes Salvadorians, Guatemalans, and Nicaraguans (plus plenty of young technocrati newcomers).
Mission Dolores, 3321 16th St., tel 415-621-8203, missiondolores.org

Brazilian Bash
The city shows off its party side for May's Carnaval. Plumed Brazilian showgirls strut their stuff, the sounds of samba fill the air, and the Grand Parade draws a crush of revelers. In the words of taxi driver and walking tour guide Jean Feilmoser, born and raised in the neighborhood, "lots

The Main Neighborhoods

Japantown
Japanese malls and pagoda occupying six blocks of the Western Addition
BEST BET: Soothing communal baths at Kabuki Springs & Spa

North Beach
Italian restaurants and cafés on and off Columbus Avenue and around Washington Square Park
BEST BET: Baonecci Ristorante's divine pesto pasta and thin-crust pizza

The Mission
Latin American restaurants and shops between Mission Dolores and the Bayshore Freeway
BEST BET: Carnaval parade and street festival (May)

Little Russia
Russian eateries on Geary between 17th and 27th Streets
BEST BET: Easter Sunday services at the Holy Virgin Cathedral

Chinatown
Chinese restaurants and shops on Grant between the Dragon's Gate on Bush and Broadway
BEST BET: Chinese New Year Parade

of feathers and skin, great Latin music, and about 400,000 viewers." Although its roots are in Rio, the two-day fest in the Mission bills itself as the biggest multicultural bash on the West Coast. On tap: lots of Latin music, arts, crafts, and street food, from tacos to Thai barbecue. *carnavalsanfrancisco.org*

Russian Richmond
Look for the golden domes to experience (and taste and drink) some authentic Russian culture—without the brutal cold and snow. The Russians are here, along a ten-block strip of Geary Boulevard known as Little Russia. Start at the 19th-century, onion-topped Russian Orthodox Holy Virgin Cathedral. Inside, vestiges of imperial Russia adorn the ornate cathedral, including the chandelier donated to the church by Tsar Nicholas II and the five bells in the towers given by Emperor Alexander III. For centuries, Holy Virgin has acted as a magnet for Russian migrants to this Richmond District neighborhood. Attend a daily English- or Russian-language service to get the full flavor, especially around Easter. "Russian Orthodox Easter is the biggest feast of the orthodox calendar, and a great many services lead up to a big midnight service on the eve of Easter Sunday and rounds of visits to homes," says Natalie Sabelnik, president of the Congress of Russian Americans and manager of the Russian Center of San Francisco. She also recommends visiting during Maslenitsa ("Pancake Week") before Lent, during which the humble *blini* (Russia's tasty answer to a crepe) takes center stage at the neighborhood's Russian restaurants. Better yet, drop in any time of year to Russian Renaissance Restaurant, in business since the 1950s. An unassuming exterior belies a cavernous chandelier-lit interior. Here, the vodka shots flow freely and the beef Stroganoff draws raves. *Holy Virgin Cathedral, 6210 Geary Blvd., tel 415-221-3255, sfsobor.com; Russian Renaissance Restaurant, 5241 Geary Blvd., tel 415-752-8558*

Costume exhibit at the **Museum of the African Diaspora** in **San Francisco**

Students at a Concordia Language Village in Minnesota

LANGUAGE IMMERSION PROGRAMS

Become a master of your linguistic domain.

■ **Weekend en Español**
Whether you're relatively new or simply rusty, you'll benefit from being immersed in Spanish for 72 hours straight with San Francisco's Weekend en Español—and have fun along the way. This San Francisco–based group also offers workshops and classes, a film club, plus immersion programs in Oaxaca, Mexico.
weekendenespanol.com

■ **Dartmouth College Rassias Center**
Intensive weekend versions of the so-called Rassias Method for all levels in a variety of languages (check schedule for which one) are offered on the Dartmouth campus in Hanover, New Hampshire. The weekend includes meals and cultural programs. This language program has been around

since the '60s, when a Dartmouth professor who was also the Peace Corps director of languages created it.
rassias.dartmouth.edu

■ **Deutsche Sommerschule am Atlantik**
The University of Rhode Island in Kingston offers an intensive seven-week residential program. It culminates in a standard Goethe-Institut certificate recognized by German universities, combines academic instructions with social events and extracurricular activities.
uri.edu/artsci/ml/german/ sommerschule.html

■ **Spanish Anders Languages**
Immerse yourself in Spanish in a city where the majority of the residents speak it: Miami, Florida. Anders Languages claims

that a week of its immersion program, which encompasses classes and activities from 9 a.m. to 10:30 p.m., is equivalent to six weeks of instruction elsewhere. After classes, night owls can partake in the city's famed nightlife and practice your newly acquired language skills.
anderslanguages.com

■ **Language Loop: Dive & Survive in Italian**
Learn the Italian way in the Windy City—and we don't mean making the deep dish. "Dive & Survive in Italian" will have you practicing Italian seven hours each day for five straight days in Chicago, Illinois, a city with a rich Italian-American heritage. The native-speaking instructors can customize the program to special needs, from hospitality to business, law

to health care. And when the weather allows it, the courses take place alfresco on the school's rooftop.
languageloopllc.com

■ **Concordia Language Villages**
Fittingly for its locations on Turtle River Lake in Minnesota, where Nordic immigrants settled in huge numbers, this comprehensive residential program offers Finnish, Norwegian, and Swedish courses as well as Chinese and French intensive retreats. Geared toward adult learners, the villages' immersion programs incorporate culture with over half a century of language instruction know-how. Most programs last a week, making it a perfect vacation from work, whether you are taking up a new language for personal enrichment or career opportunities.
concordialanguage villages.org

A gondola cruise on Lake Merritt

OAKLAND, CALIFORNIA
VENETIAN VOYAGE

Clad in straw hat and striped shirt, the gondolier deftly poles his craft across a stretch of calm water as the sun sinks on the western horizon. Although one would imagine this scene unfolding on some Venetian canal, the venue is actually Lake Merritt near downtown Oakland, California. Gondola Servizio is one of the more unusual aspects of a city more renowned for Jack London, Black Panthers, and a hard-hitting football team. "People thought I was crazy when I said I wanted to start a gondola service in Lake Merritt," says Italian-born owner Angelino Sandri, who spent summers as a gondolier in Venice. And that's where he returned for the three wooden boats that comprise his Oakland fleet.

HOW TO EXPLORE: Depending on your mood (and companion), book a tranquil ride on early morning Lake Merritt, a sun-splashed afternoon cruise, or romantic sunset outing with views across the water to downtown Oakland, the lake gardens, and the wildlife sanctuary. The standard cruise is a half hour. But you can also opt for a 50-minute wine-and-cheese voyage with Chianti or a dessert cruise that features chocolate chip cannoli, Italian cookies, and a bottle of Prosecco.

WHERE TO EAT: Continue the Venetian theme with a waterside Italian meal. Order orecchiette pasta with house-made Italian sausage at Lake Chalet Seafood Bar & Grill, right beside the gondola dock. And then stroll around the lakeshore to Gelato Firenze, where the frozen fare runs a broad gamut from cardamom to cabernet.

■ *Essentials:* Gondola Servizio, 1520 Lakeside Dr., tel 510-663-6603, gondolaservizio.com; Lake Chalet Seafood Bar & Grill, 1520 Lakeside Dr., tel 510-208-5253, thelakechalet.com; Gelato Firenze, 478A Lake Park Ave., tel 510-414-9997, facebook.com/GelatoFirenze

DIGGING DEEPER

Oakland has a long and strong Italian heritage. After the devastating 1906 San Francisco earthquake and fire, thousands of the city's displaced Italian immigrants flocked across the bay to Oakland. Today, just 2.2 percent (8,885 people) of Oakland's diverse population is of Italian descent.

You Could Be In . . . EGYPT

San Jose, California
Visit ancient Egypt in San Jose by browsing Rosicrucian Egyptian Museum's extensive antiquities collection.

BAY AREA AFGHANS

Few people outside of the San Francisco Bay Area had heard of Little Kabul until a 2003 book called *The Kite Runner* shot the neighborhood to worldwide attention. In his celebrated book, Afghan-American author Khaled Hosseini describes the suburban California community as a paradise compared to his war-torn homeland, "with no ghosts, no memories and no sins." Today, Little Kabul's mosaic of Afghan eateries and shops sit elbow to elbow with other immigrant institutions like the old Mission San José and a Shaolin-style kung fu academy.

WHAT TO EAT: De Afghanan Cuisine showcases authentic dishes like *kabob-e-gousfand* (lamb kebabs), *qabili palu* (lamb covered with basmati rice and topped with chopped carrots and raisins), and *manto* (pastry with onion and beef filling). Buy a slab of fresh-from-the-oven naan (and other south Asian bread products) at Maiwand Market.

WHERE TO SHOP: Browse for handmade silk scarves, woolen shawls, henna wraps, and Islamic jewelry at the eclectic Afghan Bazaar.

JOINING IN: Little Kabul lets loose each March during the two-week NowRoz Afghan New Year festival. Traditional foods and music are a huge part of the festivities, but for Afghan Americans, the holiday doubles as a celebration of their freedom. The biggest bash is at

INSIGHT · Tramp Stamp

Long before the first Afghans arrived in Fremont, another immigrant left his stamp on the town. British film star Charlie Chaplin arrived in 1915 to shoot five films at Essanay-West Studio in the Niles district including his famed *The Tramp*. All that remains of the studio is a row of six bungalows on Second Street where Chaplin lived. The nearby Niles Essanay Silent Film Museum shows a regular slate of Chaplin movies and other silent film classics. *nilesfilmmuseum.org*

the Alameda County Fairgrounds, 16 miles east of Little Kabul, where the offerings run a spectrum from famous Afghan singers and traditional dance troupes to naan-eating contests and egg wars.

■ *Essentials:* De Afghanan Cuisine, 37395 Fremont Blvd., tel 510-857-1009, deafghanancuisine.com; Maiwand Market, 37235 Fremont Blvd., tel 510-796-3215; Afghan Bazaar, 37422 Fremont Blvd., tel 510-791-8447; NowRoz Festival, nowrozfestival.com

Maiwand Market in Fremont sells ingredients imported from Afghanistan.

"People [in Little Kabul] don't meet on the street or bars; they meet in homes and at weddings." —TAMIM ANSARY, AFGHAN-AMERICAN AUTHOR

Fremont's NowRoz Festival, a celebration of Afghan and Persian culture

Chestnuts on an open fire for Cornish Christmas in Grass Valley

GRASS VALLEY, CALIFORNIA
CORNISH GOLD

When gold mines in Nevada County reached below the water table and began to flood, someone got the bright idea of importing Cornish tin miners from England because they were already experts at working in inundated mines. Many of these "Cousin Jacks" and their families settled in Grass Valley, northeast of Sacramento. By the 1890s, nearly two-thirds of the population was Cornish. And although that figure has dwindled, the town retains many of its Cornish ways and means.

JOINING IN: Every March, Grass Valley celebrates St. Piran's Day, honoring the patron saint of Cornwall and tin miners, with pasty-tossing contests, Cornish folk music sing-alongs, a Cornish craft fair, and Cornish cream tea. The town's other blowout is Cornish Christmas, which unfolds along Main Street every Friday night between Thanksgiving and December 25. On tap: "Street vendors sporting the Burberry-like Cornish tartan, Christmas caroling, street performers, and an open fire pit to roast chestnuts," says Leah Barretta, manager

of the town's 151 Union Square bar and restaurant. "With all the shops staying open late, it becomes a great night."

WHAT TO EAT: Don't leave town without sampling the meat- or vegetable-stuffed Cornish pasties at Cousin Jack or Marshall's. "I grew up eating traditionally Cornish pasties," Barretta says. "Most local children do."

WHAT TO SEE: Walk it off with a stroll along Main Street with its many gold rush–era buildings. And for the full flavor of the mining era, visit the second floor of St. Joseph's Cultural Center, with its charming Grass Valley Museum housing artifacts and knickknacks from the town's boomtown days, including a bathtub that belonged to a notorious Irish immigrant and exotic dancer.

■ *Essentials:* Grass Valley, grass valleychamber.com; 151 Union Sq., 151 Mill St., tel 530-205-9513, 151unionsquare.com; Cousin Jack Pasties, 100 S. Auburn St., tel 530-272-9230; Marshall's Pasties, 203 Mill St., tel 530-272-2844; Grass Valley Museum, 410 Church St., tel 530-272-4725

DIGGING DEEPER

The Cornish miners of Grass Valley had their work cut out for them. More than 5.8 million ounces of gold were removed from 367 miles of underground shafts at its Empire Mine. Visitors can explore the mine's preserved subterranean warren.

SWEET DANISH

Welcome to a Scandinavian utopia. Or at least that was the idea when three Danish immigrants landed here at the turn of the 20th century and established the Dutch community. Today, to a visitor's eye, they succeeded. Jammed with Danish touches from the fairy-tale buildings to the bakeries, Solvang screams Scandinavia—but with warm, sunny skies year-round.

WHAT TO EAT AND DRINK: Start your Solvang sojourn greeted by a graceful naked maiden carved into the front door of the Elverhøj Museum. The 18th-century, Jutland-style farmhouse tells the tale of a town and its Danish-American residents spun with exhibits, artifacts, and artwork.

Downtown, third- and fourth-generation Danish Americans create the mood: Munch almond custard *kringle*, butter cookies, and *brunekager* at Olsen's Danish Village Bakery.

WHERE TO SHOP: Browse the Scandinavian handicrafts and household items (glassware, kitchen utensils, amber jewelry) at Rasmussen's boutique. Make like a Viking and quaff *aul* (ale) at the Solvang Brewing Company with its trademark windmill.

JOINING IN: September's three-day Danish Days, one of California's oldest international festivals, features an *aebleskiver* (Danish pancake) breakfast, a Viking Beer & Wine Garden, and a traditional torchlight parade.

INSIGHT · Late Danes

Solvang's Danish look didn't actually appear until 1947. It started with an article in the *Saturday Evening Post* that described the town as a "spotless Danish village that blooms like a rose." Townsfolk decided to leverage the positive Scandinavian spin. They gave its Western-style buildings a quaint Danish makeover, renamed Main Street Copenhagen Drive, and put up windmills. "It's ironic," says Esther Jacobsen Bates of Elverhøj Museum. Though Solvang's Danish community was dwindling, "its appearance was becoming more" Dutch.

■ *Essentials:* Solvang, solvangusa.com; Elverhøj Museum, 1624 Elverhoy Way, tel 805-686-1211, elverhoj.org; Olsen's Danish Village Bakery, 1529 Mission Dr., tel 805-688-6314, olsensdanishvillagebakery.net; Rasmussen's, 1697 Copenhagen Dr., tel 805-688-6636, rasmussenssolvang.com; Solvang Brewing Company, 1547 Mission St., tel 805-688-2337, solvangbrewing.com; Danish Days, solvangdanishdays.org

The Danish community of Solvang looks the part.

ANGKOR AWAY

Signs with distinctive Khmer script attest the changes afoot in Cambodia Town. The mile-long stretch of Long Beach, California's Anaheim Avenue is slowly but surely morphing from auto-body shops and old factories into a vibrant collection of Indochinese restaurants, jewelry shops, and fashion boutiques. Waves of immigrants arrived in the 1980s, fleeing the country's Khmer Rouge regime. Today, it's one of the largest Cambodian communities outside Southeast Asia.

WHAT TO EAT AND DRINK: Make like an ancient Khmer and sip suds. In keeping with Cambodia's long tradition of beer making, Stone Temple Beer Company makes Noble Truths Ale and Kampot Pepper Black IPA. "We opened a craft beer company to share our love for beer and to also promote awareness of Khmer culture," says head brewer Maurice Yim. The brewery doesn't have a tasting room, but you can sample its product at Cambodian eateries like Pka Roam Tek Roam. Pair with popular dishes like *chruok svay* (mango salad), *lok lak* (stir-fried beef), or hot and sour fish soup with banana flowers. For a completely different take on Cambodian culture, catch saffron-robed monks praying at Khemara Buddhikaram Temple in nearby Signal Hill.

INSIGHT · Khmerican Pie

Long Beach boasts the nation's largest Cambodian-American population (ca 20,000), but it doesn't have the largest percentage (4 percent). That honor belongs to Lowell, Massachusetts, with 13 percent (13,300) "Khmericans." As with Long Beach, the immigrants began arriving after the Vietnam War and the rise of the Khmer Rouge in Cambodia. Lowell also has a Cambodia Town, numerous Asian restaurants, shops, and other businesses, and even its own Cambodian Consulate.

■ *Essentials:* For more information on Cambodia Town, go to cambodiatown.org; Stone Temple Beer Company, 625 W. Anaheim St., tel 562-999-1949, stonetemplebrew.com; Pka Roam Tek Roam Restaurant, 1360 E. Anaheim St., Suite 205 (2nd floor), tel 562-591-7300; Khemara Buddhikaram Temple, 2100 W. Willow St., Signal Hill, tel 562-595-0566

Praying over lunch at Wat Sovannasam in Cambodia Town, Long Beach

World Cup soccer fans at the Springbok Bar & Grill, Van Nuys, California

SOCCER- AND RUGBY-WATCHING

Feel transported with a game on the telly, mates by your side, and a cold pint in your hand.

■ The Springbok Bar and Grill

As to be expected from an establishment named after the antelope-gazelle that gives the South African national rugby union team its moniker, the Van Nuys, California, bar and grill is a prime location for catching a game of rugby. This humble bar with an upscale menu is decked out in rugby paraphernalia, and fans pack the house when there is a critical match. (Good luck squeezing in when South Africa battles Australia.) The staff is so dedicated that they will open early to show important games live. You can also watch cricket and soccer. *16153 Victory Blvd., Van Nuys, Calif., tel 818-988-9786, thespringbok.com*

■ Miss Favela

With a name that references Brazil's slums, this lively bodega brings together Brooklynites of all social strata for Brazilian snacks like *feijoada* bean stew and nonstop soccer viewing. *57 S. 5th St., Brooklyn, N.Y., tel 718-230-4040, missfavela.com*

■ Lucky Bar

You're right to expect a lot from a bar that claims to be Washington, "D.C.'s original soccer bar destination"—and you'll still be impressed. It's not all those fan scarves of Europe's top footy teams, but the sheer energy of watching a game with workers from all over the world that will move you. But no matter how fervent the fans, there's no need to worry about hooliganism—the capital's young professionals keep their cool: very diplomatic. *1221 Connecticut Ave. N.W., Washington, D.C., tel 202-331-3733, luckybardc.com*

■ The Globe Pub

As the name might tip you off, Chicago's Globe Pub is an internationally minded little place. It calls itself a "neighborhood destination, but with a difference"—perhaps a time difference. International soccer matches, Six Nations rugby league, and even horse races bring Chicagoans of different hometowns together. *1934 W. Irving Park Rd., Chicago, Ill., tel 773-871-3757, theglobepub.net*

■ Three Lions Pub

When Denver's Three Lions calls itself a "world football pub," it doesn't mean the American kind with padded men and tight pants. Modeled after a London pub, this convivial drinking hole is a tribute to the "beautiful game" referred to as soccer on this side of the Atlantic. With matches filling the screens nonstop, this unpretentious bar is a vacation from your daily life. *2239 E. Colfax Ave., Denver, Colo., tel 303-997-6886, threelionsdenver.com*

■ Fadó Irish Pub

Fadó may mean "long ago" in Gaelic, but this Irish-owned pub is Austin's best place for keeping up-to-date with what's happening in international sports. As you watch the English Premier League, the FIFA World Cup, American soccer matches, and rugby competitions, you can enjoy fish and chips along with a tall glass of Guinness. *214 W. 4th St., Austin, Tex., tel 512-457-0172, plus 11 other U.S. locations, fadoirishpub.com*

LOS ANGELES

Traditional fashion at the Lithuanian Fair, Los Angeles

Korean Tune Town

The karaoke machine may have been invented in Japan, but the hot spot for sing-along fun in the L.A. metro area is Koreatown. Part of the area's attraction is the karaoke scene, personified by the über-popular Palm Tree L.A. on Wilshire Boulevard. Reserve one of the 20 private lounge rooms, sort through the selection of popular Korean, Japanese, and American tunes, and start crooning. If you're feeling a tad shy, order a bottle of *soju* (Korean rice wine) to loosen the tongue. And round things off with an order of kimchi, fried squid, and spicy rice cakes from the club's Arang restaurant. For a calmer Korean outing, drop into one of K-town's many *jimjilbangs*, or Korean spas. The biggest is affordable, 24-hour Wi Spa, complete with an oak wood *bugama* and salt therapy sauna, among others. For a smaller, more chill option, try Crystal Spa, where you can escape the L.A. heat in the Ice Room. Not surprising that today's sprawling K-town, between the Santa Monica and Hollywood freeways, is fast becoming a hub of hip for young urban professionals of various ethnic backgrounds. "It's a very cool place to live," says Ja Young Jackie Park, who moved from South Korea to L.A. at age 12 and later served as performing arts manager at the L.A. Korean Cultural Center.
Palm Tree L.A., Windsor Sq., 3240 Wilshire Blvd., Suite 401, tel 213-381-3388, lsyid.com; Wi Spa, 2700 Wilshire Blvd., tel 213-487-2700, wispausa.com; Crystal Spa, 3500 W. 6th St., Suite 321, tel 213-487-5600, crystalspala.com

Mariachi Mood

In the cool of early evening, listen to a group of Mexican-American musicians play in the streetlights of Mariachi Plaza; it really does feel like you're standing in Guadalajara rather than the Boyle Heights area of East L.A. Much as they do in Mexico, mariachis have been gathering

Like L.A. as a whole, we're a suburban kind of Chinatown. The neighborhood reflects the adaptation of many different peoples who happen to be of Chinese background. You can eat Chinese food, buy Chinese art, and gain knowledge of all things Chinese at bookshops or by talking to people. It's much more a global community than when I was a kid. The main reason people come to Chinatown—including Chinese Americans who live elsewhere in L.A.—is the food. From Vietnamese pho to Mandarin-style beef noodle soup, there are many different styles of cooking among the restaurants. For instance, the Hong Kong café-style menus have grilled meats that you wouldn't find in a Cantonese restaurant. And we have a small residential community. This is where our elders lived and where many of our ancestors lived and died.

EUGENE MOY
Chinese American Citizens Alliance president

Samurai from Nagoya in Little Tokyo, Los Angeles, for Nisei Week

Leimert Park Village Music Caravan musicians, Los Angeles

at the plaza since the 1930s, auditioning their talent for those seeking musical accompaniment for birthday parties, graduation events, and *quinceañeras*. "The best time to see them perform is during the Fiesta of Santa Cecilia, usually the Saturday before November 22," says Catherine L. Kurland, co-author of *Hotel Mariachi: Urban Space and Cultural Heritage in Los Angeles*. Other mariachi hot spots: Boyle Heights Farmers Market on Friday nights or just about any night at Eastside Luv, a nightclub perched on the plaza's eastern flank. *Mariachi Plaza, mariachiplazalosangeles .com; Boyle Heights Farmers Market, 1831 E. 1st St.; Eastside Luv, 1835 E. 1st St., tel 323-262-7442, eastsideluv.com*

African-American Cool
"The black Greenwich Village" is what movie director and local resident John Singleton calls Leimert Park Village. Ella Fitzgerald and Ray Charles are among those who have lived in Leimert Park, and the area remains a fulcrum of black culture and creativity. Catch comedy or classic jazz at the Barbara Morrison Performing Arts Center. Browse Afrocentric literature from around the world or attend a weekly author event at Eso Won Books. Dig into jerk chicken, curry goat, and other Jamaican dishes at the incredibly authentic Ackee Bamboo. Or take the self-guided Leimert Park Art Walk on the last Sunday of every month for a sampling of the area's visual and performing arts.

Leimert Park Village, leimertparkvillage .org; Barbara Morrison Performing Arts Center, 4305 Degnan Blvd., Suite 101, tel 310-462-1439, barbaramorrisonpac .com; Eso Wan Books, 4327 Degnan Blvd., tel 323-290-1048, esowonbookstore .com; Ackee Bamboo Jamaican Cuisine, 4305 Degnan Blvd., #100, tel 323-295-7275, ackeebamboojacuisine .com

Thousand and One Middle Eastern Bites
Spread along Westwood Boulevard near the UCLA campus, "Tehrangeles" is mostly about eating—restaurants that serve traditional Persian cuisine to local émigrés and others who crave Middle Eastern delights. One of the oldest and most authentic

Koreatown
Restaurants on Sixth Street in Central L.A. **BEST BET:** Movies, music, and lectures at the Korean Cultural Center Los Angeles

Little Tokyo
Japanese restaurants, shops, and temples in a 13-block area just east of downtown L.A. **BEST BET:** The Grand Parade during Nisei Week (Aug.)

Tehrangeles (Little Persia)
Westwood between Wilshire and Pico **BEST BET:** Shirazi salad, eggplant, *kookoo*, and tongue sandwich at Attari Sandwich Shop

Thai Town
Six blocks in East Hollywood on Hollywood Boulevard between Normandie and Western **BEST BET:** Breakfast, including fried Chinese doughnuts, at Siam Sunset

Chinatown
Restaurants on Broadway and Hill between the Hollywood Freeway and Dodger Stadium **BEST BET:** Pork dumplings at Phoenix Bakery

is Shaherzad, named after the queen in the Persian literary classic *One Thousand and One Nights*. Start your meal with a traditional appetizer like *kashk bademjan* (eggplant topped with yogurt sauce) or *sabzi khordan* (a blend of feta cheese, walnuts, and fresh herbs), move onto a hearty *ghaimeh* (split pea stew) or rack of

lamb kebabs, and then finish off the meal with a traditional dessert like baklava or *faloodeh* (rice noodle sorbet). The city's Iranian spots started popping up after the country's violent 1979 revolution, when Iranian refugees landed in neighborhoods like Beverly Hills and created new ethnic enclaves like Pershing Square in West L.A.

Shaherzad, 1422 Westwood Blvd., tel 310-470-3242, shaherzad restaurant.com

Cities of the Angels: Bangkok in L.A.
The Thailand Plaza strip mall with a towering pink-and-gold neon sign would equally be at home in Bangkok or L.A. It is heart and soul of six-block Thai Town on Hollywood Boulevard.

L.A. has the largest Thai population outside of Thailand, and the mall's Silom Supermarket is where they shop for lemongrass, curry paste, sticky rice, and other Thai ingredients that you can't buy at your local Safeway. Browse the Dokya bookstore for books, magazines, and newspapers on Thailand, plus a selection of

Walking Map *Little Tokyo*

harbors 40 Japanese restaurants, bakeries, boutiques, and gift shops in an ambience reminiscent of rural Japan (*335 E. 2nd St., tel 213-617-1900, japanesevillage plaza.net*).

5 | Duck into Little Tokyo Mall and the wondrous world of Japanese animation and comic books at **Anime Jungle** (*319 E. 2nd St., tel 213-621-1661, animejungle.net*).

6 | Continue south along Azusa Street to the **James Irvine Japanese Garden** with its tranquil stream and waterfall (*224 S. San Pedro St., tel 213-628-2725, jaccc .org/garden.php*).

7 | Feeling hungry? Visit **Sushi Go 55**, one of L.A.'s best bets for sushi, sashimi, and tempura (*333 S. Alameda St., #317, tel 213-687-0777, sushi go55.com*).

A mosaic of exotic sights, sounds, and smells, downtown L.A.'s Little Tokyo district offers a journey into modern-day and throw-back Japan.

1 | Start your Little Tokyo walk with a browse of the **Japanese American National Museum,** one of

the nation's best immigration collections (*100 N. Central Ave., tel 213-625-0414, janm.org*).

2 | At the end of the pedestrian street outside the museum is the **Go For Broke Monument** commemorating Japanese Americans who fought and died for Allied forces during

World War II (*tel 310-328-0907, goforbroke.org*).

3 | Backtrack to 1st and visit **Marugame Monzo,** Little Tokyo's top noodle house (*329 E. 1st St., tel 213-346-9762*).

4 | Return along First Street and enter **Japanese Village Plaza,** which

Thai movies. Savor the soothing hands at Thai Sabai Massage. Or feast on papaya salad, *tom kha gai* (coconut chicken soup), pad thai noodles, and green curry at the mall's eponymous restaurant. The plaza is also integral to the annual Songkran (Thai New Year) festival. The daylong celebration includes vendors selling lots of mango sticky rice and lobster balls, a Singha beer garden, and women donning ornate Thai costumes, plus Thai music and dance, and a parade down Hollywood Boulevard. *Thailand Plaza, 5321 Hollywood Blvd., tel 323-993-9000; Silom Supermarket, 5321 Hollywood Blvd., tel 323-993-9000; Dokya, 5321 Hollywood Blvd., tel 323-464-7178;*

Thai Sabai Massage, 5261 Hollywood Blvd., tel 310-801-3912, thaisabai.com; Songkran Festival, thainewyear.com

Baltic Bash
Savor the taste of *kugelis,* join in the swirling *rateliai,* quaff some *krupnikas,* and hunt for the perfect *rupintojelis* at the annual Lithuanian Fair in Los Feliz district near Griffith Park. Held on the grounds of St. Casimir Lithuanian Catholic Church, it's the largest Baltic festival in southern California. Start the day with a traditional breakfast of potato dumplings (*kugelis*), browse the outdoor arts and crafts stalls for a "pensive Christ" statue (*rupintojelis*) and other wood carvings, down a shot or two of spicy honey liqueur

(*krupnikas*), and then partake in a traditional circle dance (*rateliai*) to the strains of Lithuanian folk tunes. Throughout the year, St. Casimir (built in 1941) serves as an unofficial community center for L.A.'s Lithuanians, hosting both religious and cultural events like visiting singers or dancers from the eastern Baltic. It's also a shrine to Lithuanian liberty; check out the courtyard statue of Bernardas Brazdžionis, whose poetry helped inspire the "Singing Revolution" of 1989 and independence from the Soviet Union. *Los Angeles Lithuanian Fair, lithuanianfair.com; St. Casimir Lithuanian Church, 2718 St. George St., tel 323-644-4660*

Not So Little Armenia
The Kardashians are

just the tip of the iceberg—Los Angeles has more Armenians (360,000) than any other city but Yerevan and Moscow. The largest concentrations are in suburban Glendale and an inner-city district called Little Armenia, wedged between Thai Town and the Hollywood Freeway. One of the most authentic activities you can do in the neighborhood is attend an Armenian-language service at St. Garabed Armenian Apostolic Church on North Alexandria Avenue, a focal point of the community for more than 40 years. Afterward, walk or drive the four blocks to Marouch Restaurant and a sumptuous lunch of Armenian delicacies like *bastourma* (veal salami), lentil soup with toasted pita bread, stuffed grape leaves, and grilled kebabs. *Little Armenia, littlearmenia.com; St. Garabed Armenian Apostolic Church, 1614 N. Alexandria Ave., tel 323-666-0507, stgarabedchurch.org; Marouch Restaurant, 4905 Santa Monica Blvd., tel 323-662-9325, marouchrestaurant.com*

Extreme Makeover, Chinatown Edition
L.A.'s oldest Asian enclave is famed for both its immigrant community and as the site of the denouement of the

Buddhist priests help mark Songkran, the Thai New Year, in Los Angeles.

Multicultural Grand Central Market, Los Angeles

Oscar-winning, 1974 namesake film. Today's Chinatown is a 1930s Hollywood version of the ideal Chinese community: a fantasyland of mock pagodas, brightly painted balconies, and upturned tile roofs decorated with mythological creatures. Admire the whimsical architecture that surrounds Old Chinatown Central Plaza. Light joss sticks and meditate for a moment at the Thien Hau Temple on Yale Street with its gleaming golden interior and glazed orange roof. And don't leave without purchasing a bag of incredibly sour Chinese candies at JC Market at the corner of Alpine and Hill. A bit of history: The area first took shape in the 1870s as Chinese migrants, many of them former gold miners and railroad workers, built homes and shops in abandoned vineyards near the old Spanish settlement. The original Chinatown was demolished in the 1930s to make way for Union Station.
Chinatown, chinatownla .com; Thien Hau Temple, 756 Yale St., tel 213-680-1860, thienhautemple .com; JC Market, 801 N. Hill St., tel 213-628-3888

Tasty Melting Pot
You don't realize the variety of foods that immigrants have brought to Los Angeles until you step inside the aromatic Grand Central Market. In recent years Grand Central has expanded its edible repertoire from mostly Hispanic to spanning the globe. Try an iconic blend of Turkish and German cuisine at Berlin Currywurst or island-style stir-fry at Hawaii BBQ. Munch fresh-from-the-sea fish tacos at Lupita's Seafood or *carnitas* done a dozen different ways at Las Morelianas. Get your Gouda or provolone cut to order at the DTLA Cheese stall. "Grand Central is now the most diverse eating place in Los Angeles," says Adele Yellin, the current owner. "The history of the market has always been that the latest immigrants to Los Angeles are the vendors who come into the market." The market also hosts all sorts of special events, from cookbook author and celebrity chef events to live world beat music and an annual visual and performance art show.
Grand Central Market, 317 S. Broadway, tel 213-624-2378, grandcentralmarket.com

The Rose, a popular hookah lounge in Little Arabia, Anaheim

ANAHEIM, CALIFORNIA
ARABIAN DAYS AND NIGHTS

There's plenty of irony in the fact that Little Arabia is just a stone's throw (2 miles) from the place where the fictional Princess Jasmine was born. In much the same way as Walt Disney, migrants from a dozen Middle Eastern countries are creating their own magic kingdom among the strip malls and palm trees of Orange County. Running through the heart of the neighborhood, Brookhurst Street is flanked by Arabian-American restaurants, grocery stores, and hookah lounges.

WHERE TO GO: Combining aspects of East and West, Fusion Ultra Lounge features artsy glass-and-brass hookahs, fusion foods, and a hip-hop/rock sound track in a hip nightclub atmosphere. Dip Middle Eastern breads—*keshek, za'atar, kofta, lahm b'ajeen*—into the marvelous *labneh* (Lebanese cream cheese) made at Al Amir Bakery.

JOINING IN: Celebrate the end of Ramadan with the joyous celebration called Eid al-Fitr. At the Center Street Promenade in downtown Anaheim, live Middle Eastern music, food stalls, carnival rides, and camel shows are part of the festivities. "Our market vendors sell a diverse array of items from attire to jewelry to ancient perfume arrangements," says festival organizer Dania Alkhouli.

INSIGHT · Arab Spring Flings

Long before Arab Americans started moving into the area, the northwest corner of Anaheim was colloquially called Little Gaza Strip, a corruption of Garza Island as the unincorporated area was officially known. But it might as well have been named after the troubled and often violent Palestinian enclave, because Little Arabia has become a hotbed of support for the Arab Spring and other Middle Eastern causes in recent years. Residents have staged demonstrations with music, chanting, and flag-waving along Brookhurst Street.

"Food dishes range from burgers to the exotic tastes of gyros, shawarma, and hummus."

■ *Essentials:* Little Arabia, littlearabia.org; Fusion Ultra Lounge, 512 S. Brookhurst St., tel 714-520-5661; Al Amir Bakery, 2281 W. Ball Rd., tel 714-535-0973, alamirbakery.com; Eid Festival, eidfestival.net

"Anaheim's Eid festival is geared at uniting the Muslim-American community in celebration." —DANIA ALKHOULI, EID FESTIVAL ORGANIZER

A communal wedding during the Mideastern Eid Festival in Anaheim

AROUND THE WORLD IN
SAN DIEGO

The Junípero Serra Museum at San Diego's Presidio

Eclectic Asian

Shop for exotic ingredients at Asian supermarkets, sing your heart out at a karaoke lounge, get your nails done at a beauty salon, or let needles cure what ails you at an acupuncture specialist. Coat of many colors is a good way to describe Convoy District, home to more than 200 Asian American–owned businesses, many of them eateries. What makes the area even more unique is the fact that it flaunts half a dozen different types of Asian cuisine rather than just one: Korean, Chinese, Japanese, Vietnamese, Thai, and Taiwanese. "It's a miniature Asia town," says resident Steve Kent, a Korean-American banker who wrote a research paper on Convoy District while a student at University of California, San Diego. "Asians first started hanging out there in the 1980s when someone opened up the first Chinese supermarket." On any given night, you can choose between kimchi and sushi, dim sum and pho noodles. Kent recommends Friend's House for truly authentic Korean cuisine. "It's where I go to have my Korean comfort or soul food." *Convoy District, convoydistrict .com; Friend's House, 4647 Convoy St., Suite 101A, tel 858-292-0499, friendshousekorean .menutoeat.com*

La Dolce Vita

Here's an offer you can't refuse: a fall film festival in San Diego that showcases the best of contemporary Italian cinema, many of the movies winners of the Nastro d'Argento (Silver Ribbon), Italy's version of the Oscar. Venues range from the Museum of Photographic Arts in Balboa Park to the old North Park Theatre, a wonderfully restored 1920s movie palace. Food is always a big part of the event. Gather with other film aficionados before or after screenings in the *ristorantes* along India Street in San Diego's bustling Little Italy district. And be on the lookout for the fest's unique food-and-film events like the alfresco Dining on the Docks and a pairing of food-oriented films and gourmet eats called CineCucina.

I grew up with my grandparents in Little Italy on Columbia Street. My grandparents started a little store, which turned into the restaurant going on 65 years now. When I was growing up, San Diego was the tuna capital of America. My grandparents would place the orders with the tuna fleet before they went out. But then they put through Interstate 5 and Little Italy got cut off from the waterfront. The neighborhood went into a slump. We started the Little Italy Association around 18 years ago, and slowly started revitalizing and rebuilding the neighborhood to what it once was, minus the tuna fleet, of course. There's a lot of new housing—condos, apartments—coming in. People want to live here because you can walk everywhere downtown. We're going gangbusters.

DANNY MOCERI
Owner, Filippi's Pizza Grotto, and vice president, Little Italy Association

Old Town's Cinco de Mayo in San Diego features vivid costumes and dancing.

San Diego Italian Film Festival, sandiegoitalianfilm festival.com; Museum of Photographic Arts, 1649 El Prado, tel 619-238-7559, mopa.org; North Park Theatre, 2891 University Ave., tel 619-239-8836, thenorthparktheatre.com

Old World Haunt
Sip a margarita amid lush tropical and tile-roofed adobe surroundings at San Diego's Old Town, founded in 1769 as the first European settlement of any kind on the west coast of what would later become the United States. Although many of the historic structures date from early American days, remnants of Spanish colonial and Mexican eras feature prominently in the state and city parks that preserve the area. And if you happen to be in

town on or around May 5, celebrate Cinco de Mayo by grooving to mariachi music on outdoor stages, browsing the lowrider car show, and chomping on tortilla chips. For another taste of the Spanish colonial past, explore the ruins of a 17th-century Spanish fort called the Presidio on a wooded hillside overlooking Old Town. You can also wander through 19th-century adobe houses (Casa de Estudillo and reconstructed Casa de Machado y Stewart), peruse artifacts and enjoy lectures and special events at the Spanish Revival–style Serra Museum, and check out the modest El Campo Santo Cemetery, where some of the city's earliest settlers are buried (and, some say, still haunting). *Old Town San Diego State Historic Park,*

4002 Wallace St., tel 619-220-5422, parks.ca.gov and oldtownsandiego. org; Presidio Park, sandiegohistory.org

Saints and Sopas
The annual Festa do Espirito Santo (Feast of the Holy Spirit) takes place in late May as Portuguese Americans commemorate a miracle that helped Portugal's Queen Isabella feed the poor during a 14th-century famine. Watch the solemn Saturday night candlelight procession between St. Agnes Catholic Church and the Portuguese Hall, or attend a special Sunday Mass during which the king and queen of the festival are crowned. San Diego's oldest ethnic festival, dating back more than 100 years, blends Portuguese

Live Irish music at the House of Ireland, Balboa Park

The Main Neighborhoods

Convoy District
Asian tearooms and cafés on Convoy between Kearny Mesa and Clairemont Mesa
BEST BET: Trying a dozen cuisines at San Diego Night Market

Old Town
Mexican eateries and shops in the Old Town neighborhood
BEST BET: Margaritas and folk dancing on Cinco de Mayo

Point Loma
Portuguese fishing outfitters at Harbor Drive's west end; St. Agnes Catholic Church and Portuguese Hall
BEST BET: Iberian fare at Seafood City Supermarket's Portuguese Hall

Mira Mesa
Filipino eateries on Mira Mesa between Scripps Ranch and Camino Ruiz
BEST BET: *Pandesal* rolls and cassava cake at Seafood City Supermarket

Little Italy
Italian eateries on India between Ash and Hawthorne
BEST BET: Alfresco food, music, and bocce during Little Italy Festa

Festa Queen at St. Agnes Church, Festa do Espirito Santo, San Diego

traditions and Roman Catholic rites that play out on the bay side of Point Loma district. "It's a big deal to 'make the Festa' and people come back from all over to be there that weekend," says Cindy Luis, who attended St. Agnes's school and was one of the festival queens in third grade. "I was in the Festa parades every year until I was 14. It's become much bigger in recent years, expanding from two days and a small parade to three days and a big parade." Over the course of the festival, you can also play traditional Portuguese games, watch Iberian folkloric dances, or listen to the Filarmónica União Portuguesa de San Diego at the Portuguese Hall, a market and café. Madeira cheeses, Iberian condiments, seafood products, and *linguiças* (smoked pork sausages) are among the items sold at the shop. The little eatery serves a variety of Portuguese fare including *bifanas* (pork cutlet) sandwiches, Sagres beer, and Sumol fruit sodas. And don't leave without sampling the homemade *sopas,* a thick Portuguese soup filled with beef, cabbage, and potatoes and served over mint-covered bread.

The neighborhood's other big bash is the Cabrillo Festival at the end of September, which honors the feats of Juan Rodríguez Cabrillo. The three-day celebration features a wreath laying at Cabrillo National Monument, a dinner/dance at Portuguese Hall, and an all-day, outdoor *festa* at nearby Ballast Point navy base.
Festa do Espirito Santo, upsesfesta.com and san diego.com; Cabrillo Festival, cabrillofestival.org

Eastern Enlightenment
Surfers flock to "Swami's" for one of the best breaks along the southern California coast. Seekers of inner peace and harmony flock to the golden-domed compound for enlightenment or maybe just to get away from it all. Perched on a bluff above the sea, the Self-Realization Fellowship ashram is one of the more recognizable landmarks along the San Diego coast. Indian guru Paramahansa Yogananda founded the center in 1936, long before Indian mysticism became popular with the flower power generation. Nowadays you can attend weekly sessions on concentration, meditation, and *kriya* yoga, as well as lessons on how to live a more balanced spiritual and

material life. Pop into the temple and listen to a Hindu *Bhagavad Gita* reading, wander the Meditation Gardens, and watch surfers riding the waves far below, or sign up for a retreat with overnight accommodation in the ocean-view Hermitage. *Self-Realization Fellowship, 1150 S. Coast Hwy. 101, Encinitas, tel 760-753-5353, encinitas temple.org*

Filipino Feast
Like nearly everything else in the Mira Mesa district, Manila Sunset Grille is to be found in the nondescript strip mall. But here, in the city's largely Filipino neighborhood, the food is out of this world: fresh *lumpia* (sautéed vegetables, lettuce, and peanuts rolled in a crepe-like wrapper), *arroz caldo* (rice porridge with chicken), *pancit malabon* (rice noodles with grilled shrimp), and various cuts of barbecued pork. You can also dig into exotic Filipino desserts like the angelic *halo-halo* (shaved ice and milk with diced tropical fruits, sweet potato, and seaweed). In a city with a large and vibrant Filipino population, the Mira Mesa district boasts the largest concentration. The neighborhood is also flush with Filipino grocery stores, fast food outlets, and restaurants. *Manila Sunset Grille, 9837 Mira Mesa Blvd., tel 858-578-6200, manila sunset.com*

Garden of Mexican Delights
Taste San Diego's most authentic Mexican cuisine—and sip some darn good margaritas—in Eden Gardens. One of southern California's oldest Hispanic communities, the ethnic enclave lies in a small coastal valley in the Solana Beach area on the north side of San Diego. Founded after World War I by immigrants working at the citrus farms of nearby Rancho Santa Fe, the hamlet was originally called La Colonia. Despite development all around, Eden Gardens has retained its Mexican flavor for nearly a century. La Colonia County Park hosts soccer games and *quinceañeras* parties, as well as the 1887 Stevens House with its small heritage museum. Sample uncommon (for San Diego) Mexican dishes like menudo (tripe and hominy soup), *pescado ranchero* (grilled fish), and nopal (prickly pear cactus) at Fidel's Little Mexico restaurant on the north side of Eden Gardens. *Fidel's Little Mexico, 749 Genevieve St., Solana Beach, tel 858-755-5292, fidelslittlemexico.com*

Mediterranean Mix
Travel back in time—and across the globe—at the "international cottages" in Balboa Park. One of the highlights of the 1935 California Pacific International Exposition was the House of Pacific Relations, a miniature village where the cultures of 32 nations were on display. Eighty years later, the cute Mediterranean-style bungalows continue to host national groups as varied as Ukrainian, Palestinian, Chinese, and Argentinian. Attend weekend club "lawn programs" between March and November to sample ethnic music, dance, crafts, costumes, and edibles. Or wait for the annual December Nights Festival, when thousands of people descend on the village for holiday season food and drink from far-off lands. *Balboa Park, 1549 El Prado, tel 619-239-0512, balboapark.org*

San Diego's Little Italy offers 30 gastronomic opportunities.

Rhinos at the
San Diego Zoo

SAFARIS

Lions and tigers and elephants and cheetahs. Venture into a slice of the Serengeti.

■ **San Diego Zoo Safari Park**
Choose how you want to interact with the San Diego park's animals: Take a cart safari to see herds of grazing giraffes and gazelles, zoom down the zip line through shady trees for a bird's-eye view of the deer and rhino enclosures, or meet a cheetah. Live out African safari fantasies with the Roar and Snore overnight option, and stay in a canvas tent near the African plains field exhibit. Open year-round. *15500 San Pasqual Valley Rd., Escondido, Calif., tel 760-747-8702, sdzsafaripark.org*

■ **Safari West**
A slice of the Serengeti nestled in the heart of California's wine country, Safari West in Santa Rosa is a private African wildlife preserve and tent camp. Cheetahs, giraffes, and lemurs are only some of the animals guests encounter on their excursions. The adults-only Wild Nights in Wine Country package combines glamping (luxury camping) in imported South African tents with wine tasting at the Francis Ford Coppola Winery. *Safari West, 3115 Porter Creek Rd., Santa Rosa, Calif., tel 707-579-2551, by reservation only, safariwest.com*

■ **African Lion Safari**
At this park in Hamilton, Canada, lions, kangaroos, gibbons, and elephants roam free for tourists caged in their vehicles. Seven game reserves, divided by region of origin, host more than 1,000 local and exotic birds and animals. *1386 Cooper Road, Hamilton, Ont., tel 519-623-2620, open May–Oct., lionsafari.com*

■ **Lion Country Safari**
The 4-square-mile park in Loxahatchee, Florida, brings the African safari experience to American weekend vacationers. The place is home to over 900 animals including lions, white rhinos, chimpanzees, zebras, and giraffes. Take the *Safari Queen* on Lake Shanalee to visit island-dwelling siamangs and spider monkeys, pan for gems, or cool off in the water park. *2003 Lion Country Safari Rd., Loxahatchee, Fla., tel 561-793-1084, lioncountrysafari.com*

■ **The Wilds**
The Wilds's conservation center in Cumberland, Ohio, protects 31 rare and endangered species, including the world's first fourth-generation rhinos born in human care. With nearly 10,000 acres of grasslands, woodlands, wetlands, and lakes, visitors can take in the expansive grounds by car, mountain bike, horseback, or zip line. *14000 International Rd., Cumberland, Ohio, tel 740-638-5030, thewilds.org*

■ **Fossil Rim Wildlife Center**
Inquisitive ostrich and giraffe regularly visit vehicles at this exotic game ranch turned conservation center in Glen Rose, Texas. More than 125 cheetahs were born here, the result of successful breeding programs. Stay at the swanky lodge to see animals at dawn (when they are most active), take a biking safari, or engage through day and overnight camps at the adjacent Wolf Ridge Nature Camp. *2299 County Rd. 2008, Glen Rose, Tex., 254-897-2960, fossilrim.org*

You Could Be In . . . THE SOUTH PACIFIC

Kauai, Hawaii
Fiji has nothing on the tropical foliage and spectacular sunsets over Kee Beach in Hawaii.

AROUND THE WORLD IN
HONOLULU

**A hula show on
Kuhio Beach,
Honolulu**

**Aloha, *Talofa, Kaoha,*
Etcetera**
Tie on a dancing skirt
and rock those hips
to the wild beat of the
drums in Tahiti, weave
your own palm-leaf
sun hat in Samoa, and
take up the challenge
of *lafo*—shuffleboard
on steroids—in Tonga.
Travel on to Fiji, Hawaii,
the Marquesas, Rapa Nui
(Easter Island), all in one
day at the Polynesian
Cultural Center. Enthu-
siastic Brigham Young
University students
from around the Pacific
earn their tuition by
sharing their native cul-
tures, each in their own
authentic village tucked
into 42 acres bursting
with exotic flora. Stay
for the evening luau and
sample a lavish buffet of
Pacific specialties. Try
haupia coconut pudding.

Don't say "aloha" before
the dramatic evening
show, full of music,
dances, and an erupting
volcano.
*Polynesian Cultural Cen-
ter, 55-370 Kamehameha
Hwy. (Hawaii 83),
Laie, tel 800-367-7060,
polynesia.com*

**Ama-zen Japanese
Temple**
Stroll into a Zen dream-
scape of koi-filled
streams and ponds. In
the serene Byodo-In
Temple, a reproduction
of a temple of the same
name in Uji, Japan,
you'll feel all that stress
slip away. Begin by
bonging the Bon-sho, a
three-ton brass bell. The
deep sound reverber-
ates against the green
cliffs of the Ko'olau
Mountains. According
to tradition, you'll find

happiness and long life.
Light incense before
the largest carved Bud-
dha outside Asia, and
then climb a hill to the
Meditation Pavilion
where your serenity may
be punctured by the
screeches of resident
peacocks. The streams
and ponds in the gar-
dens swarm with hun-
dreds of prize koi.
*Byodo-In Temple, 47-200
Kahekili Hwy. (Hawaii
83), Kaneohe, tel 808-239-
8811, byodo-in.com*

Dance With the Dead
Put on your *happi* coat,
cotton kimono, or just a
headband will do, and follow the hypnotic beat of
the *taiko* drums. Dance to
honor the souls of ances-
tors. Summer is Japanese
obon season with festivals
at Buddhist centers like
Honpa Hongwanji Hawaii

When my son,
David, went off to
university in Texas,
he had so much
trouble adjust-
ing to American
culture that they
let him join the
foreign students'
club. He missed
our sprawling old
house in Kahala
and long palmy
Kahala Beach
where Nalu, our
95-pound retriever,
swam with him.
They often hiked
up Diamond Head
to survey the surf
break. That's what
he missed the most,
those long rolling
waves. The part I
didn't know: There
was a tiger shark
the kids called Big
Sam who liked
to surf the same
break, and when
Big Sam was in the
hood, he owned
the waves. I wish
I could say David
missed my cooking
(vegetarian) but it
was slurping *saimin*
[noodle soup] at
Zippy's, followed by
a coconut "napple,"
a flaky turnover,
that he longed for.

RITA ARIYOSHI
*Writer, photographer,
hula dancer*

The Syrian Room
in Doris Duke's
Shangri La home,
Honolulu

Betsuin, and Moiliili Hongwanji and Haleiwa Shingon Missions. It's a bit like line dancing without the boots and *yee-haws*. Munch mochi, cone sushi, and teriyaki meat stick, and send a paper lantern out to sea.
Honpa Hongwanji Hawaii Betsuin, 1727 Pali Hwy., tel 808-522-9200, hongwanjihawaii.com; Moiliili Hongwanji Mission, 902 University Ave., tel 808-949-1659, moiliili hongwanji.org; Haleiwa Shingon Mission, 66-469 Paalaa Rd. Haleiwa, tel 808-637-4423

Hot Scots
The haunting wails of the bagpipes usher in the Annual Hawaiian Scottish Festival and Highland Games every April at Ala Moana Beach Park. Are you ready to try the Widow-maker, a tossing contest involving a 50-or-so-pound weight? Perhaps a little swordplay? Easier yet, get good whiskey (and Hawaiian pupus) on the Grand Scotch Tour.
Ala Moana Beach Park, 1201 Ala Moana Blvd., tel 808-768-4611, scots hawaii.org

Tropical St. Paddy's
On St. Patrick's Day, Hawaii's capital island, Oahu, becomes an Emerald Isle in more than its botany. Everyone who has a drop of Irish blood, and those that wish they did, celebrates. The day gets off to a rousing start with a parade of pipes and drums, floats and bands through Waikiki. The party goes on into the night at a giant block party and pub crawl through the China-town section of down-town Honolulu where a trio of Irish pubs offer imported stout, whis-key cakes, and fish and chips. The street music is pure Irish, unless you hula to "Lola O'Brien, the Irish Hawaiian." No blarney.
Friends of St. Patrick, fosphawaii.ning.com

Arabian Escape
Stroll through the Syrian Room, Mughal Garden, and Isfahan courtyard amid thousands of art treasures from the Islamic world at the late Doris Duke's Honolulu home, Shangri La. The impressive 2,500-item collection spans coun-tries—Spain, Morocco, Egypt, Syria, Iran, India—and centuries. Don't for-get to look outside and watch the waves roll onto the Diamond Head shore from the five-acre ocean-front estate.
Shangri La Center for Islamic Arts and Cul-tures, 4055 Papu Circle, tel 808-734-1941, shangri lahawaii.org

Kilts and bagpipes at Honolulu's Hawaiian Scottish Festival and Highland Games

The varied terrain of Kualoa Ranch in Oahu, Hawaii

FOREIGN MOVIE AND TV SETS IN HAWAII

Discover Hollywood's tropical back lot.

■ Raging Dinos

In the mega-monster movie *Jurassic Park,* the Hawaiian island of Kauai was cast as the fictional Isla Nublar off the coast of Costa Rica. That waterfall in the opening sequence is Kauai, Hawaii's Manawaiopuna, now popularly known as Jurassic Park Falls. Director Steven Spielberg and his stars, Richard Attenborough, Laura Dern, and Jeff Goldblum, had been filming on the island for three weeks when Hurricane Iniki, the most powerful storm to hit Hawaii to date, slammed into Kauai. The camera crew gallantly shot footage of the hurricane while the cast hunkered down with stranded tourists in the ballroom of the Westin Kauai resort. Afterward, the final shoot had to move to Oahu.

■ Lost in Paradise

Hawaii doubles as so many other places in the blockbuster TV series *Lost,* it's no wonder the cast was confused. Daniel Dae Kim's character, Jin-Soo Kwon, thought his home was in Korea, but it was really at the Ilikai Hotel in Waikiki. Naveen Andrews's character suffered a really nasty flashback to his days with Iraq's Republican Guard, but he needn't have worried, because the dry side of Diamond Head stood in for Iraq. The Hawaii Convention Center served as an Australian airport, and the *Lost* survivors' primitive encampment was located at Oahu's Kualoa Ranch with a handy 7-Eleven nearby plus some cute boutiques and art galleries.

■ Gorillas in Love

Imagine the terror of a young honeymoon couple camping in remote, idyllic Kalalau Valley, Kauai, when they were awakened by a 25-foot mountain gorilla crashing through the underbrush. It turned out to be Jessica Lange's hairy sweetheart, King Kong, on location for the 1976 remake of the eponymous film. A more diminutive gorilla, barreling in at a mere 16.5 feet, also made an unlikely appearance in Hawaii—in Oahu's Ka'a'awa Valley for the 1998 movie *Mighty Joe Young.* This time, the object of affection was Charlize Theron.

■ Fire and Virus

In 1995, for the film *Outbreak,* a thatched village was built at a struggling tourist attraction along Kauai's Wailua River. It was supposed to be Zaire. To prevent the spread of the deadly Motaba virus, Donald Sutherland and Morgan Freeman burned the whole place down. The tourist attraction was never rebuilt, but the movie grossed $190 million (according to *imdb.com*).

■ Hollywood Roundup

Cows take a backseat to the stars at Kualoa Ranch, a 4,000-acre working cattle ranch on Oahu's windward coast. The vast and varied terrain has appeared in *Lost, Hawaii Five-O, Pearl Harbor, Godzilla, Windtalkers, 50 First Dates,* and more, passing as Africa, Asia, Ireland, Mexico, and even Atlantis, among others. Visitors can sign up for a movie tour. *Kualoa Ranch Tour, 49-960 Kamehameha Hwy., Kaneohe, Hawaii, tel 808-237-7321, kualoa.com*

For more information on Hawaii film location tours, go to Hawaii Movie Tour, tel 800-831-5541, hawaiimovietour.com

Hula dancers perform at Hawaii Volcanoes National Park.

HAWAII VOLCANOES NATIONAL PARK, BIG ISLAND
GODDESS COUNTRY

It is said Pele, the jealous Polynesian fire goddess who hurled lava at her rivals, still lives among the flames of Kilauea, one of the world's most active— and the only drive-up—volcanoes. Giving the goddess a little berth, Hawaii's Polynesian settlers considered the whole area, now Hawaii Volcanoes National Park, to be Pele's domain.

WHAT TO SEE: The best way to experience what those early Polynesians felt is to walk around and see red. Hula groups often come on pilgrimage. Look for offerings to Pele left all over the park by island visitors, from rocks wrapped in ti leaves and red blossoms to, occasionally, a bottle of gin. Listen to some of the rarest birds in the world, including endangered large gold-and-white Palila finches and Hawaii's state bird, the two-foot-tall nene goose. Hike across a crater where the ground is toasty beneath your feet. Walk through an old lava tube. Take

time to sniff the sulfur. Stay until evening when the flames and rivers of lava are most dramatic. Visitors claim to see powerful Pele in the tamer flames of the fireplace at Volcano House, a historic hotel on the lip of Kilauea crater. Lucky diners may see her pyrotechnics shooting from the Halema'uma'u Crater while dining on *lilikoi* cream puffs.

For another view of the goddess, stop by the park's Thomas A. Jaggar Museum, where dramatic murals of a fire- and lava-haired goddess greet visitors. Pele's slightest tremor is monitored on multimillion-dollar seismographs. Jump, and they will register you too.

■ *Essentials:* Hawaii Volcanoes National Park, Hawaii Belt Rd. (Hawaii 11), tel 808-985-6000, nps.gov/havo; Volcano House Hotel, Crater Rim Drive, Hawaii Volcanoes National Park, tel 866-536-7972, hawaiivolcanohouse.com

DIGGING DEEPER

Explore how the ancient Polynesians got to Hawaii using their star compasses at Imiloa Astronomy Center. The interactive exhibits and planetarium shows weave Polynesian culture and early Hawaiian knowledge with today's science.

Smoldering
lava flow in
Hawaii

CHAPTER 5
NORTHWEST

Reenactors "battle" at Viking Days in Seattle, Washington.

SERBIAN HOLIDAYS

A century ago, a fifth of Butte's residents were Serbian. These days, says Father Russell Radoicich, "It's still taken for granted that Serbian culture is mainstream here."

Radoicich oversees Holy Trinity Orthodox Christian Church, where Serbian culture continues to leave its mark on everyday life. The city's sanitation workers don't collect Christmas trees from the streets, for instance, until after the Orthodox Church celebrates the holiday on January 7. In fact, Orthodox Christmas is a citywide celebration, when the rest of Butte is invited to join Father Radoich's congregation for a feast of *sarma* (cabbage roll) and Serbian sausage.

"In order to preserve a heritage, you have to bring it into the New World and translate it, or else it will perish when the connection to the old country dies," Father Radoicich says. Though most Serbian Americans in Butte don't speak the language anymore, they keep the culture going by maintaining traditions like their "extremely diligent tradition of hospitality" in welcoming others.

WHAT TO SEE: For his part, Radoicich spends at least eight hours a week giving tours of his church. The highlight? The colorful frescoes that line the walls. Created in 2006 by six iconographers from Belgrade, the paintings depict images of the major events of salvation history. You don't have to be a believer or Serbian to visit the church. In fact, even the congregation is made of people of various backgrounds, from Serbian to Greek to Irish.

■ *Essentials:* Holy Trinity Orthodox Christian Church, 2100 Continental Dr., tel 406-723-7889, holytrinitybutte.org

INSIGHT · Serbian Yuletide

Come January, Christmas may be over for most celebrants, but not in Butte. For many in the city's Serbian community, Christmastime actually begins January 7, following the Gregorian calendar. Visitors are invited to join three days of services and feasting at the Serbian Holy Trinity Orthodox Christian Church. Traditionally, Serbian Christmas feasts are meatless and include dishes such as *bakalar* (salted cod fish) with potatoes, *prebranac* (a layered bean-and-onion dish), and cookies made without dairy and eggs. *"Prijatno!"* is how you say *bon appétit.*

Holy Trinity Serbian Orthodox Church, Butte

Basque dancers perform in front of Boise's Basque Museum.

BOISE, IDAHO
BASQUE BLOCK

A Basque farmhouse in the foothills of the Rocky Mountains is not necessarily what you'd expect in rugged southwestern Idaho. Yet the region boasts over 15,000 residents of Basque ancestry. Their cultural hub is the so-called Basque Block in the heart of downtown Boise.

WHAT TO SEE: The Anduiza Hotel, once a boarding house for Basque shepherds, is now home to an indoor court for playing pelota, a Basque cousin of squash. Down the street, you'll find the brick-and-timber *baserri* (farmhouse) of the Basque Center, a gathering place for the community. You can also sample the famous beef tongue and Basque wine at Bar Gernika, or admire the outdoor mural portraying Boise's acclaimed Oinkari Basque Dancers, a typical sheep camp, and a rendition of Picasso's "Guernica," the famed masterpiece depicting the bombing of the namesake Basque town. At the Basque Market, which claims to have the largest collection of Spanish wines in the Northwest,

pick up traditional fare like olive tapenade, port-poached figs, *croquetas* (croquettes), or squid in ink.

Learn about the uniqueness of Basque culture and history in the American West at the Basque Museum and Cultural Center. The largest exhibition in the United States about Basque culture includes an extensive archive of photographs, videos, and oral histories. And stop by the museum's shop on your way out: It stocks authentic items from the Basque regions of Spain and France—red *gerriko* scarves, laced *abarkak* shoes, cuff links bearing the enigmatic *lauburu* cross.

■ *Essentials:* The Basque Block, thebasqueblock.com; Anduiza Hotel, 619 Grove St.; Basque Center, 601 Grove St., tel 208-342-9983; Bar Gernika, 202 S. Capitol Blvd., tel 208-344-2175, bargernika.com; The Basque Market, 608 W. Grove St., tel 208-433-1208, thebasquemarket.com; Basque Museum and Cultural Center, 611 W. Grove St., tel 208-343-2671, basquemuseum.com

> *"We are proud to share our culture with the public."*
> —PATTY MILLER, DIRECTOR OF BOISE'S BASQUE MUSEUM AND CULTURAL CENTER

You Could Be In . . . THE SERENGETI

American Prairie Reserve, Montana
Northern Montana's American Prairie Reserve mirrors the vast expanses of the Serengeti grasslands.

AROUND THE WORLD IN
PORTLAND

The Paradosis dance group awaits its entrance at Portland's Greek Festival.

My Neighborhood

LITTLE ITALY

Chinese Hideaway
Stroll among the curved-roof pavilions. Amble about the reflective still waters of the lily pad–dotted koi pond. Channel the quiet Zen of the carefully laid stones, and cross a series of footbridges that will transport you to ancient China. In other cities, they pave paradise to put up a parking lot; in Portland, Joni Mitchell would be tickled to see that in 2000 a parking lot became Lan Su Chinese Garden, a classical Chinese garden that takes up a whole city block. This urban oasis also hosts special events like tea ceremonies, food lectures, and outdoor summer concerts.
Lan Su Chinese Garden, 239 N.W. Everett St., tel 503-228-8131, lansugarden.org

Japanese Garden of Good
Not to be outdone, the Japanese community also has a garden of its own—a 5.5-acre, well-manicured grounds in the hills of western Portland. When you walk through the traditional wooden gate, you'll be transported to a mystical land of moss-covered stone lanterns, enthralling waterfalls, and blooming flowers.
Portland Japanese Garden, 611 S.W. Kingston Ave., tel 503-223-1321, japanesegarden.com

Pho Real
Don't be deterred by the rough-around-the-edges feel of Portland's 82nd Avenue corridor. This is where locals in the know head for authentic Vietnamese eateries like Lanvin, which elevates

Vietnam's Francophone baking tradition with its crispy *bánh mì*, flaky croissants, and sweet *pains au noix*. Pho Van, as the name suggests, excels in the art of Vietnamese noodle soup—as well as the vermicelli and grilled staples of Vietnamese cuisine. My Brother's Crawfish, a Vietnamese-owned shellfish shack, puts an Asian spin on its seafood boils with fiery hot sauces—much like the kind you'll find at Cajun Vietnamese joints down in Louisiana. Ha & VL, an unassuming little place, serves an array of comforting soups, best for combatting the Northwest gloom.
Lanvin French Bakery, 8211 N.E. Brazee St., tel 503-252-0155; Pho Van, 1919 S.E. 82nd Ave., tel 503-788-5244, phovanrestaurant.com;

I grew up with my grandparents in Little Italy on Columbia Street. My grandparents started with a little store which turned into the restaurant going on 65 years now. When I was growing up, San Diego was the tuna capital of America. There were three canneries, all the tuna boats were there. Right across the street the fishermen would be fixing their nets right there on the sidewalk. My grandparents would fulfill the food orders for the tuna fleet before they went out. But then they put through Interstate-5 and Little Italy got cut off from the waterfront. The neighborhood went into a slump. We started the Little Italy Association around 18 years ago and slowly started revitalizing and rebuilding the neighborhood to what it once was, going gangbusters.

DANNY MOCERI
Owner Filippi's Pizza Groto Restaurant

Lan Su Chinese
Garden, downtown
Portland

My Brother's Crawfish, 8220 S.E. Harrison St., tel 503-774-3786, mybrotherscrawfish.com; Ha & VL, 2738 S.E. 82nd Ave., 503-772-0103

Mediterranean Bazaar

Sample homemade pork souvlaki, gyros, feta pastries, and spit-roasted lamb when Portland struts its far-flung Mediterranean roots at the three-day Greek Festival. Greek immigrants have been settling in the Pacific Northwest since the late 19th century, and Holy Trinity Greek Orthodox Church, which throws the bash, remains the community's anchor. Its annual festival, which started back in the '50s as a simple bazaar of handicrafts and food, has grown to be one of the most popular celebrations in Portland, with over 15,000 guests attending each year.
Portland Greek Festival, portlandgreekfestival .com; Holy Trinity Greek Orthodox Church, 3131 N.E. Glisan St., tel 503-234-0468, portlandgreekfestival .com

Slavic Scene

Sword fights, accordions, and oompah bands lend the laid-back city streets an oddly fun Bavarian vibe at the annual Slavic Festival. Or maybe not so odd. Southeast Portland is home to many recent immigrants from Russia and Ukraine. The celebration of the city's eastern European culture includes plenty of music, sword fight demonstrations, and cookouts featuring *plov*, made with rice and lamb. "The latest festival drew over 5,500 people from as far as Alaska and Florida," says Galina Nekrasova, president of the Oregon chapter of the Association of Slavic Immigrants. "The festival is all about enjoying oneself, immersing your person in Russian culture, and experiencing the joys of a peaceful day at the park." For a consistently good little piece of Russia, the beloved grocery Good Neighbor stocks fresh produce, handmade piroshki, and imports from Mother Russia (like jarred herrings).
Slavic Festival (Association of Slavic Immigrants), tel 503-332-2798; Good Neighbor, 4107 S.E. 82nd Ave., tel 503-771-5171

The World on the Go

You could say you can eat around the world by chasing Portland's food trucks, which reflect the city's incredible culinary diversity. Among the best of Portland's mobile, global eats: Burrasca has gained national fame, with its ever changing fare handcrafted by Florentine chef-owner Paolo Calamai, like wine-soaked squid, chicken, potato croquettes in tomato sauce, and fresh pasta. Nong Poonsukwattana from Bangkok made a name for herself with her herb-laden poached chicken at Nong's Khao Man Gai. And Tal Caspi, hailing from Israel, serves *sabich,* the traditional pita sandwich stuffed with fried eggplant, at Gonzo.
Burrasca, burrascapdx .com; Nong's Khao Man Gai, kmgpdx.com; Gonzo, iheartfalafel.com

A Japanese maple in a blaze of fall color, Portland Japanese Garden

Fruit still on the vine, St. Josef's Winery, Camby, Oregon

EUROPEAN-STYLE WINERIES

Wein, vin, vino . . . Whatever you call it, savor a sip of Europe at these wineries.

■ **St. Josef's Estate Vineyards & Winery**
Descending from winemakers of Hungary and educated in the Riesling country of southern Germany, Josef Fleischmann created St. Josef's Bavarian-style winery complete with timbered buildings half an hour south of Portland, Oregon, in the Willamette Valley. Come October, you can stomp grapes with his family in ten-foot (3 m) oak barrels to the sounds of Bavarian music. *28836 S. Barlow Rd., Canby, Ore., tel 503-651-3190, tastings on Sat. year-round; stjosefswinery.com*

■ **Vignoble Ste.-Pétronille**
As far as European experiences go, it doesn't get much more authentic than the postcard-ready Île d'Orléans outside of Quebec City, with its mansard-roofed farmhouses and family farms. Stop at Vignoble Sainte-Pétronille for the region's ice wine. *1 Chemin du Bout-de l'Île, Ste.-Pétronille, Que., tel 418-828-9554, vs-p.ca*

■ **Belhurst Castle**
The 19th-century castle-by-the-lake, built with materials from Europe, harks back to the old continent. Wine tastings are held in the wine and gift shop. *4069 West Lake Rd., Geneva, N.Y., tel 315-781-0201, belhurst.com*

■ **Raffaldini Vineyards & Winery**
"*Audentes Fortuna Iuvat*," or "Fortune favors those who dare," is the Latin motto of this stylish Italian-style winery in North Carolina. But you don't have to be daring to visit Villa Raffaldini, the gymnasium-size tasting room inspired by villas in Italy's Mantua, from where the Raffaldini family hails. "Our focus in today's world is not only to make great wine, but to share with our guests the Italian ideals of family, good food, and self-reflection," says Jay Raffaldini, owner and winemaker. Combining Italian dolce vita with stupendous views of the Blue Ridge and Brushy Mountains, this winery is a perfect spread for sipping handcrafted wine made from the estate's Montepulciano grapes. *450 Groce Rd., Ronda, N.C., tel 336-835-9463, raffaldini.com*

■ **Chateau Montelena Winery**
The terroir may be distinctly Napa, but the ambiance at California's Chateau Montelena Winery throws back to Europe, with ivy-covered stone buildings dotting the picturesque vineyard by Jade Lake, among Napa Valley's most beautiful nature preserves. *1429 Tubbs Ln., Calistoga, Calif., tel 707-942-5105, montelena.com*

■ **Jordan Vineyard & Winery**
Reminiscent of the rolling hills of Gironde near Bordeaux, northern California's Sonoma Valley is without a doubt a romantic getaway. Visit the chateau-style buildings and sun-drenched courtyard at Jordan Vineyard & Winery, which spans over 1,200 acres. Tours and tastings require reservations, but you can always drop by if you want to marvel at the undulating vineyards from the winding, tree-lined driveway. *1474 Alexander Valley Rd., Healdsburg, Calif., tel 800-654-1213, jordanwinery.com*

TILLAMOOK COUNTY, OREGON
JAPANESE WASABI

As the name would suggest, the *wasabia japonica* plant is native to Japan, but it found an unlikely new home on the cool, misty Oregon coast. Between Pacific City and Tillamook, Jennifer Bloeser and Markus Mead of Frog Eyes Wasabi Farm grow *sawa*, or water-grown, wasabi—the kind that fetches top dollar from gourmet chefs. The area's gentle temperatures, clean water, and little sunlight make the adopted plant thrive.

"We were intrigued by the plant and the culture around it," Bloeser says. "It's a fascinating plant—particular, but hardy. It has a huge number of health benefits—people use it to treat allergies, and there have been studies about its antibacterial and anticarcinogen qualities."

JOINING IN: Come to the farm to try your hand at harvesting and cooking wasabi. The rhizome is grated to make the familiar green paste; the stems and leaves are pickled in salt and sugar for as little as 15 minutes, or sautéed like kale.

"Most people have never tasted real wasabi," Bloeser says. "Most store-bought wasabi is just horseradish with dye in it, and has little or no real wasabi. Visitors are surprised when they try it for the first time." Fresh wasabi made from a real plant has a much more broad and complex flavor, with lingering sweetness and spiciness.

■ *Essentials:* Frog Eyes Wasabi Farm, tel 503-475-8311, tours are by appointment only, but the farm is in the process of setting up regular hours, thewasabistore.com

DIGGING DEEPER

Wasabi isn't just for sushi. Some think of it as just horseradish of a different hue, but when freshly grated, the green plant makes a versatile condiment that lightens cream-based sauces, lends artichoke-like freshness to meat dishes, and adds a whole new dimension to vegetables.

CENTRAL POINT, OREGON
EUROPEAN CREAMERIES

Robust blue cheese, milky mozzarella, musky chèvre ... Taste *Old*—really, really old—Europe by biting into ripe artisan cheese. At southern Oregon's Rogue Creamery, you can entertain your palate with a gamut of cheeses that range from farm fresh to pungently ripe.

WHAT TO DO: At Rogue Creamery's tasting room, watch cheese makers transform local nonstandardized milk and hand-form it into fresh balls of mozzarella before your eyes.

It's not just look but don't touch. In the shop, you can sample 100 different cheeses—some made on-site, others from similar artisans across the United States. European products include excellent Gruyères from Switzerland and whole wheels of supreme Parmigiano-Reggiano.

Some hometown favorites include Smokey TouVelle, cold smoked over hazelnut shells that give it a chocolaty flavor, and award-winning Oregonzola, a tangy blue cheese reminiscent of the best of Gorgonzola, with an added touch of fruitiness.

But the creamery doesn't just try to emulate Europe. One of the most popular items at the shop? Its good ol' American grilled cheese sandwich, only made with fancy cheese.

"We're in a unique position," says cheese shop manager Tom Van Voorhees. "We share our parking lot with two other businesses, Lillie Belle Farms and Ledger David Cellars." The craft chocolate maker and the acclaimed wine tasting

MORE · Destination Cheese

Beecher's. Known for authentic, traditional cheese making (try its signature Flagship, semihard curd aged for 15 months), Beecher's also sells mac and cheese. *Seattle and New York City, beechershandmadecheese.com*

Cypress Grove. One of America's goat cheese pioneers, this chèvre maker is a must-visit for fans of its distinctive, vegetable ash–covered Humboldt Fog Grande. *Arcata, Calif., cypressgrovechevre.com*

Vermont Creamery. Taste sustainably created crème fraîche, cultured butter, and German-style Quark in the meadows of the Green Mountains. *Websterville, Vt., vermontcreamery.com*

room form a gourmet triumvirate, making it a well-rounded destination for sybarites of all persuasions.

■ *Essentials:* Rogue Creamery, 311 N. Front St. (Hwy. 99), tel 866-396-4704, roguecreamery.com; Lillie Belle Farms, 211 N. Front St., tel 541-664-2815, lilliebellefarms.com; Ledger David Cellars, 245 N. Front St., tel 541-664-2218, ledgerdavid.com

Lovingly crafted cheeses at Rogue Creamery, Central Point

WILLAMETTE VALLEY, OREGON
TRUFFLE HUNTING

Down a thicket of Douglas fir goes Charles Lefevre with a canine companion, trained specifically to sniff out truffles. Under the moist soil await precious fungi that can whip gourmands and chefs into a frenzy. The buried treasures, which can fetch upwards of thousands of dollars per pound, are often associated with European haute cuisine. But this is not Italy's Piemonte, France's Périgord, Croatia's Istria, or any other region famous for truffles. You are in Oregon, whose Willamette Valley harbors no less than four different native species of truffle.

IN THE KNOW: "Oregon truffles used to have a bad reputation, for being weak," says Lefevre, who became interested in truffles while getting his Ph.D. in forest mycology. It turned out it wasn't the quality of the truffles, Lefevre explains, but premature and unprofessional harvesting that was giving the Oregonian tubers a bad rap. "When they're at their best, the Oregonian ones can be as powerful as the European sorts."

JOINING IN: Truffles are finicky, and are hard to preserve. So you have to be there to taste them at their best. In 2006, to raise the prominence of American truffles, Lefevre and his wife, Leslie Scott, founded the annual Oregon Truffle Festival, the first of its kind in America. Combining talks

INSIGHT · Foodies' Best Friend

Even the most seasoned truffle hunter can't detect the prized delicacies alone. Truffles burrow deep underground, and only pigs and dogs can sniff them out. Your pooch, too, can be trained to help you unearth the edible treasures. Each year a two-day long Dog Training Seminar is offered as part of the Oregon Truffle Festival. After theory instructions and exercises, participants hit the ground running—literally. And yes, you do get to keep the truffles if your canine companion is successful.

by prominent scholars as well as cooking demonstrations and tasting sessions, the festival has become an important culinary happening. Today, prominent Oregon chefs congregate once every winter to experiment with the so-called black gold. (Pricier white truffles, too, are showcased.)

■ *Essentials:* Oregon Truffle Festival, 503-296-5929 (voice mail), oregontrufflefestival.com

Canine truffle training at the Oregon Truffle Festival in Willamette Valley

SCENT K-9

"Compared to hunting for truffles in Europe,
there's no competitiveness in Oregon. We all help out here."
—DR. CHARLES LEFEVRE, PRESIDENT AND FOUNDER OF NEW WORLD TRUFFIERES

Truffle desserts
lined up at the
Oregon Truffle
Festival

An alpenhorn
at Oktoberfest
in Leavenworth

LEAVENWORTH, WASHINGTON
GERMAN OOMPAH

Timbered homes, oompah bands, freely flowing beer—no, you're not in Bavaria. This is Leavenworth, a mountain hamlet modeled after a quaint Teutonic village. But this is no average tourist trap. Hundreds of recent German immigrants as well as German Americans offer a taste of the old country, right in the Pacific Northwest.

WHERE TO EAT: German-owned Café Mozart is an upscale, authentic dining experience, with its meats and sausages freshly delivered from a German butcher in eastern Washington. Andreas Keller with dozens of German beers, exemplifies *Gemütlichkeit,* or coziness. Master baker Bert Timmerman makes treats like stollen and pretzels at Bavarian Bakery.

JOINING IN: "If you come here during Christmastime, Leavenworth is the most authentic thing you'll see," says Richard Zucktriegel, a 20-some-year Leavenworth business owner who originally hails from Bavaria. "The lighting, the tree, the atmosphere—everything is just like in Germany."

Leavenworth's Oktoberfest is also among the best in the United States, with six to eight bands brought in from Germany and South Tirol. But can this tiny fleck in the middle of the mountain *really* hold a candle to Germany?

"Leavenworth has the same good skiing as the Bavarian Alps, and I have my German beer and breakfast white sausages here, too," Zucktriegel says. "I go to Bavaria once a year to see family, but it's too crowded for me. Leavenworth has more room."

■ *Essentials:* Café Mozart, 829 Front St. (upstairs), tel 509-548-0600, cafemozartrestaurant.com; Andreas Keller, 829 Front St., tel 509-548-6000, andreaskellerrestaurant.com; Bavarian Bakery, 1330 Hwy. 2, tel 509-548-2244; Oktoberfest, leavenworth oktoberfest.com

DIGGING DEEPER

With a cry of *"O' zapf is!"* or "It is tapped," Oktoberfest kicks off every harvest season in Bavaria—and in Leavenworth, where the keg-tapping ceremony marks the beginning of the popular weekend feast of hearty pork, musical performances, and of course, lots of beer.

If it's a brat you want, North America has options.

BRATWURST

Why cross the ocean for a wurst when you have these winners close to home?

■ **Uli's Famous Sausage**
Uli Lengenberg, trained master sausage maker from Westphalia, runs a popular sausage joint in Seattle's lively Pike Place Market. Savor them with a view of the Pacific Ocean. *1511 Pike Place, Seattle, Wash., tel 206-838-1712, ulisfamoussausage.com*

■ **Altengartz Authentic Bratwurst**
The Wittkopp family's ancestors left Germany in 1878, but they passed down their Old World sausage recipes. In addition to supplying gourmet restaurants in the Portland, Oregon, area, the family runs a food truck popular with late-night crowds. *Corner S.W. 10th and Alder Sts., Portland, Ore., tel 503-699-4962, germanbratwurst.com*

■ **Weeping Radish**
At North Carolina's oldest microbrewery, Weeping Radish, the on-site German butcher prepares all meats, including bratwurst made with its award-winning beer. Even the sausage-making equipment at this Grandy brewery was brought in from Germany. *6810 Caratoke Hwy., Grandy, N.C., tel 252-491-5205, weepingradish.com*

■ **Bratwurst Festival**
Charming Bucyrus, Ohio, is so proud of its authentic bratwursts that they have been throwing an annual party dedicated to juicy sausages. Dirndl-clad townsfolk add to the campy German atmosphere. *bucyrusbratwurstfestival.com*

■ **Schnitzelbank**
Jasper, Indiana, boasts a predominantly German-American population, and the Hanselman family has been running the well-known Schnitzelbank since 1961. Save your appetite for the Wurstplatter, which heaps three different kinds of house-made sausages on a bed of sauerkraut. *393 3rd Ave., Jasper, Ind., tel 812-482-2640, schnitzelbank.com*

■ **Charcoal Inn**
Be prepared to be overwhelmed by the number of restaurants serving fresh wursts in Sheboygan, Wisconsin, the self-proclaimed Brat Capital of the World. In this tidy city on Lake Michigan, no respectable eatery would do without a charcoal grill, considered the only proper way to cook sausages. Begin your sausage expedition with Charcoal Inn's double brat sandwich consisting, as the name would suggest, of two brats nestled in a roll. *1313 S. 8th St. and 1637 Geele Ave., Sheboygan, Wis., tel 920-458-6988, charcoalinn.com*

■ **Gene's Sausage Shop**
Beginning as a Chicago Polish deli, Gene's Sausage Shop & Delicatessen may have expanded to two locations but doesn't neglect what made the family business a hometown favorite in the first place: over 40 sorts of sausages handmade daily. *4750 N. Lincoln Ave. and 5330 W. Belmont Ave., Chicago, Ill., tel 773-728-7243, genessausageshop.com*

■ **Wurstküche**
Traditionell it's not, but Wurstküche, a sausage specialist with a hipster following, serves inventive links (think mango jalapeño or pheasant) that have won over discerning Los Angelinos. *800 E. 3rd St., Los Angeles, Calif., and 625 Lincoln Blvd., Venice, Calif., tel 213-687-4444 (ext. 2), wurstkuche.com*

AROUND THE WORLD IN
SEATTLE

Viking Days at the Nordic Heritage Museum, Seattle

My Neighborhood

BALLARD

My family migrated from Iceland to Ellis Island in 1952 by ship, and my grandfather and father were given a job on a fishing boat in Ballard. I remember as a child going down to the Ballard Locks to watch and welcome them back from a long fishing season.

My grandparents, their children, and their grandchildren made Ballard their new home, absorbing new cultures and incorporating their Old Icelandic heritage. Ballard is a Nordic microcosm, with immigrants from Norway, Sweden, Denmark . . .

We all still live and work here. It's one of Seattle's fastest-growing neighborhoods, with an eclectic range of restaurants with some of the best food in Seattle. It also remains the center of the Seattle fishing industry, and Scandinavian heritage is still felt and enjoyed by visitors and locals alike.

DEBERA RIGGLE
Co-owner, Hotel Ballard

Nordic Cool

It's not often that you stumble onto a lutefisk-eating contest on the street in America. Ballard, once a humble working-class enclave of canneries, sawmills, and salmon ladders, may be on a fast track to gentrification, but this salt-tinged neighborhood remains the incontestable center of the Pacific Northwest's Nordic heritage.

Scandinavian immigrants, perhaps attracted to the Pacific Northwest's forests, fjords, and fisheries, settled in scores in Seattle, becoming the largest ethnic group in Washington State by 1910.

Today, you can find remnants of Ballard's Scandinavia in the Historic Landmark District around the intersection of Market Street and Ballard Avenue N.W. The Nordic Heritage Museum, the only such educational establishment in the United States, is a window to Nordic civilization and history. In this redbrick schoolhouse, you will find not only Scandinavian artifacts dating back to the Viking days, but also contemporary pieces by working artists in the Nordic region. A bonus: You can also pick up some phrases at the language institute on site.
Nordic Heritage Museum, 3014 N.W, 67th St., tel 206-789-5707, nordicmuseum.org

Walk the Walk

Seattle's Chinatown has morphed into the International District—not just a politically correct moniker, but descriptive: It's more diverse than ever. This vibrant home of Vietnamese, Laotian, and other Asian immigrants not only is iconic with its dragon-motif lampposts and red eaves, but also its tumultuous history during the world wars.

Join a walking tour by the Wing Luke Museum of the Asian Pacific American Experience, which casts an unflinching look at the neighborhood's past and present. "The tour strives to connect everyone to the rich history, dynamic cultures, and art of Asian Pacific Americans through vivid storytelling and inspiring experiences," says Doan Nguyen, who runs the museum's tour program. "Seattle's story cannot be told without Asian Pacific American history." By visiting neighborhood shops, landmarks off the beaten path, and meeting old-time residents, the tour takes you through the neighborhood's past from the gold rush era through

Japanese internment up to the multicultural present. *Wing Luke Museum of the Asian Pacific American Experience, 719 S. King St., tel 206-623-5124, wingluke .org*

Bento and Ball Pens
Sure, most American cities now boast Asian groceries, but few can be as comprehensive and impressive as Uwajimaya, a venerable Japanese supermarket whose history reaches back to 1928. Uwajimaya Village, the original flagship of what has evolved into a regional business empire, carries not only every thinkable Asian delicacy, but also a good selection of manga, both in original Japanese and translation. After a bento lunch, stock up on cutesy stationery and the latest Asian pop music.

Umajimaya Village, 600 5th Ave., tel 206-624-6248, uwajimaya.com

Out of Africa
Experience the depth and variety of Africa's culinary diversity right in southeast Seattle. In recent years, immigrants from Ethiopia, Eritrea, Somalia, and other African nations have settled here and revitalized the vicinity of the Columbia City light-rail station. Steps from the station is La Teranga, a beloved Senegalese eatery that serves simply grilled fish and meat with sweet, mustardy sauce alongside baobab juice and ginger nectar. Nearby Meskel, a homey mom-and-pop eatery with a patio, serves the typical Ethiopian feasts of *wat* stews and spicy beef *tibs* atop *injera* bread. And Jane Kagira from Kenya single-handedly runs Safari Njema Restaurant, where panfried goat and chili-powered chicken stew satiate compatriots from the East African nation. "Walk in, and you'll feel like you're in a restaurant in the middle of Nairobi," Kagira says. "I even play the latest pop songs from Kenya." She's especially proud of her citrusy and woodsy Tsavo Spice Sauce, combining habanero with secret Kenyan ingredients. But she will never reveal her recipe, even if you ask nicely. *La Teranga, 4903 Rainier Ave. S., tel 206-725-1188; Meskel, 2605 E. Cherry St., tel 206-860-1724, meskelrestaurant.com; Safari Njema Restaurant, 5041 Rainier Ave. S., tel 206-926-3833*

Samba in Seattle
Samba in . . . Seattle? Sure. The Northwest's Brazilian population is small but growing, and a one-day celebration named BrasilFest brings out the community and their friends for a day of all things Brazilian, from high-kicking capoeira to shake-it samba, grilled meats to cheesy *pão de queijo*. "We go beyond keeping traditions alive, and combine traditional and contemporary Brazilian expressions," says Eduardo Jorge de Mendonça, one of the organizers. And the Brazilian party is not the only one. Seattle Center's series of year-round, multicultural fests include Vietnamese New Year and Tibetan theater. *BrasilFest, brasilfest .com; Seattle Center, 305 Harrison St., tel 206-684-7200, seattlecenter.com/ festal*

Preserved Chinatown hotel part of Wing Luke Museum, Seattle

You Could
Be In . . .
PROVENCE

Sequim, Washington
Experience the
essence of Provence's
famed purple fields
by visiting a lavender
farm in northwest
Washington's Sequim.

RUSSIA COLONY

Anxious for sea otter and fur seal pelts to trade with China, Russians landed in the Tlingit village of Sitka in 1804, an event that would forever change the lives of the Native American people who had lived there for centuries. The story of this one-time Russian colonial capital is, by no means, a gentle one—it includes harsh treatment of and battles with the native people who lived there. The descendants from that era are of mixed Tlingit and Russian heritage. Modern-day Sitka offers a relaxed pace (and excellent kayaking), but wander through town and it's not difficult to imagine the "last days of Holy Russia," says Ana Dittmar, historian (and bell ringer) at Sitka's Russian Orthodox St. Michael the Archangel Cathedral. "There's plenty of residue of Russian culture."

WHAT TO SEE: Three original buildings remain from Sitka's Russian-run days, including the Russian Bishop's House—now a National Park Service museum featuring exhibits about the Russian days of Sitka. Throughout the summer season, the New Archangel Dancers perform traditional Russian dances in just as traditional costumes.

The existing cathedral—its dome and bell tower an easy way to orient yourself pretty much anywhere around town—is a faithful reproduction of the original 1844

INSIGHT · The Battleground

Alaska's oldest federally designated park, Sitka National Historical Park was designated on June 21, 1890. Here, Russian invaders fought indigenous Tlingits in 1804 and based their Russian Orthodox Church, at Bishop's House, from 1842 until 1969. The National Park Service took over the near collapsed Russian building and, after 16 years, returned the mustard yellow, spruce-walled structure to a state that would have been recognizable to residents circa 1853.

building, which burned down in 1966. The walls are lined with sailcloth to improve acoustics and as a memorial to local fishermen lost to the sea.

■ *Essentials:* sitka.org; Sitka National Historical Park, nps.gov/sitk; St. Michael the Archangel Cathedral, 240 Lincoln St., tel 907-747-8120, oca.org/parishes/oca-ak-sitsmk; New Archangel Dancers, 208 Smith St., tel 907-747-5516, newarchangeldancers.com

New Archangel Dancers celebrate Russian heritage in Sitka.

Sons of Norway
Hall, Petersburg

PETERSBURG, ALASKA
LITTLE NORWAY

Lured by waters rich in salmon, halibut, and her ring, Norwegian fishermen first started settling down in Petersburg more than a century back. Named for Peter Buschmann, a Norwegian man who homesteaded and built the area's first cannery in the 1890s, Petersburg is "definitely more like Norway than Alaska," says Sally Norheim Dwyer, the president of the Sons of Norway Lodge whose family settled in the area in 1903. "It's ingrained in everybody's everyday life." The town's location at the tip of Mitkof Island—a fjordish view—offers suitably Scandinavian surroundings, as does the traditional rosemaling on buildings around town. The town sounds Norwegian too. The most popular saying in Petersburg? Definitely *uff da*, says Dwyer, which can be put to use for anything from "oh my" to exclamations much stronger.

WHAT TO SEE: Nordic traditions old and older await around town, including the Trading Union store's 36-foot-long rosemaling piece, painted by the local decorative painting club, the Muskeg Maleriers. The Sons of Norway Lodge, built in 1912, and a replica Viking ship sit out over Hammer Slough.

JOINING IN: Started in 1958, May's annual Little Norway Festival celebrates Norway's Constitution and the arrival of the fishing season. Some locals dress in Norwegian costumes—there are Vikings and Valkyries aplenty. Traditional dancing, a parade featuring the Viking ship, and lots of *lefse* (flatbread spread thick with butter and sugar) make for a sweet weekend.

■ *Essentials:* petersburg.org; Sons of Norway, petersburgsons.org; Trading Union, 401 N. Nordic Dr., tel 907-772-3881, tradingunion.com

DIGGING DEEPER

Norwegians do beautiful cookies. Step inside the Java Hus at the Scandia House Hotel for a *krumkake* (with designs reminiscent of the morning's tour of rosemaling) or a *skorpe* (think Norwegian biscotti). *scandiahousehotel.com*

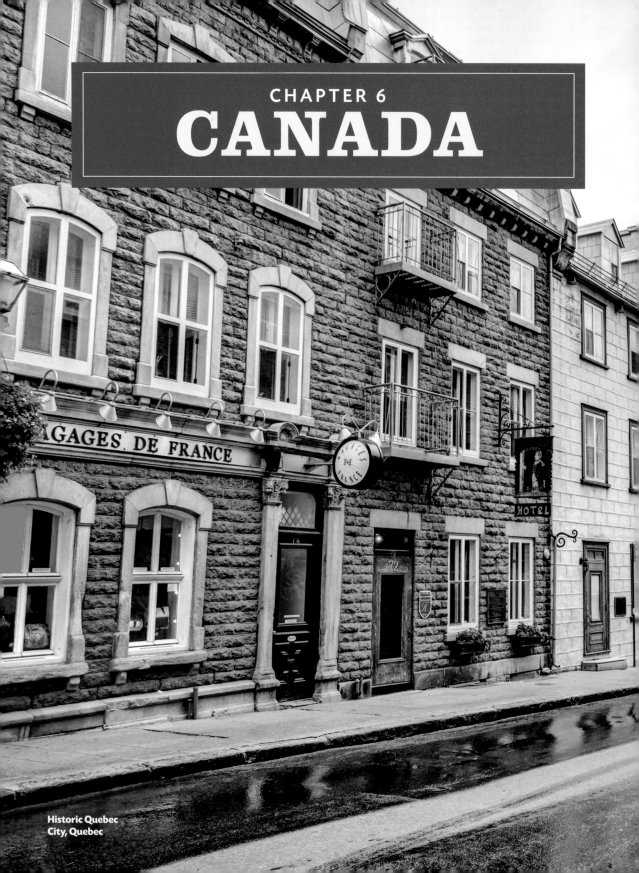

CHAPTER 6
CANADA

Historic Quebec
City, Quebec

CAPE BRETON, NOVA SCOTIA

GAELIC RESURGENCE

Step into Mabou's Red Shoe Pub on a Friday night and you'll be caught up in a whirlwind of fiddling, dancing, and comfort food—Gaelic style. You're in the heart of Celtic country, where the Scottish Gaelic language, music, dance, and stories are alive and well.

IN THE KNOW: Gaels landed in Cape Breton in 1773, following Scotland's Highland Clearances, the eviction of the Gaels known as *Fuadach nan Gàidheal*. Today, the province's 15 public schools teach Gaelic, and a dedicated Gaelic College in St. Ann's offers Cape Breton fiddle, step dancing, and piping. As Jeff Macdonald, Gaelic field officer for Gaelic Affairs, explains, "The Gaels of Nova Scotia are reawakening to who they are and to what their future can be. It's a testament to the tenacity of the Gaels that their language and their culture are experiencing a revitalization here in the 21st century."

WHERE TO GO: On Cape Breton's Cabot Trail, towns like Ingonish and Inverness preserve the influence of Scottish settlers. If you want to hear fiddle music, stop into any of the co-ops or small stores and ask where the closest ceilidh is that evening. At the Glenora Inn & Distillery in Glenville, many of the desserts are spiked with their signature whiskey.

JOINING IN: Bond over the bonfire at the Féis An Eilein, the first held outside Scotland and one of the largest

INSIGHT · The Beat Goes On

Although the name brings to mind skipping through a field, the highlight of a "milling frolic" happens around a table with traditional Gaelic work songs sung while beating a length of newly woven cloth to soften and shrink it. This practice, called *waulking* cloth in Scotland, is mesmerizing when accompanied by the beat-driven songs that increase in tempo as the cloth becomes more pliable. Milling frolics occur today across Cape Breton Island, including Johnstown and the Highland Village Museum in Iona.

annual Gaelic festivals held on merry Christmas Island, near the Bras d'Or lakes. Year-round, enjoy workshops in Gaelic traditions.

■ *Essentials:* Red Shoe Pub, 11573 Rte. 19, Mabou, tel 902-945-2996, closed mid-Oct.–May, redshoepub.com; Gaelic College, gaelic.novascotia.ca; Glenora Inn & Distillery, 13727 Rte. 19, Glenville, tel 902-258-2662, glenoradistillery.com; Féis An Eilen, feisaneilein.ca

A Gaelic milling frolic at Highland Village Museum in Cape Breton

The Buddy
Macmaster
School of Fiddling,
Nova Scotia

ALL THINGS SCOTTISH GAELIC

Experience this vibrant culture at a ceilidh, a party filled with song and dance.

■ **Rare Bird Pub**
At the Rare Bird Pub's ceilidh in Guysborough, Nova Scotia, watch the performance from the rooftop deck with captivating views of the Atlantic Ocean and lobster boats. Local Doug Anweiler of Authentic Seacoast Resorts says, "There are proud grandparents in the audience watching the next generation on the fiddle. This ceilidh is something done for the local people."
80 Main St., Guysborough, N.S., tel 902-533-2128, rare birdpub.com

■ **Celtic Music Interpretive Centre**
If you're looking for more than a party, check into the Celtic Music Interpretive Centre in Judique, Nova Scotia, where you can immerse yourself in the full Celtic experience. Live music demonstrations

lead to learning your way in the Buddy MacMaster School of Fiddling, a weeklong program where ten different instructors teach their own style of fiddle playing. You can also step to the beat with interactive fiddle and step dancing lessons Wednesday and Thursday evenings as well as on Sunday afternoons, another fun aspect to this lively culture. And if that's not enough, just sit back and enjoy a complete roster of ceilidhs with live traditional music; check the website for local venues and dates.
5471 Nova Scotia Trunk 19, Judique, N.S., tel 902-787-2708, celticmusiccentre.com

■ **Prince Edward Island Ceilidhs**
P.E.I. is noted through and through for its ceilidhs. The Crane Family plays the fiddle, piano, and guitar to the tunes

of traditional maritime music, folk, and pop for a foot-stomping *craic* held in picturesque St. Andrew's Chapel in Mount Stewart; stop by any Tuesday at 7:30 p.m. throughout the summer. Other gatherings: the Ceili at the Olde Dublin Pub in Charlottetown, as well as the College of Piping in Summerside. Ask at the local tourism office for additional guidance.
St. Andrew's Chapel, just east of Mount Stewart on Rte. 2, Mount Stewart, P.E.I.; Olde Dublin Pub, 131 Sydney St., Charlottetown, P.E.I., tel 902-892-6992, oldedublin pub.com; College of Piping, 619 Water St. E., Summerside, P.E.I., tel 902-436-5377, collegeofpiping.com

■ **U.S. National Mòd**
Immerse yourself in all things Gaelic at the U.S. National Mòd in Ligonier, Pennsylvania, an annual

three-day celebration of Gaelic song, literature, art, and culture built on a series of formal competitions (including choral events and traditional music, spoken word, and storytelling) and workshops. Native Scottish Gaelic speakers and newcomers alike are welcome to soak up as much Gaelic as they can at this annual gathering of the clans.
usmod.wordpress.com

■ **Beinn Seanair**
Renowned Gaelic singers and storytellers teach all levels of Scotland's ancient language through interactive classes and evening activities including ceilidh at this weeklong event in Banner Elk, North Carolina, organized by the American Scottish Gaelic Society.
acgamerica.org/events/grandfather-mountain

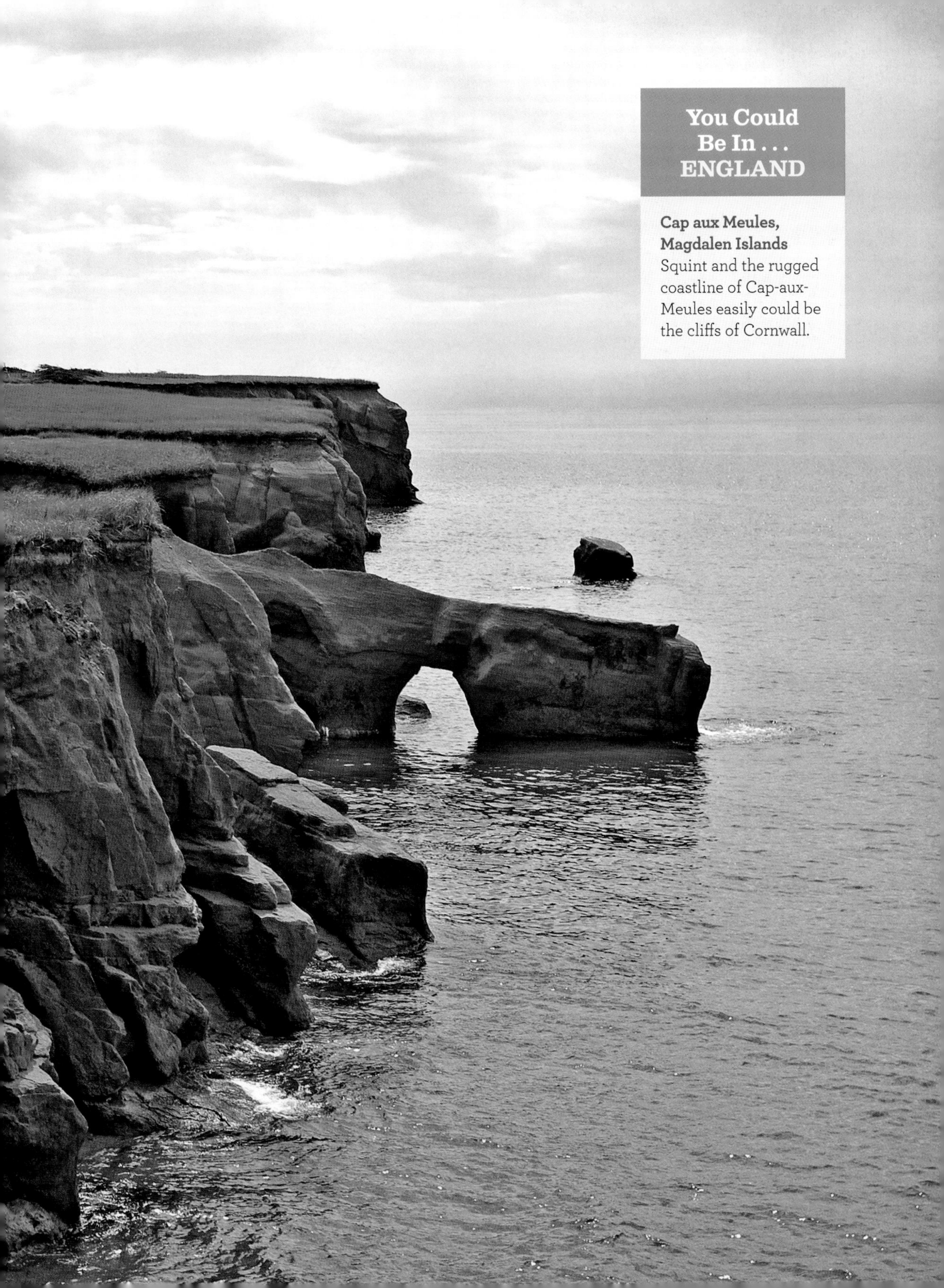

You Could Be In . . . ENGLAND

Cap aux Meules, Magdalen Islands
Squint and the rugged coastline of Cap-aux-Meules easily could be the cliffs of Cornwall.

AROUND THE WORLD IN
MONTREAL

Jean-Talon
farmers market
in Montreal's
Little Italy

My
Neighborhood
PARK EXTENSION

I live in Park Exten-
sion, one of the
densest neighbor-
hoods in Canada,
with about 400 peo-
ple per square kilo-
meter (the national
average is under 4).
It's a place of immi-
grants, now mostly
from South Asia.

The area feels
very different from
the English-speaking
enclave where I grew
up, Montreal West.
Here in Park Exten-
sion, I hear people
speak Urdu, Bengali,
Singhalese ... Eng-
lish is often many
people's third or
fourth language.

I love that I'm
a minority in my
neighborhood. It
helps me not be
complacent—I find
that healthy. You see
kids everywhere, and
there's a lot of life. If
you came for a visit,
I'd take you to Ave-
nue Ogilvy, parallel
to the main artery of
Jean-Talon, where
businesses catering
to South Asians,
Latin Americans,
and North Africans
line the street.

CHAD LUBELSKY
*Philanthropic
foundation program
officer*

Folly to Be Wise

Along Old Montreal's
cobblestone streets,
restaurant tables cluster
on bustling sidewalks,
harking back to a scene
you'd recognize on the
old continent. Even if
French culture is dominant
(and therefore taken for
granted) in Montreal, you'll
marvel at the city's distinct
old European flavors. The
colorful Vieux-Port harbors
historic Chapelle Notre-
Dame-de-Bon-Secours,
where sailors prayed
before setting to sea. The
Marché Bonsecours is
an open, indoor market
of eateries and made-in-
Quebec boutiques. Look
for hidden squares, like
the one at Gibby's. Then
join in the fun at the
annual FrancoFolies de
Montréal, which brings
together more than a
thousand French-language
music performers from all
around the world, making
it among the largest
music events *en français*.
Held each summer, the
festival is a welcome
opportunity to experience
the best of contemporary
Francophone culture.
*Notre-Dame-de-Bon-
Secours, 400 St.-Paul
St. E., tel 514-282-8670;
Marché Bon Secours,
350 St.-Paul St. E.,
marchebonsecours.qc.ca;
francofolies.com*

Quartier Chinois

Montreal's ethnic
neighborhoods are like
a timeline stacked along
St. Laurent Boulevard,
commonly known as
The Main, arranged in
the order the cultures'
communities arrived.
The ethnic enclave
closest to Old Montreal
is Chinatown, established
by transcontinental
railroad workers in the
1880s. Thanks to a steady
influx of immigrants from
China and Vietnam, the
vibrant quarter has stayed
true to its Asian origin,
but with a decidedly
Francophone appearance.
(When a movie about New
York's Chinatown was shot
here, the film crew had to
cover up or replace all the
French signs.) Start the
morning with dim sum at
Maison Kam Fung—you
don't have to speak French
or Cantonese, just point at
what you want and enjoy.
*Maison Kam Fung, 1111
rue St. Urbain, tel 450-462-
7888, restaurantlamaison
kamfung.com*

Mocha and ...
Mussolini?

Home to Canada's second
largest Italian community,
Montreal has a *Piccola*

Window-
shopping in
Vieux Montreal

Italia of its own, with street names like Milano and Dante to remind you that Italians make up the city's third largest linguistic group, after the French and the English. At the Church of the Madonna della Difesa, which continues to give more services in Italian than French or English, carefully survey the ornate fresco—you might spot Benito Mussolini on horseback in the apse. (To the church's defense, it was painted before WWII.) For a less ecclesiastic experience, lounge at Café Italia, a resting spot that does the namesake country proud with its strong espresso, touted to be among the city's best. *Church of the Madonna della Difesa, 6800 av. Henri-Julien; Café Italia, 6840 blvd. St.-Laurent, tel 514-495-0059*

Hellenic Beat

On Greece Independence Day (March 25), flag-waving Greek Montrealers spill onto Park Avenue between Mount Royal and Van Horne Avenues. Soccer victories are another occasion for revelry. This is Montreal's unofficial Greektown, or Quartier Hellénique, a commercial and cultural hub of more than 60,000 locals of Greek descent. You'll discover restaurants, groceries, and other Greek businesses all along the 1.2-mile stretch. "Many of the Greeks have moved to Laval outside the city, but Park Avenue is where the immigrants built their community when they first arrived over a century ago," says Paris Petrou, a Greek-Canadian journalist. For quieter ruminations, head to one of the six Greek Orthodox churches that welcome visitors, Koimisis tis Theotokou Church, among the most historical. Decipher the religious paintings on the church's gilded iconostasis, the highly symbolic screen of religious paintings that embodies the evolution of Eastern Christian liturgical traditions. *Koimisis tis Theotokou Church, 7700 av. de L'Épée, tel 514-273-9888*

Petit Maghreb

Among the newest Montrealers are the community of French- and Arabic-speaking North Africans who have settled near the St. Michel Metro station along rue Jean-Talon. The neighborhood, referred to as Petit Maghreb, is a low-key community of halal butchers, Moroccan restaurants, family grocers, and exceptional sweetshops. The Algerian proprietress of the bite-size bakery Pâtisserie Les Trésors Sucrés re-creates recipes from her mother, using generous nuts, honey, and flower water. Stop in for Algerian treats like pistachio-filled ice-cream cones and *ghribia*, buttery semolina cookies. *Pâtisserie Les Trésors Sucrés, 3640 rue Jean-Talon E., tel 514-223-2174*

Street Meat

Shish taouk is Montreal's street-meat staple. It's a local variation of chicken *shawarma*—marinated, boneless chicken, roasted on a vertical spit and then sawed off and piled on a pita with pickled veggies and hummus—and it is ubiquitous in the city. There's some confusion over the naming of the dish—shish taouk and shawarma mean different things in different parts of the Middle Eastern dining diaspora these days—so be sure to clarify what you're ordering. If you just ask for "shawarma," you're likely to be served beef.

Classic Haitian

Tassot is a classic Haitian dish, made with jerked goat or beef, marinated in citrus juice. As Montreal's Haitian community continues to grow, tassot is increasingly available, along with other staples of French Caribbean and Creole cuisine. One favorite Haitian option is Ange & Ricky, a no-frills spot near Jean-Talon Market. Grab a platter of tassot, rice, and fried plantains to go. *Ange & Ricky, 95 rue Jarry Est, tel 514-385-6094*

Frescoed apse of the Church of the Madonna della Difesa, Montreal

Autumn in Baie-St.-Paul, Charlevoix, one of Quebec's oldest towns

CHEMIN DU ROY, QUEBEC
COUNTRYSIDE À LA FRANÇAISE

With ancient forests, imposing mountains, and even a pristine fjord, Quebec's countryside is the great Canadian outdoors at its best—with a decidedly French twist. *Allez-y,* and you'll find petit villages, artisan food, and expansive wineries.

IN THE KNOW: Since 1737, le Chemin du Roy, or the King's Highway, has threaded through the countryside between Quebec City and Montreal, keeping the province's Francophone heart beating. Marked by the unmistakably French fleur-de-lis white crown, the highway passes through some of Quebec's most picturesque villages, including Neuville, Cap-Santé, Deschambault, and Ste.-Anne-de-la-Pérade. The entire length is some 160 miles, and much of it is flat, making it a breeze to bicycle as well.

WHERE TO GO: Neuville, dating back to 1665, is a handsome farming village perched on three terraces overlooking the St. Lawrence River. Stop for a picnic with a glass of robust rosé at the Domaine des Trois Moulins winery. Cap-Santé, with its *magnifique* 18th-century church and leafy squares, is a place to linger, especially during the salmon migration season in summer and fall when the Atlantic fish return to climb the fish ladder at the mouth of the Rivière Jacques-Cartier. Deschambault, with its remarkable collection of stone-and-wood mansions protected by the historic registry, is a good place to browse antique furniture and vintage kitchenware. The township of Ste.-Anne-de-la-Pérade's population rises each winter when colorful huts pop up to accommodate ice fishers who flock to catch Tommy cod from December to February.

■ *Essentials:* lecheminduroy.com; Domaine des Trois Moulins, domainedes3moulins.com; Antiquités Deschambault, antiquitesdeschambault.ca

DIGGING DEEPER

Befitting a former French colony, Quebec is a *fromage* lover's dream come true, where dairies practice the age-old art of cheese making. Visit award-winners FX Pichet, du Presbytère, Le Détour, S.C.A l'Île-aux-Grues, and de l'Abbaye St.-Benoît-du-Lac.

QUEBEC CITY, QUEBEC
TOUT FRANÇAIS

With its steeple-punched skyline, warren of cobblestone alleys, horse-drawn calèches, and four-centuries-old ramparts, Quebec City is a dollop of the old continent in the middle of Canada's open nature. One of North America's oldest settlements (founded in 1608), a vibrant, painstakingly preserved, open-air exhibition of Canada's Francophone glory, the town has earned the approval of UNESCO as a World Heritage site.

WHAT TO SEE: Fold away the map and lose yourself in Vieux Québec's history and romance. In Basse-Ville, or "lower town," rub shoulders—literally—with other pedestrians under a canopy of walkways and clotheslines on charming rue Sous-le-Cap, the city's narrowest street. Climb the well-trodden stairs (or ride the funicular) to the cliff-perched Upper Town, where the guard-changing ceremony at the star-shaped citadel is an age-old summer ritual. Make an essential pit stop at Chez Temporel, on the dogleg rue Couillard, for a little French folk music and a bowl of café au lait. Seek out the wonderful Musée de l'Amérique Francophone, which chronicles French history in North America through its invaluable paintings and antiques. Fairmont Le Château Frontenac is an unmistakable symbol of the city, its copper roof and fairy-tale turrets gracing many postcards; sit in the oak-paneled bar sipping

INSIGHT · Le Frosty

Bonhomme, short for *bonhomme de neige*, or snowman, is the de facto symbol for both the Winter Carnival and the city of Quebec. You'll find souvenirs bearing his image in shops all year long. When the festivities kick off during the coldest months of the year, the mayor hands Bonhomme the key to the city, putting him in charge of all the merrymaking. Always smiling and prone to dancing, he's more than a mascot—he's an embodiment of the province's joie de vivre.

a Pierre Elliott Trudeau (a combo of vodka, triple sec, and Campari), and gaze over the riverfront where the history of New France began.

■ *Essentials:* Chez Temporel, 25 rue Couillard, tel 418-694-1813; Musée de l'Amérique Francophone, 2 côte de la Fabrique, tel 866-710-8031, www.mcq.org/en; Fairmont Le Château Frontenac, 1 rue des Carrières, tel 418-692-3861, fairmont.com/frontenac-quebec

Master sculptures from blocks of snow, Quebec Winter Carnival

"Come in winter; enjoy drinking Caribou (a cocktail), and visit the Bonhomme Chateau." —HÉLÈNE FRECHETTE, TELECOMMUNICATION TECHNICIAN

Le Château Frontenac defines the Quebec City skyline.

TORONTO

The Gerrard India Bazaar in Toronto

Caribbean Corner

You won't find a designated neighborhood, but Caribbean culture pops up throughout Toronto. Every July, the Scotiabank Caribbean Carnival (formerly Caribana) explodes onto Exhibition Place as drummers and dancers in bejeweled costumes parade onto the closed-off Lake Shore Boulevard to the rhythms of reggae and soca music. For a taste of these laid-back islands try the spicy jerk chicken at The Real Jerk, or the homemade tropical soursap ice cream at Ali's West Indian Roti. At the Haitian-inspired Rhum Corner, stop in for some *accra* and salt cod patties served alongside rum and colas; background music straight from the islands and bright murals on the walls will make you feel like you're on holiday. *torontocaribbeancarnival .com, The Real Jerk, 842 Gerrard St. E., tel 416-463-6055, therealjerk.com; Ali's West Indian Roti, 1446 Queen St. W., tel 416-532-7701, alisroti.ca; Rhum Corner, 926 Dundas St. W., tel 647-346-9356, rhumcorner.com*

Little India

Finger richly colored silks and textiles, ogle exquisitely crafted gold bangles, and breathe in the rich aromas of Eastern spices and incense at the six-block-long Gerrard India Bazaar in Toronto's East End, a South Asian marketplace imported to Canada. Among dozens of shops, music stores, and art galleries awaits Rang Home Décor, one of the bazaar's real jewels.

Here bead-embellished silk pillows and throws blaze in shades of hot pink, bright green, and cerulean blue, transport you to the crowded and steaming—yet glamorous—marketplaces you'd stumble upon in Mumbai. *Gerrard Street between Coxwell and Greenwood, gerrardindiabazaar.com*

Koreatown Karaoke

The term "karaoke" is derived from the Japanese words *karappo,* meaning "empty," and *okesutura,* or "orchestra" . . . meaning, use your lungs to put some vocals to that accompaniment! The activity is as popular as K-pop in Toronto's Koreatown, and it's a treasured source of after-hours hilarity in the neighborhood's *noraebangs,* or singing

As a kid, my father's law practice had an exclusively Hong Kong immigrant client base, so we logged some serious meals in Chinatown. Dim sum on Sundays at Bright Pearl, dinners at Real Peking (long departed), and New Year's banquets in lavish rooms filled with gold dragons. Spadina Avenue is getting a facelift from new restaurants like People's Eatery—from the folks behind my favorite bar, 416—and the new bun concept from Banh Mi Boys. But what unites them all is a deep and abiding love for the flavor and wild nature of Chinatown, which remains the edible heart of Toronto, regardless of what's happening outside its streets.

DAVID SAX
Author of
The Tastemaker

The Caribbean Carnival (Caribana), Toronto

Deep-fried meats and fish cakes at Toronto's Asian Night It Up! market

rooms. BMB Karaoke is one of the city's largest, located on the Bloor West strip, and instant noodles are served alongside your karaoke machine. At XO Karaoke you can sip on *soju*, a Korean alcohol, as you belt along to any of the bar's vast catalogue of 500,000 tunes, including new ones in Korean, Japanese, and Chinese. Or rent a room in Toronto's comfortable old karaoke classic, the 20-year-old Freezone Karaoke, to stage your "Gangnam Style" moment. *BMB Karaoke, 593 Bloor St. W., tel 416-533-8786; XO Karaoke, 693 Bloor St. W., tel 416-535-3734; Freezone Karaoke, 721 Bloor St. W., tel 416-530-2781*

Chinatown
As Toronto expands and gentrifies, its Chinatown, radiating from the corner of Spadina Avenue and Dundee Street West,

is experiencing rapid change. You'll still find it teeming with vendors selling fruit, bustling crowds speaking Cantonese, and nooks for after-hours "cold tea" (read: cold beer) and hearty Szechwan. But perhaps the best place for an authentic Chinese experience is T&T Supermarket, where more than 15,000 Asian products are colorfully packaged and stacked high on shelves, including teas, noodles, frozen dumplings, and specialty items like taro buns and Taiwanese star fruit. There's a food court too. *T&T Supermarket, 222 Cherry St., tel 416-463-8113, tnt-supermarket.com*

Asian Night Markets
The South Asian population's strong presence in Greater Toronto makes the popularity of dim sum

and night markets no surprise. One weekend every July, you can join the hungry swarms at Night It Up! market, where alfresco vendors selling ethnic food evoke the chaotic, lively street cultures of Hong Kong and Taiwan. Try the famous Taiwanese stinky tofu, a fermented dish that gives off a pungent, distinctive odor, followed by the sweet Hong Kong Puffle, a mini egg waffle topped with gooey ingredients like chocolate and marshmallows. Then nudge your way through the crowds to play games like fishing in swimming pools (with prizes), in the kind of zaniness you'd find in the parking lots of Taipei or Tainan. *nightitup.com*

French Kiss
Quebec may be the true enclave of French culture and heritage in

The Main Neighborhoods

Little India
Gerrard Street East between Coxwell and Greenwood
BEST BET: Chat houses and colorful silks at Gerrard India Bazaar

Koreatown
Karaoke bars and restaurants along Bloor Street West, between Bathurst and Christie
BEST BET: "Real" Korean food at Buk Chang Dong Soon Tofu

Chinatown
Shops, restaurants and spas along Spadina Avenue
BEST BET: Lion dances during Chinese New Year festival

Little Italy
Restaurants, bakeries, and shops on College Street between Euclid and Shaw
BEST BET: Wine and appetizers at Trattoria Taverniti

Greektown on the Danforth
Cosmopolitan restaurants, cafés, and stores on Danforth Avenue between Chester and Dewhurst
BEST BET: August's Taste of the Danforth food festival

Canada, but you can find a corner of Paris at Nadège Pâtisserie in Toronto's Queen West neighborhood. Sleek and urbane, the shop channels a trendy Parisian café and produces confections worthy of one too. Owner Nàdege Nourian, a world-renowned baker from Lyon, France, is best known for her decadent *macarons*, jewel-toned, crispy shells filled with moist ganaches in eclectic flavors like salted caramel, cotton candy, and mojito. What's gone in two swallows takes Nadège a day or two make, a careful

ritual of measuring, baking, and assembly that melts on your tongue. *Nadège Pâtisserie, 780 Queen St. W., tel 416-368-2009, nadege-patisserie .com*

Italian Renaissance
Toronto has a distinct Little Italy district, but some of the city's best restaurants are in trendy areas such as Dundas West, Parkdale, and King West. Bar Buca, in the Fashion District, puts a modern spin on the Old World Italian practice of finding culinary use for every last part of a pig's

anatomy. If it's offered, try the *migliaccio,* or Tuscan-style crepes—the batter is mixed with pig's blood and the pancakes stuffed with chocolate and figs. The result will surprise you; a slightly salty, tangy flavor complements the sweet fillings of the crepe. Chef Rob Gentile even works pig parts onto his drink menu: Order a Caesar with brunch, and you'll find it's not far off from a Bloody Mary, with a garnish of fried pork jowls instead of celery. *Bar Buca, 75 Portland St., tel 416-599-2822, barbuca .com*

Greektown Delight
Toronto's Serano Bakery is a shrine to Greek baking, with glass cases and racks loaded with homemade pastries, breads, and *syropiasta—* Greek concoctions like baklava dripping with honey and syrup. The Takas brothers brought traditional recipes and baking techniques with them from their homeland when they opened their Greektown shop 20 years ago. You can partake in a bit of Greek Easter all year with the bakery's *tsoureki,* or Easter Bread, infused with *mahlepi,* a

Walking Map *Kensington Market*

The world is at your feet in Kensington Market.

1 | On the edges of **Kensington Market,** stop by for a steaming smoked meat sandwich at classic

Jewish deli **Caplansky's** *(kensington-market.ca; 356 College St., tel 416-500-3852, caplanskys.com).*

2 | Stroll down to Augusta and stop in at **Le Ti Colibri** for Creole *bokit.*

(291 Augusta Ave., tel 416-925-2223, leticolibri.com).

3 | Neighboring **Perola's Supermarket** is your pit stop for Latin American goods from piñatas to Jarritos soda from Mexico. **Emporium**

Latino is known for its pupusas. **Pancho's Bakery** sells Kensington's best churros along with Mexican hot chocolate *(247 Augusta Ave., tel 416-593-9728, perolasuper market.com; 243 Augusta Ave., tel 416-351-9646; 214 Augusta Ave., 416-854-8770, panchos bakery.com).*

4 | More diverse flavors can be found at **Seven Lives Tacos** for southern California tacos *(69 Kensington Ave., tel 416-666-6666).*

5 | For a break, try Swedish-inspired **Fika** for their indulgent lavender white hot chocolate *(28 Kensington Ave., fika.ca).*

6 | Backtrack to **Global Cheese** and take home a taste of the market *(76 Kensington Ave., tel 416-593-9251).*

spice extracted from the Mahaleb cherry native to the Mediterranean. Purists opt for the traditional loaf, but for a twist, try the bread dipped and drizzled in dark or white chocolate. *Serano Bakery, 830 Pape Ave., tel 416-462-2735, seranobakery.com*

Sakura in High Park

Each April and May, throngs fill High Park, reveling in the blossoming of some 2,000 cherry trees, with the largest concentration along High Park Trail and around Grenadier Pond. They date from 1959, when Toru-Hagiwara, Japan's ambassador to Canada, presented them as thanks for Toronto's acceptance of Japanese-Canadian refugees after World War II. To avoid the crowds, come midweek if you can, and early, when the delicate petals are set against a pale sky and the park is relatively peaceful. *1873 Bloor St. W., tel 416-338 0338, sakurainhighpark.com*

Filipino Rising

Foodies love the Mabuhay! Philippines Festival on the Harbourfront Centre, where each August top chefs try to come up with the most original take on traditional Filipino dishes. Or if fashion is more your thing, attend Canada Philippine Fashion Week to critique the looks coming down the runway, all brainstormed by Filipino designers. Then head downtown to where Lamesa Filipino Kitchen adds fusion concepts to traditional Filipino recipes such as the Ginataan Sundae, which combines yam-based *ube* ice cream and a coconut soup called *ginataan* with the decidedly contemporary garnish of caramel corn. The dessert is unexpectedly delicious. *Harbour Front Centre, harbourfrontcentre.com; Canada Philippine Fashion Week, canadaphilippine fashionweek.com; Lamesa Filipino Kitchen, 669 Queen St. W., tel 647-346-2377, lamesafilipinokitchen.com*

Little Ethiopia

Toronto doesn't have a Little Ethiopia, though proponents have nominated a stretch of Danforth Avenue. Here you'll find Desta Market, a great stop for essential Ethiopian spices like *berbere, mitmita,* and *beso bela* as well as *injera,* the spongy traditional flatbread used to grasp food. If you want your Ethiopian food prepared for you, Lalibela, with locations on Danforth and on Bloor Street, has a reputation for delicious lamb dishes including *ye'beg key wat,* which *Toronto Life* magazine described as "luscious hunks of meat smothered in a mellow berbere sauce." Or head over to Rendez-Vous for the vegetarian platter, a colorful, spicy jumble of lentils, chickpeas, beans, and salad, rumored to be as good as anything you'll find in Africa. *Desta Market, 843 Danforth Ave., tel 416-850-4854; Lalibela, 869 Bloor St. W., tel 416-535-6615 or 1202 Danforth Ave., tel 416-645-0486; Rendez-Vous, 1408 Danforth Ave., tel 416-469-2513*

Little Malta

Although a halt in immigration has created an ebb in Toronto's once robust Maltese community, the Malta Bake Shop, run for 30 years by husband-wife duo Charles and Antoinette Buttigieg, still anchors the old neighborhood—a vivid mural of Malta's Mediterranean setting makes it easy to spot. Stand in line for your *pastizzi,* a traditional Maltese baked good served hot, stuffed with cheese and veggies, and wrapped in layers of hand-stretched, home-baked pastry. And lest you forget whose culture you're savoring, a live stream of the Grand Harbour in Valletta, Malta, is broadcast into the café. *Malta Bake Shop, 3256 Dundas St. W., tel 416-769-2174*

Japanese Cherry blossoms in Toronto's High Park

Trolling the merchandise in Toronto's Chinatown

Pho, a Vietnamese
noodle soup with
herbs and meat

PHO

Slurp your way across North America with this aromatic noodle-and-broth Vietnamese dish.

■ **Hanoi 3 Seasons**
When Canadian author Vincent Lam wrote his Vietnam-based novel *The Headmaster's Wager,* he simply relied on frequent visits to his favorite local Toronto pho shop to get in the mood. The pocket-size Hanoi 3 Seasons isn't just known for atmosphere. Its superb Vietnamese beef noodle soup broth is made North Vietnamese–style, meaning simpler and a bit saltier than usual.
Hanoi 3 Seasons, 588 Gerrard St. E., Toronto, Ont., tel 416-463-9940, hanoi3seasons.com

■ **Pho Lien**
This is Quebec, where you'll spot *soupe tonkinoise* (not necessarily "pho") on awnings of busy, real-deal noodle shops. And the tastiest of its beef noodle soups rank up with Vietnam's best. For a little extra comfort—nothing fancy, but deck chairs on a nice day beats being inside—Pho Lien serves great bowls from a street of several pho options, on the west side of Park Mont Royal.
Pho Lien, 5703 Chemin de la Côte-des-Neiges, Montreal, Que., tel 514-735-6949

■ **Pho 88**
Orlando's Vietnamese community centers around the ViMi, or Mills 50, a thriving neighborhood near downtown. There are scores of dining options, but a winner for a family-run, quite authentic noodle shop is Pho 88.
Pho 88, 730 N. Mills Ave., Orlando, Fla., tel 407-897-3488, pho88orlando.com

■ **Pho Lien Hoa,**
You know you're in Oklahoma City's thriving Vietnamese neighborhood—the state's biggest Asian group—when you see a giant milk bottle atop a squat redbrick building. It's a Route 66 survivor, but now serves up the best Vietnamese *bánh mì* sandwich in OKC's "Asian District." In all directions you'll find good pho options (along with Vietnamese groceries and dim sum restaurants). A longtime favorite, Pho Lien Hoa is run by a Vietnamese family who came to Oklahoma in 1992.
Pho Lien Hoa, 901 N.W. 23rd St., Oklahoma City, Okla., tel 405-521-8087

■ **Pho Bang**
The air is practically soupy inside Pho Bang, the family-run dive located in a strip mall in the heart of the local Vietnamese community of this northeast Dallas suburb. It's a simple spot, even with its recent makeover, but it's worth a Texas-size detour for fresh beef noodle soup that simmers overnight, every night. It's best at noon.
Pho Bang, 3565 W. Walnut St., Garland, Tex., tel 972-487-6666

■ **Pho Thanh Lich**
The dining options run thick in Orange County's Little Saigon, offering many specialties that are tough to find outside of Vietnam. For pho, the tucked-out-of-the-way, cash-only Pho Thanh Lich wins the most loyal following.
Pho Thanh Lich, 14500 Brookhurst St., Garden Grove, Calif., tel 714-622-8652

Historical attire (and battle stance), Icelandic Festival of Manitoba

GIMLI, MANITOBA
NEW ICELAND

Icelanders escaping the Arctic conditions and volcanic eruptions of their homeland fled to the lakeside town of Gimli in 1875, settling on land granted by the Canadian government. Today the town boasts the second largest Icelandic community outside of Iceland. As Cameron Arnason, president of the local Icelandic Festival, declares, "Fishing and being by water is in our blood."

WHAT TO SEE: The New Iceland Heritage Museum preserves its history with exhibits, period rooms, and daily tours (with the option of an Icelandic translator) along Gimli's waterfront. Check out the collection of 350 rocks that relay Iceland's rock-and-ice history. In season, stop by the Reykjavik Bakery for a Christmas *vinaterta*, a layered shortbread torte traditionally filled with prunes—though here you'll find it with rhubarb, native to Iceland.

JOINING IN: Islendingadagurinn, the Icelandic Festival of Manitoba, has been celebrated on the first weekend of August since 1890 with mock Viking battles, arts and crafts, and the wearing of the traditional Fjallkona (Maid of the Mountain) costume: a white gown, crowned headdress, and white veil. A fan-favorite event is the Islendingadunk, which pits two sack-wielding competitors perched on a soap-covered beam against each other. The sacks are filled with sponges; the "battle" involves whacking each other with the sack, and the winner is whoever doesn't slide off the beam into Gimli Harbour. As Arnason says, the festival is "an affirmation of our loyalties to family and friends and our love for Iceland."

■ *Essentials:* New Iceland Heritage Museum, 94 1st Ave., tel 204-642-4001, nihm.ca; Reykjavik Bakery, J-41 Center St., tel 204-642-7598; Icelandic Festival of Manitoba, icelandicfestival.com

DIGGING DEEPER

Raymond Sigurdson, a former politician in the area, remembers, "My grandparents came here [from the northeast of Iceland] in 1891 and I was born on my parents' farm. My mother kept correspondence with her relatives in Icelandic for 50 years. We try to keep the culture alive."

You Could Be In . . . SCOTLAND

South Glengarry, Ontario
St. Raphael Roman Catholic Parish in Ontario is as evocative as any ruin in the Scottish Highlands.

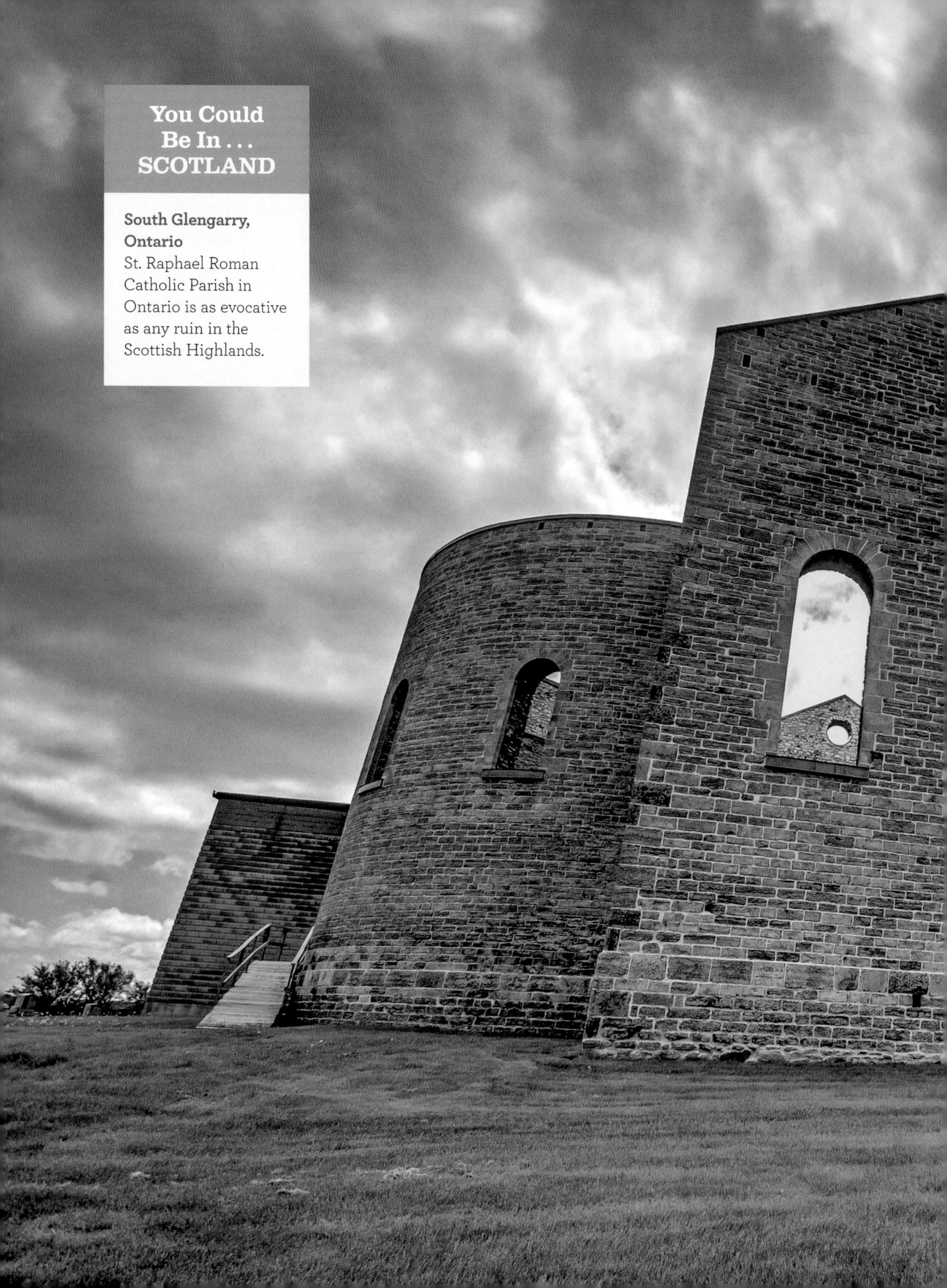

AROUND THE WORLD IN
OTTAWA

Gilded Pakistani bus at the Canadian Children's Museum

Shawarma Shakedown
With tens of thousands of Arabic speakers in the region, it's no wonder there's an increasing number of shawarma shops popping up in Ottawa. Best known for its delicious spiced and stacked meat carved off a rotating spit, this street food may be enjoyed along with kebabs at Shawarma Palace on Rideau Street, or at Shawarma House on Carling Avenue, which offers eat-in and take-out options. If you're here in July, join the Lebanese community's annual festival with cultural dances and performances, and tasty treats of course.
Shawarma Palace, 464 Rideau St., tel 613-789-9533, shawarmapalace.ca; Shawarma House, 3059

Carling Ave., tel 613-667-2020, shawarmahouse carling.com; Ottawa Lebanese Festival, ottawa lebanesefestival.com

Italian Pace
A stroll along Preston Street in the heart of Little Italy will likely include an encounter with a set of older Italian men, sitting outside cafés, nursing their espressos. Join them or continue on to Pasticceria Gelateria Italiana for gelato or a latte and a chat with owner Joe Calabro, as time stands still.
Pasticceria Gelateria Italiana, 200 Preston St., tel 613-233-2104, pasti cceria.ca

Pomp and Circumstance
Witnessing the Changing of the Guard

in Ottawa is the next best thing to being at Buckingham Palace. A tradition here since 1959, dozens of soldiers in red uniforms and black bearskin hats parade through city streets to set foot on the lawn of Parliament Hill precisely at 10 a.m. Hundreds crowd to see the half-hour free spectacle, complete with a band trumpeting beneath the Canadian flag. If you miss the morning tradition, check out the Ceremonial Guard at Rideau Hall, home and workplace of the Governor General, the Queen's representative in Canada. Led by a piper, the two regiments that form the Ceremonial Guard—the Canadian Grenadier Guards and the

As a teenager, driving through Little Italy was like screening a foreign film. Old Italian men sitting at bistro tables in front of cafés, deep in conversation, complete with flying hand gestures—these men fueled my desire to travel to La Dolce Vita. I can now vouch that my Little Italy experience was indeed like the old country.

Giovanni's on Booth Street maintains that Old World charm. Italian men still lounge out front. Inside, the decor is updated yet reminiscent of Italy. Jars of Italian candy line the counter and Moretti beers sit on the shelves. Being there on game day with the locals cheering team Italia brings me back to the Pasticceria Serena café in Massarosa. It's the Giovanni's of my childhood; only now I can order my coffee and sandwich in Italian.

NATHALIE HARRIS
Photographer

Governor General's Foot Guards—proudly switch places each hour on the hour from late June to late August.
Rideau Hall, 1 Sussex Dr., tel 866-842-4422, gg.ca

Churchill Reincarnated

Some of the most fascinating remnants of British history reside in the present in the most subtle ways. Nicknamed the third chamber of Parliament for the number of politicians who regularly roam its corridors, the historic Fairmont Chateau Laurier in the heart of Ottawa displays a portrait of a former guest, British Prime Minister Winston Churchill. In his famous "Some chicken! Some neck!" speech in Ottawa, Churchill declared his view of Canada as the "linchpin of the English-speaking world." His distinctive image is also preserved in the works of celebrity and portrait photographer Yousuf Karsh, who lived at the Chateau for 18 years and operated his studio on the sixth floor. Some of his work remains in the hotel's Reading Lounge and the Karsh Suite.
Fairmont Chateau Laurier, 1 Rideau St., tel 613-241-1414, fairmont .com/laurier-ottawa/ hotel-history

A Drink for Scotland

Home to homesick Scots and whisky connoisseurs alike, The Highlander Pub is Ottawa's only gold-level, single malt scotch bar. More than 200 single malt scotches are available, including such selections as Balvenie 30 and the Glenmorangie Pride, distilled in oak casks for 18 years and hundreds of dollars for a sipping portion. Ottawa Valley's large Scottish contingent celebrates Robbie Burns Day and St. Andrews Day here as well.
The Highlander Pub, 115 Rideau St., tel 613-562-5678, thehighlanderpub .com

Un Pique-nique and a Play

There is nothing more French than a street-side picnic, whether along the banks of the Seine, on a bench, or in the park. The Ottawa chapter of Le Cordon Bleu, the respected French culinary school and famous restaurant, has partnered with the Odyssey Theatre to provide summer patrons with a picnic of bread and cheese, pasta salad, and a *macaron* to be enjoyed while watching a theater performance in Strathcona Park, along the banks of the Rideau River.
Odyssey Theatre, 2 Daly Ave., tel 613-232-8407, odysseytheatre.ca

Relieving the sentries at Rideau Hall, Ottawa

UKRAINIAN CONNECTION

The homemade pierogies and dill-rich borscht proffered at this historic village might taste like something you'd find in the old country. Instead, you're on a patch of Canadian prairie in Alberta, at the Ukrainian Cultural Heritage Village. The center re-creates life as it was between 1892 and 1930, when Ukrainian immigrants flocked to this part of the world. The interesting part is that many of the reinterpreters are of Ukrainian heritage themselves, and may well break out into fluent Ukrainian.

WHAT TO SEE: Walk or hop on and off a free horse-drawn wagon to visit the living history museum's 30-plus buildings, from the onion-domed churches to a sod-home *burdei*, where Ukrainians lived until they could establish themselves on the land. You can also help the farmers till the historically accurate gardens and bring their crop to the functioning grain elevator. Natalya Vanovska, who came to Edmonton from the Ukrainian city of Ternopil some four years ago, plays the role of a young immigrant fresh off the train, circa 1892, complete with white kerchief wrapped around her head. "People here are friendly, always willing to help," she says. "And here in Edmonton there is such a huge Ukrainian community—so many of them speak Ukrainian and they are always there for you."

INSIGHT · The First Ukrainians

The Ukraine was a desperately poor region that had suffered decades of oppression when peasant farmers began to immigrate by the droves to western Canada in 1891. Their lives weren't easy on this side of the Atlantic either: Most arrived with almost no capital, the climate was unfamiliar, and initially they could do little more than subsistence farm to feed their families. The bloc communities the pioneers formed were incredibly important for sustaining them, psychologically and physically, through these early privations.

IN THE KNOW: Looking at the region's endless wheat fields beneath a blue sky, patches of birch forest, and rampant vegetable gardens, it's no wonder Ukrainians settled here—if you didn't know it, you could be in Ukraine itself.

■ *Essentials:* Ukrainian Cultural Heritage Village, Hwy. 16, tel 780-662-3640, history.alberta.ca/ukrainianvillage

A wagon ride at the Ukrainian Cultural Heritage Village

A *burdei,* or dugout-style hut, at Alberta's Ukrainian Cultural Heritage Village

Francophone Tour de l'Alberta, a multiday cycling race across the province

EDMONTON, ALBERTA
FRANCO-ALBERTANS

French culture and whispers of the French language are everywhere in Edmonton. You'll hear them at the University of Alberta's Campus Saint-Jean in Bonnie Doon, the only Francophone university campus west of Manitoba, and see them at a theater performance at L'Uni Théâtre, Alberta's only professional Francophone theater company, and among artists at La Société Francophone des arts visuels de l'Alberta. The Franco-Albertan flag waves high and proud, a western emblem of Canada's bilingualism.

WHAT TO SEE: Striking examples of Franco-Canadian architecture offer a glimpse into the town's early influences. The Fairmont Hotel Macdonald, a grand, château-style building that evokes a French castle, was built a century ago and has been carefully restored to its former elegance. Come to the hotel's Royal Tea & Tour, offered on weekends, for a historical tour of the hotel's opulent interior and ballrooms. About a mile west in Edmonton's Oliver neighborhood, the redbrick Gothic Revival St. Joachim's Roman Catholic Church is a historic monument to the early Catholic Francophone community. Go to a Mass there today, and you'll find yourself immersed in a service conducted entirely in French.

WHERE TO EAT: "There's a *Mad Men* quality to the sparse black, white, and silver interior," *Avenue* (Edmonton) magazine once remarked of Marc Restaurant, but the no-frills dining room belies the carefully prepared French bistro-style dishes the kitchen serves up. Be sure to order the beignets; they're the French cousins to doughnuts, and lightly sugared balls of pastry fried to a crispy gold are delivered warm to your table with caramel and vanilla dipping sauces.

■ *Essentials:* L'Uni Théâtre, 8627 rue Marie-Anne-Gaboury (91 St.), Suite 126, tel 780-469-8400, lunitheatre.ca; La Société Francophone des arts visuels de l'Alberta, 9103 95 Ave., tel 780-461-3427, savacava.com; Fairmont Hotel Macdonald, 10065 100 St., tel 780-424-5181, fairmont.com/macdonald-edmonton; St. Joachim, 9924 110 St. N.W., tel 780-482-3233; Marc Restaurant, 9940 106 St., tel 780-429-2828, themarc.ca

DIGGING DEEPER

Breeze by the yellow canola fields of the Francophone towns of St. Albert, Legal, and more of rural Alberta in the Tour de l'Alberta, an homage to the Tour de France. Alberta's biggest one-day bike ride offers six distance options so the whole family can get involved.

BUNNOCK CHAMPIONSHIPS

"**A**ll you need is a piece of ground—a roadway without gravel is perfect," says Rudolph Stang, chairman and co-founder of the World Bunnock Championships in Macklin, Saskatchewan, just east of Alberta's borders. In this bone-tossing game, brought to Saskatchewan by Russian-German immigrants in the early 20th century, teams take turns tossing horse anklebones at the opposing teams' row of bones. The first to knock down all 52 bones in a specific order wins. Described as a cross between bowling and curling, bunnock is also known as the "game of bones."

JOINING IN: The game can be played anywhere outdoors, with the major event being the World Bunnock Championships, held every long weekend in August—an event that attracts more than 300 teams and some 1,500 people to compete for over $30,000 in cash and prizes.

IN THE KNOW: The game is believed to have originated in Siberia in the early 19th century when bored Russian soldiers couldn't drive horseshoe spikes into the cold, hard ground. Instead they discovered horse bones could stand on their own. "Our forefathers would be pleased to see what we're doing. It has put our community on the map," says Stang.

INSIGHT · Make No Bones About It

You know you've arrived in Macklin when the world's largest bunnock statue looms into view on Highway 14; shaped like an anklebone, the 32-foot-tall structure, which houses the information booth, is made of fiberglass. But the game uses real horse anklebones, 52 in various sizes. The eight heaviest are designated as *Schmeiser* (throwers), used to knock down the others in a match of accuracy and skill. You can buy your own painted set for $150 at Macklin's Baier's Boutique.

Bunnock really goes back to family. "It doesn't matter what age you are, from 3 to 83," says Kim Gartner, coordinator of the championships. Stang agrees. "The championship is like a family reunion. Family atmosphere is the key to the success of this championship."

■ *Essentials:* World Bunnock Championships, macklin.ca/bunnock.html

Tossing a horse bone in the World Bunnock Championships, Macklin

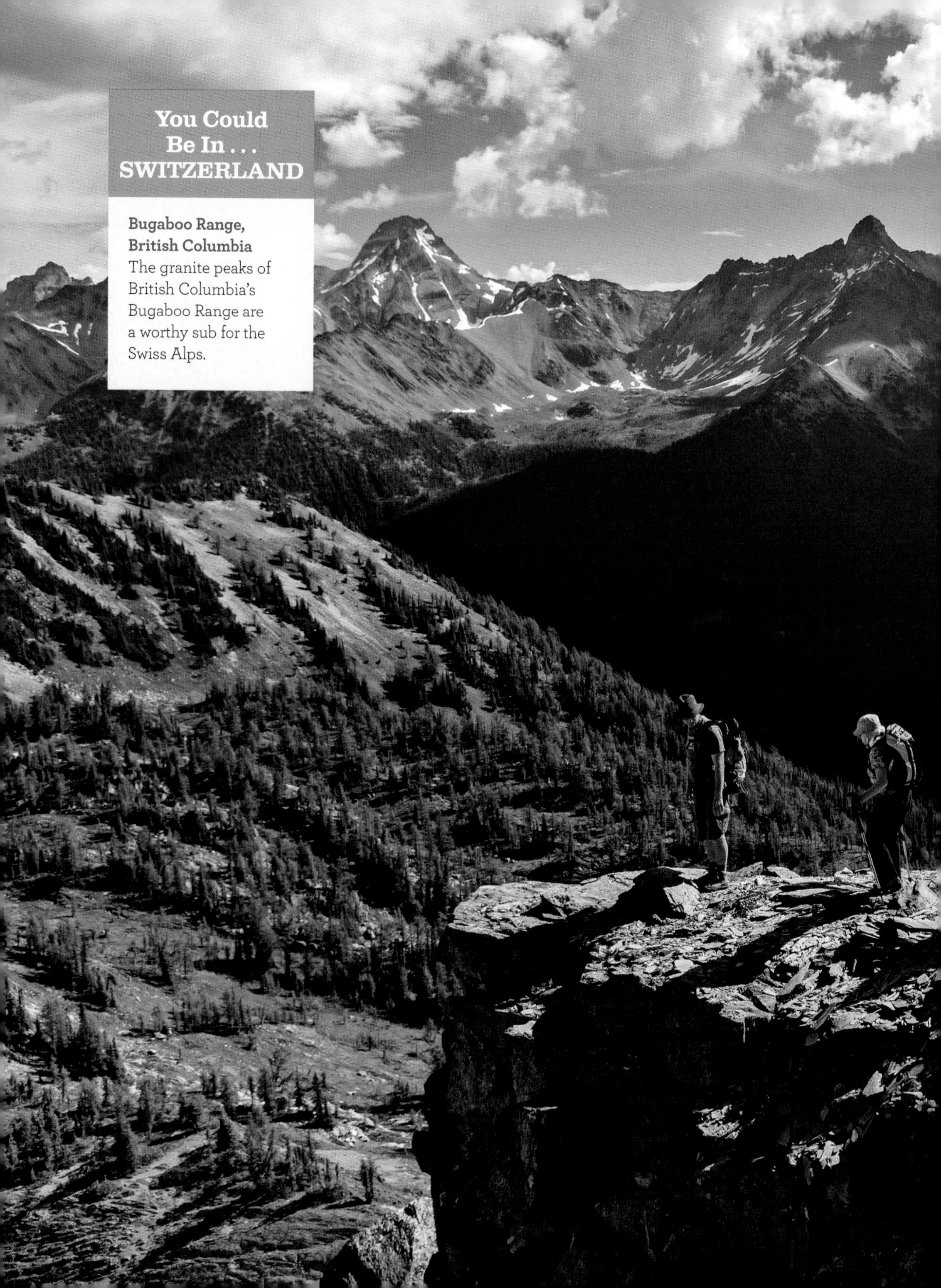

You Could Be In . . . SWITZERLAND

Bugaboo Range, British Columbia
The granite peaks of British Columbia's Bugaboo Range are a worthy sub for the Swiss Alps.

VANCOUVER

Nitobe Memorial
Garden, University
of British Columbia,
Vancouver

I was born and have always lived here. Honestly, I didn't like it as a kid because as a working-class neighborhood, Strathcona didn't have a great reputation. But as I grew older, I started to appreciate it more.

Strathcona has a lot of history—it was one of the first settlements in British Columbia. The elementary school I attended is Vancouver's oldest. There's a lot of diversity, with immigrants from Asia—like my parents. Where Jimi Hendrix's grandmother lived, on the corner of Union and Main, there's a shrine dedicated to the musician.

Things are changing fast. We're attracting a lot of attention, and even hipster businesses are moving in. Craft beer bars, sausage parlors, and creative agencies are replacing Chinese herb stores, bringing a new vibe. I'm excited to witness how these changes will shape the future of Strathcona.

IRIS LUONG
*Community funding
adviser*

Big Fat Greek Parties

The Pacific's frosty waters may be a far cry from the inviting Mediterranean, but thanks to East Vancouver's vibrant Greek community, you can have a Hellenic good time in the Pacific Northwest. The Greek community of Kitsilano rallies together every summer to put on not one but two festivals for Vancouverites and visitors alike. The jubilant Greek Summerfest, held for ten days from late June through early July, combines musical performances with great food. The aroma of spit-roasted lamb wafts between booths decked out in the colors of the Greek national flag, and you can catch festivalgoers breaking out in impromptu *tsamiko* circles to the sound of folk music. "It's all about the food, the music, the dancing, and gathering with all of our neighbors,"

says Rania Hatzioannou, president of the Cyprus Community of British Columbia. "We Canadians of Greek heritage are proud to host our friends of all backgrounds." The food-centric Greek Day, usually also in late June, brings food, beverage, and jewelry vendors together to create an Athenian agora, complete with cooking demos and entertainment for kids. Some 100,000 Vancouverites turn out for this one-day event. *Greek Summerfest, vancouvergreeksummer fest.com; Greek Day, greekday.com*

Japanese Culture High and Low

Sakura trees cover numerous streets with pink canopies during the annual Cherry Blossom Festival in April, and the moss-

covered tranquillity of the Nitobe Memorial Garden can easily compete with the finest of Kyoto's manicured yards. But upscale Alberni Street, once catering to Japanese tourists with its authentic restaurants, has become less Little Ginza and more Little Rodeo Drive, its original businesses replaced with luxury boutiques. Does that mean Japanese culture is out of favor in Vancouver? On the contrary—grub pub *izakayas* and deluxe *omakase* tasting menus have become part of the mainstream palate, making Japanese cuisine more ubiquitous than ever. The proof positive is Japadog, the mobile hot dog stand that took the city by storm long before Twitter-fueled food trucks became de rigueur. The Japanese-owned business

A performance
at the Greek
Summer Festival,
Vancouver

is now a veritable citywide phenomenon with six locations and counting. With the audacious mission statement of "making the world happy and alive through hot dogs," Japadog gives wieners complete Japanese makeovers, with flavors like teriyaki, *tonkatsu*, and miso. After all, what's more ingeniously Japanese than adapting a Western classic and improving it many folds? *Cherry Blossom Festival, vcbf.ca; Nitobe Memorial Garden, 804 S.W. Marine Dr., tel 604-822-3928, botanical garden.ubc.ca/nitobe; japadog.com*

Chinese New Year
Though many recent Chinese immigrants have opted to set up shop in the newer malls of neighboring Richmond, Vancouver's Chinatown (see p. 270), occupying a handful of blocks of prime real estate in central Vancouver,

remains the community's historic and cultural heart. To experience Chinatown at its most vibrant, come out for the Chinese New Year celebration that ushers in the beginning of each lunar year with an energetic parade. Amid fireworks, dance, and music, the mile-long parade route fills with partygoers wishing one another *gong hei fard choy*. The rest of the year, stop by Dr. Sun Yat-Sen Classical Chinese Garden, showcasing exquisite Ming-style courtyards and gardens that transport you to the serenity of the Suzhou; covered walkways make this a good rainy-day choice. *Chinese New Year, vancouver-chinatown .com; Dr. Sun Yat-Sen Classical Chinese Garden, 578 Carrall St., tel 604-662-3207, vancouverchinesegarden .com*

Commercial Break
Café-hop down the most caffeinated street of Vancouver. Settled by Italian immigrants, Commercial Drive has been spared the kind of homogenization by chain stores seen in other popular districts. While natural food suppliers, reggae record stores, and vintage clothing boutiques have descended upon this pleasant street, the demitasse-size coffee shops run by Italians remain the neighborhood's pillar. "Many of the noted Italian cafés are a place older Italian immigrants call home away from home," says neighbor Nick Pogor. "It is simply the place to go for the best espresso outside of Italy." Renzo's is a bright little gem at a street corner with park views. Whether you root for Juventus or

The Main Neighborhoods

Kitsilano
The seaside neighborhood in the west is home to a sizeable Greek population that established businesses around West Broadway.
BEST BET: Deli items like marinated octopus and dolmades from the family-owned Parthenon Supermarket

Chinatown
North America's third largest Chinese enclave.
BEST BET: Dr. Sun Yat-Sen Classical Chinese Garden

Punjabi Market
A go-to for good curries, the South Asian enclave is one of the favorite getaways for locals.
BEST BET: Ross Street Gurdwara, a Sikh temple designed by Vancouver's own Arthur Erickson

Grand Avenue
The influx of hipsters can't erase the indelible marks left by original immigrants of Little Italy.
BEST BET: Watching an Italian league soccer match on Commercial Drive

Prado Café, Vancouver—serving up authentic cappuccino and a hip vibe

South Asian music at the Indian Summer Festival, Vancouver

A. C. Milan, you can find common grounds with old-timer signori who gather to watch soccer at Caffé Roma, proudly displaying an awning in the color of the Italian flag. If you like panini, calzones, and knockoffs of famous Florentine sculptures, you'll feel at home at Café Calabria, touted to serve some of the city's best mugs of joe. And the neighborhood's newer, hipper residents congregate at minimal-cool Prado Café.
Renzo's, 1301 Commercial Dr., tel 604-253-8721; Caffé Roma and Lounge, 1510 Commercial Dr., tel 604-251-7586, cafferoma .ca; Café Calabria, 1745 Commercial Dr., cafecalabria.ca; Prado

Café, 1938 Commercial Dr., tel 604-255-5537

French Bliss
Vancouver may be on the opposite end of the country from Canada's Francophone province of Quebec, but its French-speaking population remains active by congregating every June for its Festival d'été francophone de Vancouver. Now over a quarter century in existence, the summer festival showcases French cultures of the Americas and beyond, with appearances by artists of Quebecois, Louisiana Acadian (Cajun), Haitian, and other traditions. For a week, performances by musicians such as

the zydeco performer Zachary Richard entertain concertgoers.
Festival d'été francophone de Vancouver, lecentre culturel.com/festivaldete

Bhangra Love
Centered around Main Street between 48th and 51st Avenues is the area affectionately known as Punjabi Market or Little India, a multicolored neighborhood in every shade of jangly gold bracelet and billowing sari. Authentic eateries imbue this bustling district with tantalizing spices, and several colorful festivals like November's Festival of Lights, April's Vaisakhi Day (Indian New Year), and the nascent Indian Summer Festival electrify the lively

enclave's atmosphere. The most exciting of the celebrations is the annual City of Bhangra festival, which takes over Vancouver with shimmy-inducing beats for ten days. The largest of its kind in North America, the joyous celebration showcases music and dance of the Punjab regions in India and Pakistan. The infectious music pulses on in parks, clubs, indoor venues, outdoor stages—and even the steps of the Vancouver Art Gallery, inviting guests of all ages to join in on the fun, whether they have two left feet or know the latest Bollywood moves by heart.
City of Bhangra festival, vibc.org

Full house at the Vancouver Asian Film Festival

FOREIGN FILM FESTIVALS

Travel the world from the comfort of your neighborhood theater.

■ **Vancouver Asian Film Festival**
As Canada's oldest Asian film festival, this annual event celebrates the accomplishments by North American film-makers of Asian heritage as well as artists from Asia, affording a glimpse at the transpacific zeit-geist through a range of narrative and experimental films.
vaff.org

■ **Montreal World Film Festival**
Travel around the world via 400 films from 80 countries or more. Since its founding in 1977, this event has been North America's only film competition recognized by the International Federation of Film Producers Associations, on par with the likes of Cannes. Its prestige draws the crème de la crème of contemporary films from around the world.
ffm-montreal.org

■ **Toronto International Film Festival**
With its Oscar-like power to generate industry buzz and Cannes-like critical clout, this prestigious Canadian festival has been the launching pad of many successful careers for actors and directors. Hundreds of films representing more than 60 countries take you around the world—and you may even spot a celebrity or two.
tiff.net

■ **New England Festival of Ibero American Cinema**
A slate of feature films, documentaries, and shorts from Latin America, Spain, and Portugal connect book-smart New England with the film scenes of the Hispanic and Lusophonic world. Hosted by Brown University in Providence, Rhode Island, and Yale University in New Haven, Connecticut, with screenings at other college campuses, the festival transports you to the world of Romance language.
nefiac.com

■ **Israeli Film Festival of Philadelphia**
A celebration of Israeli culture, this nonprofit festival aims to both entertain and inform. For almost two decades, this festival has carefully curated films that examine contemporary social issues in Israel.
iffphila.com

■ **Chicago Palestine Film Festival**
Started as a grassroots project by a small group of students and professionals, this independent festival provides a rare chance to catch Palestinian films on a big screen.
palestinefilmfest.com

■ **Indian Film Festival of Houston**
Nearly 9,000 miles separate Houston from Bollywood, but this Texan celebration brings in a wide array of Indian films to the Lone Star State, from musical comedies to serious cinema.
iffhinc.org

■ **Berlin & Beyond Film Festival**
Get a glimpse at today's German culture in the heart of the Castro district in San Francisco. Since 1996, the Berlin & Beyond Film Festival has become a premier German-language cinema festival, hosting VIPs such as Fatih Akin, Moritz Bleibtreu, Daniel Brühl, and Wim Wenders with its eclectic slate of German, Austrian, and Swiss movies.
berlinbeyond.com

RUSSIAN SPIRIT WRESTLERS

Doukhobors, or "spirit wrestlers," left their Russian homeland in the late 1800s in search of religious freedom, settling in the wilderness of the Kootenay Rockies in eastern British Columbia. Today, their descendants spread the spiritual group's pacifist, antimaterialistic message from the town of Castlegar, where you can experience the life of Doukhobor homesteaders who arrived here more than a century ago.

WHAT TO SEE: Doukhobor Discovery Centre is a reconstructed village that demonstrates the everyday life of the Doukhobor people at the turn of the 20th century. Perched on a bank high above the Columbia River, the open-air museum displays structures like a *banya* steam sauna and a *pech,* a kind of hand-built oven. You can walk through a typical communal home filled with personal objects such as furniture and spinning wheels, as well as handwoven attire, needlepoint bed linen, antique farming instruments, and wooden kitchen utensils. "I grew up with the culture, so I take it for granted that aspects of our culture are different from others," says Lisa Poznikoff, the museum's administrator. "We don't live in communal homes anymore, but we still have a communal mind-set."

A tour led by a descendant of the original settlers sheds light on the distinct culture, as visitors move from

INSIGHT · Russian L'oven

The so-called Russian oven, or *pech,* is a multifunctional wonder of domesticity, used to heat the home, bake breads, and dry food for preservation. Designed to stay warm for long periods of time, the enormous pech channels air and smoke through a maze of passages, keeping the brick encasing (and therefore those sitting around or on top of it) toasty. There are variants around the world wherever a Russian community gathered, but one thing seems constant: The pech brings people together.

a preserved blacksmith workshop full of metal-forging equipment to sheds and barns that contain many traditional agrarian tools. At the gift shop, you'll find an array of crafts, books, videos, and music. And you can even taste typical dishes like borscht and *pyrohi* (vegetable tarts) at the café.

■ *Essentials:* Doukhobor Discovery Centre, 112 Heritage Way, tel 250-365-5327, doukhobor-museum.org

A communal kitchen at Doukhobor Discovery Centre

ASIAN NIGHT MARKETS

A wave of recent immigrants from the Chinese-speaking world has transformed Richmond, a once sleepy suburb of Vancouver, into a destination in its own right. The city now looks much like a genuine Asian city, with such impressive Buddhist sanctuaries as the Guan Yin International Buddhist Temple, a sprawling complex modeled after Beijing's Forbidden City, and the Ling Yen Mountain Temple, with a 10,000-strong congregation.

WHERE TO GO: To meet your more earthly needs, Richmond is home to Hong Kong–style megamalls (that is, Hello Kitty and K-pop galore!) and hundreds of Asian restaurants. The four-block span between the Aberdeen and Lansdowne SkyTrain stations—known as the Golden Village—is packed with supermarkets and specialty shops. Alexandra Road, dubbed Wai Sek Kai or "food street," features 200-some restaurants in every price category and regional tradition.

NIGHT MARKETS: A crash course in Richmond's gastronomic zeitgeist is its two night markets. Every weekend May through September, 20,000 diners descend upon the International Summer Night Market; with over 60 culinary vendors, it's consistently voted as one of the world's best night markets. Not to be outdone, the original Richmond Night Market has returned from a hiatus, with a similar spread of nearly 90 affordable food stalls. Traverse Asia

INSIGHT · You Say Potato

Fresh street food is a can't-miss component of any trip to Asia—or Richmond. Spicy barbecue abalone, Vietnamese summer rolls, tapioca bubble tea, Korean seafood pancakes, Taiwanese fried chicken, stinky tofu, hand-pulled noodles, Japanese octopus balls, shaved ice topped with red beans . . . you name 'em, you'll likely find them here. Among the most popular items is a decidedly New World one: the Rotato, a potato cut into a long swirl, skewered, battered, deep-fried, and seasoned with your choice of toppings.

from Malaysia to Korea, China to India at this sprawling marketplace on summer weekends from May until mid-October. Confused about which one to visit? They're both good, so you might as well try them both.

■ *Essentials:* richmond.ca/home.htm; Guan Yin International Buddhist Temple, 9160 Steveston Hwy., tel 604-274-2822, buddhisttemple.ca; Ling Yen Mountain Temple, 10060 Number 5 Rd., tel 604-271-0009; International Summer Night Market, summernightmarket.com; Richmond Night Market, richmondnightmarket.com

Visitors pack the food court area at the Night Market in Richmond, B.C.

Zen meditation in Canada's great outdoors

MEDITATION CENTERS

Achieve enlightenment without venturing (too far) from home.

■ **Paradise Found Yoga**
Paradise is found—near Vancouver. Located on one of the Gulf Islands in the Strait of Georgia between Victoria and mainland British Columbia, this sanctuary hosts a series of diverse programs such as kundalini yoga workshops and silent retreats, as well as private couples' getaways. Its small size guarantees individual attention, and the private dock and outdoor hot tub are a plus. *paradisefound.ca*

■ **Gampo Abbey**
This Shambhala Buddhist monastery welcomes enlightenment seekers to the raw wilderness of Cape Breton Island, Nova Scotia. Since 1984, the forested Kalapa Valley has been home to Gampo Abbey, a place where you can meditate or hike near waterfalls.

Whether the meadow is blanketed in snow or dotted with wildflowers, you will leave feeling purified by the *lhasang* (a Tibetan smoke ceremony) and long stretches of contemplation. Casual visitors can also take a guided tour to take in the splendor of the sacred basin. *kalapavalley.shambhala.org*

■ **Gonzaga Eastern Point Retreat House**
Buddhists don't have a monopoly over meditation, of course. Following the teachings of St. Ignatius, this Jesuit-run retreat in Gloucester, Massachusetts, provides time and space for silent contemplation to the hypnotic sound of ocean waves dowsing the rugged coastline nearby. From a weekend to a month, retreats bring you closer to your spiritual self. *easternpoint.org*

■ **Southern Dharma Retreat Center**
Here, you can cultivate your inner landscape against the stunning backdrop of the Blue Ridge near Asheville, North Carolina, as an experienced teacher guides you through periods of meditation and Noble Silence, when ordinary conversation is not permitted. *southerndharma.org*

■ **Green Gulch Center**
Also known as Soryu-ji (Green Dragon Temple), this northern California farm follows the Japanese Soto Zen tradition, with classes and retreats of varying periods as well as training in organic farming. You can join educational workshops, silent retreats, or, on Sundays, drop in for a *zazen* (meditation) session open to the public, followed by lunch made with vegetables grown on-site. *sfzc.org/ggf*

■ **The Palolo Zen Center**
Clear your mind with a session of *sesshin,* or intense meditation, in balmy Hawaii. This retreat center includes a tranquil *zendo* (meditation hall) and simple living quarters, but most of its 13-acre grounds are lush and wide open, teeming with thousands of songbirds. Commune with nature in the surrounding winding Waimao Valley. *diamondsangha.org*

■ **Breitenbush Hot Springs**
Heal yourself by poaching in natural hot springs, losing yourself in a labyrinth, or receiving Breema bodywork, a cross between Thai massage and yoga. Not for silent ascetics, this rural Oregon retreat also welcomes families. *breitenbush.com*

AROUND THE WORLD IN
VICTORIA

The Gate of Harmonious Interest, entry to Victoria's Chinatown

Victorian Tea

Stately Victoria properly puts the "British" in British Columbia, with its imposing colonial buildings and English gardens. Some locals claim their dignified little town is more English than England. Join in with a quintessentially British experience: afternoon tea. The Fairmont Empress has the fanciest set, its tradition of sips and scones going back over a century. And the tour of the English antique-filled Point Ellice House culminates with an elegant tea of quiche and trifle in its wicker chair–dotted garden. *Fairmont Empress Hotel, 721 Government St., tel 800-257-7544, fairmont.com/empress-victoria; Point Ellice House, 2616 Pleasant St., tel 250-380-6506, pointellicehouse.ca*

Victoire, Victoria

Lest you forget: Canada is

a bilingual nation, with most elementary schools in Victoria offering French immersion programs. Victoria's Francophone community celebrates Saint-Jean-Baptiste Day, Quebec's National Day, with games and outdoor concerts—*en français, naturellement.* The annual event, taking place on June 24, culminates with the singing of and dancing to international Francophone music around a bonfire. *Société Francophone de Victoria, francocentre.com*

Chinese Know-How

Canada's first—and, until 1902, biggest—Chinatown offers a compact and charming introduction to the city's pioneering Chinese community. Here you may sample roasted duck at historic Loy Sing Meat Market.

Or test Carlos Chan of I-Kyu's claim to bring "over 100 years of noodle making" know-how into practice at I-Kyu Noodles. Next head to Fan Tan Alley, said to be Canada's narrowest street, where kitsch shops, fruit vendors, and a barbershop have taken up residence in former bachelors' apartments and opium dens. "For both the Chinese community and others, Fan Tan Alley represents the hardship and discrimination that those who came encountered, but also the hopes and dreams that they brought for a better life for their families," says Charlayne Thornton-Joe, third-generation Chinese Victorian. *Loy Sing Meat Market, 554 Fisgard St., tel 250-383-9934; I-Kyu Noodles, 564 Fisgard St., tel 250-388-7828*

Victoria has a reputation for being an old England—and there's definitely that distinct flavor. But being a gold rush town, the city has been shaped by the diverse presence of the First Nations, French, Chinese, black, Jewish, and other peoples. Historic Chinatown is remarkable. Even though the Chinese community has long completely integrated, this historic district has maintained its character as the only port of entry in British Columbia in the 19th century. I lead heritage and history tours, and I just love it. In Chinatown, I like to show visitors buildings with their distinct features like the swallow-tailed eaves, recessed balconies, and red accents. You'll see how the culture is kept alive through rituals at the Buddhist temple, and the classes at the Chinese school, built in 1909 with red pagoda roofs.

JOHN ADAMS
Local historian and tour guide

The Fairmont
Empress,
Victoria's place
for British
afternoon tea

**You Could Be In
. . . AN ENGLISH
GARDEN**

**Bentwood Bay,
British Columbia**
Roses form a canopy at
The Butchart Gardens
outside Victoria, British
Columbia.

LIST BY HERITAGE

INDEX

ACKNOWLEDGMENTS

CONTRIBUTORS: Rita Ariyoshi, Sheila Buckmaster, Maryellen Duckett, Olivia Garnett, Elaine Glusac, Michael Kennedy, Chaney Kwak, Sophie Massie, Meghan Miner, Robert Reid, Jenna Schnuer, Natalie Taylor, Suzanne Wright, Joe Yogerst

ILLUSTRATIONS CREDITS

Front cover: UP, Marcell Puzsar Fine Art Photography; LO (Left to Right), Chris Cheadle/All Canada Photos/Corbis; Enzo Figueres/Getty Images; Tenley Fohl Photography; blueeyes/Shutterstock; Back Cover (left to right): Dennis Frates/Alamy; Nancy Kennedy/Shutterstock; Orhan Cam/Shutterstock; Andrei Tselichtchev/Dreamstime.com; 2-3, Angela Amaral; 4, tropicalpix singapore/iStockphoto; 6, Chris Cheadle/Getty Images; 8-9, Matt Conti; 10, Derek Davis/*Portland Press Herald* via Getty Images; 11, Courtesy National Park Service; 12-13, Michael Blanchette; 14, Colleen Ellse; 15, Azorean Maritime Heritage Society; 16, AP Photo/Steven Senne; 17, Matt Conti; 18, f11photo/Shutterstock.com; 19, Andrew Lichtenstein/Corbis; 21, Yale Center for British Art, Paul Mellon Collection; 22, Diana Delucia Photography; 23, Mike Marsland; 24-25, Nancy Kennedy/Shutterstock; 26, Steve Tsividakis; 27, Richard Levine/Demotix/Corbis; 28, Scott Houston/Corbis; 30, littleny/iStockphoto; 31, Zygmunt Bielski; 32, Kevin Desouza; 33, Harry Prott Photography; 34, © 2014 Michael Karas/Northjersey.com; 35, Snowflake Studios Inc./the food passionates/Corbis; 36, Mary Jane Bent/CIDDE/University of Pittsburgh; 37, Randy Strothman; 38, Songquan Deng/Shutterstock; 39, Courtesy Winterthur Museum, Fraktur Room/Photo taken by Jim Schneck; 40, George Widman Photography LLC; 41, Racheal Grazias/Shutterstock.com; 42-43, The Barnes Foundation; 44, Dino Frangos; 45, Visit Baltimore Baltimore.org; 46-47, Orhan Cam/Shutterstock; 48, Yassine El Mansouri; 49, spirit of america/Shutter stock; 50, AP Photo/Jacquelyn Martin; 52, Maridav/Shutterstock; 53, Tod Marks; 54-55, Roadside America .com; 56, © Copyright hamarisite.com; 57, HelveticWV.com; 58, Casey Chalmers; 59, Nathan Morgan/*Bowling Green Daily News*; 60, Margarita Borodina/Shutterstock; 61, Jade Broadus with Vagabond3.com; 62-63, James Bulebush/Flickr Vision/Getty Images; 64, Gordon Munro; 65, Mjudy/iStockphoto; 66, Alan Hawes; 67, Micheline Callicott/www.Piwakawaka Photo .com; 68, Plaza Fiesta; 69, MISHELLA/Shutterstock; 70, St. Augustine, Ponte Vedra & The Beaches VCB; 71, © Walter Bibikow/JAI/Corbis; 72, iShootPhotosLLC/iStockphoto; 73, Tatiana Mironenko/iStockphoto; 74, Sponge Docks.net; 75, Sean Pavone/Shutterstock.com; 76, Juanmonino/iStockphoto.com; 77, Joe Skipper/Reuters/Corbis; 78, Songquan Deng/Shutterstock; 79, Chloe Herring/WLRN-Miami Herald News, All Rights Reserved; 80, Michele Eve Sandberg/Corbis; 82, Photo by Jonathon Smith; 83, AP Photo/Rogelio V. Solis; 84-5, Spirit of America/Shutterstock; 86, sandoclr/iStockphoto; 87, Linda Vartoogian/Getty Images; 88, Paige Prather; 89, annaaddison photography.com; 90, Renphoto/iStockphoto.com; 91, Vernonrd/iStockphoto;

92-93, Paul Denny/Tuliptime.com; 94, Bockfest/Brewery District CURC; 95, Joe Valencic; 96, Dublin Irish Festival; 97, Dane Hillard; 98, Kathy Korzinek/intuitivedesignsllc.com; 99, Thomas Barrat/Dreamstime.com; 100, fotohmmm/iStockphoto; 101, Jim West/Alamy; 102, Franklin County Tourism; 103, Photo courtesy of *The Herald-Tribune*, Batesville, Indiana; 104, chicagoview/Alamy; 105, CopernicusCenter.org; 106, Ralf-Finn Hestoft/Corbis; 108, Stefania Rossitto/Dreamstime.com; 109, Photographs by S Miller/Shutterstock; 110, Altamish Osman/http://altamish .com; 111, Kristin Szremski/CNN; 112-113, Ira Block/National Geographic Society/Corbis; 114, ©VISIT Milwaukee; 115, © Conventual Franciscans, Basilica of St. Josaphat. Used with permission; 116, Bobby Tanzilo; 117, Courtesy of the Wisconsin Department of Tourism; 118, Darren Hauck/Getty Images; 119, Courtesy of Mount Horeb Area Chamber of Commerce; 120, Sue Moen; 121, Sue Moen; 122, John Michael Kohler Arts Center; 123, Jon Jarosh/Door County Visitor Bureau; 124, © Marlin Levison/*Minneapolis Star Tribune*/ZUMAPRESS.com; 125, Paul Crosby Photography; 126, Minneapolis Park and Recreation Board; 127, Bob Christofferson; 128, Courtesy of Odysseyresorts.com; 129, Jen Deraspe; 130, Tom Wallace/*Star Tribune*/Minneapolis-St. Paul 2014; 131, Pam Imerman; 132, America/Alamy; 133, Christopher Jones https://www.flickr.com/photos/bilikenhawkeye; 134, Charlie Langton, courtesy Vesterheim Norwegian-American Museum; 135, Courtesy of John D. McGurk's Irish Pub; 136, George Denniston; 137, www.stonehillwinery.com; 138, Courtesy of the Missouri Division of Tourism; 139, Jim Richardson; 140-1, Rudy Lopez Photography/Shutterstock; 142, Courtesy of the Omaha Convention & Visitors Bureau; 143, Ramon Amaya; 144-145, Glenn Asakawa; 146, Raindrop Turkish House; 147, Alan Warren/Houston Community Newspapers; 148, Houston Parks and Recreation Department; 149, Keith Levine; 150, Debbie Sultemeier; 151, Matt Bynum; 152-153, Alisa Abecassiss exploreall50.com; 154, Image provided by Paciugo Gelato Caffè; 155, Joe Miller/Sophienburg Museum; 156, Jessica Rinaldi/Reuters/Corbis; 157, Arnold Drapkin/ZUMAPress/Corbis; 158-159, ElementalImaging/iStockphoto; 160, Danita Delimont /Alamy; 161, Parker Haeg/Demotix/Corbis; 162, Janelle Dessaint Kimura; 163, Linda & Dr. Dick Buscher; 164, Bob Rink; 165, Desert Botanical Garden; 166, Kathryn Scott Osler/The *Denver Post* via Getty Images; 167, Glenn Asakawa; 168, Zermatt Resort; 169, Jason Olson, *Deseret Morning News*, © Deseret News Publishing Company; 170, Isaac Brekken/The *New York Times*/Redux; 171, St. Garabed Armenian Apostolic Church; 172, Michelle Hammond; 173, Valerie Wheeler; 174, CONSTANT44/Shutterstock; 175, Kobby Dagan/Shutterstock.

com; 176, San Francisco Tourism; 178, San Francisco Tourism; 179, Liz Hafalia/*San Francisco Chronicle*/Corbis; 180, Photo courtesy of Concordia Language Villages; 181, Kelly Patrick Dugan; 182-183, Richard Cummins/Robert Harding World Imagery/Corbis; 184, Lianne Milton; 185, Naeem Azizian; 186, Kevin Minto; 187, Tenley Fohl Photography; 188, Jeff Gritchen/*Long Beach Register*/ZumaPress; 189, © *Los Angeles Daily News*/ZumaPress.com; 190, Casey Kazlauskas; 191, Jose Gil/Dreamstime; 192, Tuesday Conner; 194, LHB Photo/Alamy; 195, Neil Setchfield/Alamy; 196, Rose Café; 197, Rashad al-Dabbagh; 198, Courtesy SanDiego.org; 199, Casa Guadalajara; 200, Scott Linnett/U-T San Diego/Zuma Press; 201, Eduardo Contreras/U-T San Diego/ZumaPress; 202, 145/David Madison/Ocean/Corbis; 203, San Diego Zoo Safari Park; 204-205, Dennis Frates/Alamy; 206, Ray Smith; 207, Doris Duke Foundation for Islamic Art; 208, Mike Medeiros; 209, Malgorzata Litkowska/Shutterstock; 210, Jay Robinson, NPS; 211, Gardendreamer/Dreamstime; 212-3, Allyce Andrew; 214, Joe Vukovich; 215, steve bly/Alamy; 216-217, Dennis Lingnhr; 218, Benjamin Brink/The *Oregonian*; 219, Peter French/Design Pics/Corbis; 220, tvphoto/iStockphoto; 221, Bud Fawcett; 222, Markus Mead; 223, Rouge Creamery; 224, David Barajas; 225, Langdon Cook; 226, John V. Hedtke; 227, Uli's Famous Sausage; 228, Jason Brooks; 229, Bettina Hansen/The *Seattle Times*/Copyright 2013, Seattle Times Company. Used with permission; 230-231, blueeyes/Shutterstock; 232, Roberta White; 233, Blaine Harrington/age fotostock/SuperStock; 234-235, Ronniechua/iStockphoto.com; 236, Scott Munn; 237, Image courtesy of www.celticmusiccentre.com; 238-239, Allen McEachern/Getty Images; 240, © Tourisme Montréal, Stéphan Poulin; 241, Tracey Whitefoot/Alamy; 242, © Tourisme Montréal; 243, Baie-Saint-Paul/Annie Bolduc; 244, Hemis/Alamy; 245, orava/iStockphoto; 246, Gerrard India Bazaar; 247, Andrei Tselichtchev/Dreamstime; 248, Kevin Chow of Convergence StudioWorks; 250, The Canadian Press/Graeme Roy; 251, yelo34/iStock photo.com; 252, Kumikomurakamicampos/Dreams- time; 253, Terrance Klassen/Alamy; 254-255, Richard McGuire; 256, © Canadian Museum of History; 257, George Kroll/Dreamstime; 258, David van Heyst; 259, Photo courtesy Ukrainian Cultural Heritage Village; 260, Jim Kelcher/Dreamstime; 261, Macklin Bunnock Association; 262-263, Jonathan Irish/National Geographic Creative; 264, Xuanlu Wang/Shutterstock; 265, Branko Popazivanov; 266, Angela Pavuk for Angela Grayce Design; 267, Krista Edwardson; 268, Julian Fok Photography; 269, John Elk III/Alamy; 270, Ken Lambert/mct/ZumaPress.com; 271, martinedoucet/iStockphoto; 272, Doug Schnurr/Shutterstock.com; 273, meunierd/Shutterstock.com; 274-275, Michael Wheatley/Alamy.